The Book of Three

by Diana G. Gallagher and Paul Ruditis

Simon & Schuster, London

Special thanks to the following people:
Aaron Spelling, E. Duke Vincent, Brad Kern, Phyllis Ungerleider, and Risa Kessler

Bridget McCabe, Lisa Donovan, Lauren Forte, Russell Gordon, O'Lanso Gabbidon, Tricia Boczkowski, Wendy Wagner, Nan Sumski, Julie Swartsley, Renate Kamer, Theodore Sofianides, Jim Conway, Jon Paré, Tim Jacobson, Stephen Lebed, Roger Montesano, Paul Staheli, and Todd Tucker.

Designed by Lili Schwartz

Editors: Micol Ostow and Elizabeth Bracken

Simon & Schuster U. K. Ltd.
Africa House
64-78 Kingsway
London WC2B 6AH
www.simonsays.co.uk

Manufactured in the United States of America

ISBN 0-689-86111-7

Acknowledgments

Diana Gallagher would like to thank:

Everyone connected with *Charmed* at The WB is to be commended for five years of inspired entertainment: the creator of the series, Constance M. Burge, and the marvelous actresses and actors who brought the *Charmed* characters to vibrant life: Alyssa Milano, Holly Marie Combs, Rose McGowan, Brian Krause, Julian McMahon, and Shannen Doherty.

As with any extensive work, people too numerous to name contributed to the process. My gratitude to all, but most especially to the following:

For her confidence, Micol Ostow, an editor of extraordinary patience and expertise, and her assistant, Elizabeth Bracken; my agent, Ricia Mainhardt, for encouragement, unfailing support, and opening all the doors; and for always being there to talk, Ricia's invaluable other half, A. J. Janschewitz.

For Latin and Gaelic translations on demand, my husband, Martin R. Burke (all mistakes are mine); for too much to list over many years of fond friendship, Betsey Wilcox; and for helping me watch five seasons of *Charmed*, Kristina Grabowski.

As always, my entire family deserves applause for unwavering faith and dealing with my tight deadlines.

Paul Ruditis would like to thank:

Brad Kern and the cast and crew of *Charmed* with special notes of thanks to Jim Conway, Jon Paré, Julie Swartsley, Tim Jacobson, Stephen Lebed, Roger Montesano, Paul Staheli, Todd Tucker.

Everyone at Spelling Entertainment, especially Aaron Spelling, E. Duke Vincent, Renate Kamer, Theodore Sofianides, and Nan Sumski.

Micol Ostow and Elizabeth Bracken at Simon & Schuster.

Everyone at Viacom Consumer Products, especially Phyllis Ungerleider and Risa Kessler.

Dedications

With love for
Bethany A. Gallagher,
my charming grand-darling
—D. G.

For Michele,
my charmed sister with the
power to rewrite the world.
—P. R.

Table of Contents

Special Introduction

BY AARON SPELLING

Our first three beautiful women in television were *Angels* (as in *Charlie's Angels*).

Then came the *"CHARMED"* ones . . . Phoebe, Piper, and Paige. A trio of beauty and brains mixed with a whimsy of magic.

Oh, by the way, you had better love the show because these three lovelies are *not* angels! They are *witches.* I don't want to frighten you, but I would be scared to death if any of you disliked them. Because, if they heard about it, they would be less than "CHARMED" with you!

By the way, I love these three witches!!

FOREWORD

"Well, it was fun while it lasted. . . ." That was the phone call we got from a network executive the morning before the premiere aired. In other words, call your agent, start looking for your next gig, because this show's never going to make it. Needless to say, we were all pretty depressed. Cut to the next morning, though, when we awoke to discover that *Charmed* had shattered the record for the highest ratings ever for a WB series. A week later, the ratings were equally strong, and this time when the network called, they did something they'd never done before: They picked up the show after only two airings for the entire season!

Well, six seasons later, we're still on the air, thankfully, and still going strong. Actually, it's not a knock on the network that they didn't have much faith in our future; rather, it speaks to how difficult the show was for us to envision at the outset. I mean, it's one thing to do a pilot episode about three sisters who one day discover they're witches, but then what are the characters supposed to do every week after that? It's not like we'd created a cop show where a crime is committed every episode and the fun is watching the cops figure it out. Or a law show, where the drama is always what the verdict will be. Or even *Buffy the Vampire Slayer*, where the title of the show itself made its direction clear. *Charmed* didn't have a "franchise," a template for each episode, which meant we, collectively, had to figure one out. Fast.

Problem was, it took a little longer to figure out than most people know. Early on, we were somewhat inconsistent with our episodes, producing some really good ones ("Dead Man Dating," "That '70s Episode," "Déjà Vu All Over Again," "Morality Bites"), along with a few clunkers ("Wedding from Hell," "How to Make a Quilt out of Americans"). Honestly, if it wasn't for our talented stars and their on-screen chemistry, I'm pretty sure I'd be writing for another show right now instead of writing this foreword. From the beginning, they sold their characters, made us believe in the magic, and convinced us that they were really sisters. In short, they were the common thread that bought us time in order for us to hit our creative groove, to "find" the show.

It remains a continuing challenge to create new, mythological worlds for the girls to visit each and every week, especially after so many episodes. Yet, that's also the fun for all of us involved: to use our imaginations, to find new situations that will make our audience laugh, or cry, or wonder. Because at the end of the day, the only thing that matters is whether or not the fans still enjoy the show. No question about it, we wouldn't be *Charmed* without them.

Blessed be.
Brad Kern
Los Angeles, California

Charmed

BOOK OF THREE

Book of Three

Charmed Characters

PHOEBE HALLIWELL

Six months after Grams dies, Phoebe Halliwell returns home to San Francisco from New York. She is drawn to the attic of her family's old Victorian house and finds the magical Book of Shadows. A rebellious free spirit, Phoebe has an established pattern of acting before thinking, which prompts her to recite the spell that restores the sisters' Charmed powers. She instantly accepts the Halliwells' magical heritage but must convince her skeptical sisters that they have been endowed with powers. Although her priorities are boys and fun, she likes being a witch who has visions of past and future and quickly accepts her Charmed duty to protect Innocents. After she's turned evil by the Woogy, she worries that she's more susceptible to the dark side than her sisters, a fear that haunts her in spite of a defined sense of purpose and direction for good.

Unable to find a job, Phoebe returns to college and graduates with a degree in psychology. When an Innocent she saves quits her job writing a newspaper advice column, Phoebe steps in and finds a new career.

Phoebe finds herself uncontrollably in love with the half-demon, half-human Cole Turner, despite the fact that they met because he was trying to kill Phoebe and her sisters. She loves the good in Cole, as well as being attracted, somewhat, to the evil. Her devotion to Cole briefly leads to her reign as his Queen of the Underworld. But her inherent devotion to good brings Phoebe back to her sisters and to her destiny as a Charmed One—a destiny that ultimately includes vanquishing Cole and the evil he embodies. His inability to resist the forces of evil killed Phoebe's love for him—and himself, as well.

With Cole gone, Phoebe turns her attention to other things. She becomes the primary mentor for Paige's studies in witchcraft. She dotes on nephew Wyatt. And she is very successful outside of the "family business" as her advice column really takes off. Finally, Phoebe realizes that evil doesn't control her. Content and confident, she risks another romance, with Jason Dean—her handsome, ambitious boss. She's saddened when he leaves for six months in Hong Kong, but she won't sit home and wait. Life and Phoebe go on with hope, joy, and gusto.

PIPER HALLIWELL

Piper Halliwell, the middle sister, has two concerns about being a witch who freezes things, and though she soon dispels the idea that she's evil, she never stops wanting to be normal. To stay sane, she pursues an ordinary life that incorporates fighting evil only as necessary. Luckier in magic than love, Piper has brief romances with a warlock, a ghost, and her neighbor, Dan Gordon. She finally finds true love with her Whitelighter, Leo Wyatt. But the Elders forbid it and order Leo to stay away from Piper. When Piper's anger over losing Leo almost loses an Innocent, she realizes her Charmed duties are more important than her personal happiness, and the Elders send Leo back to her. After proving to the Elders that their magical duties won't suffer if they marry, Piper ironically almost cancels the wedding. But Elders, rules, and even a rampaging Astral Prue can't stop what is meant to be.

Piper is an accomplished chef and successful businesswoman. After a year of managing the restaurant Quake, Piper opens her own nightclub, appropriately called P3, for the three sisters who are co-owners. But she never forgets her main job is being a Charmed One. Piper's powers grow so that she can not only freeze things, but also blow them up. She initially rejects the new gift—until she gets the hang of it. She also rejects the responsibilities of being the oldest sister when Prue dies, but later eases into it when she needs to help Paige adjust. Piper truly accepts her destiny when she refuses a legitimate offer to give up her powers for a normal life, because she knows she can't stop being who she is.

Pregnancy brings joy and panic because of Piper's old fear that the worst happens when everything seems to be going right. However, since baby Wyatt can protect himself, she focuses on being a loving wife and mother—until her fears are realized. Leo's destiny leads him to become an Elder, causing him to leave his family. For Wyatt's sake, Piper allows Leo to erase her pain. She returns home to face life without him, and seemingly ready to take whatever fate has in store.

PRUE HALLIWELL

The oldest of three sisters, Prue Halliwell was always the strong one. She calls on that strength when the girls' grandmother dies and powers are restored to the Charmed Ones. Serious and responsible, she rejects her magical identity until it is proven the Halliwells each have a power and a purpose. Prue adapts to her telekinetic ability and accepts that the professional, personal, and magical elements of the Halliwells' lives are neither inseparable nor easy to manage. Joining with her sisters to protect Innocents helps her mend her strained relationship with Phoebe. But fighting evil doesn't erase all old wounds. Prue cannot easily forgive their father for walking out on his daughters when they were just children. Although she eventually reconciles with Victor, it takes time for her to allow him to fully be a part of her life again. Prue's ongoing issues with trust also cause her to feel betrayed once again by Phoebe, when the half-demon Cole enters the picture.

Like her sisters, Prue finds romantic relationships and being a Charmed One a difficult mix. She rekindles a flame with old beau, Andy Trudeau, only to have it thwarted by secrecy, suspicion, and ultimately, his death. Prue learns to accept her fate and stoically embraces her destiny. She is an expert on art and antiques but quits her job at Buckland Auction House after vanquishing her demon boss and being unable to accept the unethical business practices of the new owners and her new boyfriend/coworker, Jack Sheridan. Prue's talent as a photographer lands her work for *415* magazine, finally fulfilling her true career aspirations.

Shortly before The Source's assassin, Shax, ends her life, Prue recognizes that she's often driven by pride, and comes to terms with the inevitability of death.

PAIGE MATTHEWS

Adopted as a baby, Paige Matthews has always felt oddly drawn to the Halliwells. She is magically called to Prue's funeral when Piper casts a spell to find a lost witch. Unknown to all but Grams, Patty Halliwell had a fourth daughter by Sam Wilder, her Whitelighter. Although initially tempted by evil, Paige chooses good, and the Power of Three is reconstituted. Suddenly having the power to orb, and an instant family, Paige resists her identity and responsibilities at first. She feels pressured to be as good as Prue, a self-inflicted measure of worth. Once she accepts the fundamental essence of being Charmed—the Innocent always come first—Paige's common sense and instincts prove invaluable. Still, she takes no pleasure in being right about Cole's renewed demonic nature.

Paige quits her job as a social worker in order to be a full-time witch. She attacks learning the Craft with passion and stops competing with Prue when she conjures a dove, a feat Prue never mastered. She hesitates to accept Grams, but forgives Sam for abandoning her. Because of his selfless act, she's had two wonderful families—her parents and her sisters. She learns, like her sisters, the difficulty in balancing a personal life with a magical one. But Paige will keep looking for Mr. Right—no matter how many Mr. Right-Nows it takes. Paige is nothing if not upbeat, and she strives to achieve the balance she knows a superwitch can attain—love, family, friends, and a satisfying career.

LEO WYATT

A World War II medic, and gentle soul, Leo Wyatt died at Guadalcanal. He enters the Halliwells' lives as a "heavenly handyman" when their powers are restored. He returns Piper's romantic interest, but love between a Whitelighter and a witch is forbidden. They can't deny their feelings, but they face many obstacles. Piper can't handle Leo's demanding schedule. He leaves but loses his wings when he breaks the rules to save Piper from Oroya fever. He competes with Dan Gordon for her affections, then forfeits human happiness by reclaiming his powers to save Prue. However, his and Piper's devotion to duty finally convinces the Elders to let them marry.

Leo is the buffer between sisters when Paige joins the family, and she helps him put some misguided wartime guilt into perspective. He adjusts to normal behavior for husbands of pregnant wives and learns that the "crying thing" is real when he and Piper swap powers and symptoms. After Wyatt's birth, he takes paternity leave to lighten Piper's load, and copes with feeling secondary to everything. Through it all, he's the doting father, loving husband, and calm voice of reason that holds everyone together—until he becomes an Elder to save the family and future from the Titans. His last act is to assign Chris Perry as the Charmed Ones' new Whitelighter.

Based on an earlier sojourn to the future as well as Halliwell history, everyone assumes Leo and Piper's unborn child is a girl. While still in the womb, the baby displays powers that foretell his strength, wisdom, and an affinity with the forces of good. His mother's injuries are healed from within, her power to explode objects is converted into harmless flowers and fireworks, and a Darklighter's arrow is dissolved before impact. To heal a parental rift, the baby swaps Leo's and Piper's powers until they learn to appreciate each other's problems and perspective.

Born on February 16, 2003, in swaddling orbs, Wyatt Matthew's twice-blessed birth on a day when magic is suspended, lights dance in the sky, and the planets align was prophesied by an apothecary centuries before. A magical force-field protects him, and can only be breached by those he loves or trusts. Threatened by Wyatt's immense power, the Underworld passes a law making it a crime punishable by death to harm the Charmed child. In a Wiccaning ceremony conducted by his great-grandmother, he is blessed with the guidance and goodness of his Halliwell ancestors.

COLE TURNER

Half-human with a demonic side called Belthazor, Cole Turner's job as an assistant district attorney is a cover for a mission to kill the Charmed Ones. Instead, he falls in love with Phoebe and kills the Triad that hired him. Driven by a sincere desire to be with Phoebe, Cole tries to overcome his evil nature. Fate, however, is unrelenting in what seems to be a cosmic conspiracy to deny him redemption and love.

Pursued by The Source's bounty hunters, Cole helps the Charmed Ones with information and his powers. He not only fights a battle between good and evil within, but he must constantly prove his good intentions to Phoebe and her sisters. He becomes fully human when Belthazor is vanquished, which makes true love and life with Phoebe possible. However, when he absorbs the Hollow to help the witches vanquish The Source, he unknowingly commits to becoming the new Source.

Cole tries to give The Source's power to a wizard, but Phoebe unwittingly interrupts the spell. She briefly reigns as his queen, but her innate goodness forces her to vanquish him. Cole dies loving her and survives demonic purgatory because of his love. Love prompts him to use Paige's potion to strip his indestructible powers and forces him to take the powers back to save the witches from Barbas. Rejecting a known future as leader of the Underworld, Cole alters history to be with Phoebe only to be vanquished finally and forever by her hatred.

DARRYL MORRIS

As Andy Trudeau's partner and friend, Darryl is skeptical of Andy's belief in the paranormal and concerned that his relationship with Prue Halliwell interferes with his job. Although it's obvious Andy is hiding something, he is killed before Darryl finds out what. Married, with a young son, Darryl doesn't want to know more than necessary when he learns that the Halliwells are witches. Still, he doesn't hesitate to ask them for help with his more bizarre cases and repeatedly demonstrates incredible courage in the face of extraordinary weirdness.

After they bond fending off a Grimlock attack, Darryl tells Leo he thinks of the witches as sisters. His inclusion at Halliwell gatherings leaves no doubt that they consider him family too. When Inspector Cortez threatens to expose Piper and Phoebe as witches after Prue's death, Darryl puts his job on the line to protect them. He runs interference for Phoebe during an investigation into Cole's disappearance and warns them about a witch-hunting FBI agent. When an escaped suspect, who's actually a demon from ancient Egypt, jeopardizes Darryl's career, Leo repays his many favors by impersonating the criminal for Darryl to recapture. Piper throws a party at P3 to celebrate Darryl's promotion to lieutenant, a much-deserved reward for heroic deeds way above and beyond his duty as a cop.

PENELOPE "GRAMS" HALLIWELL

A strong-willed witch with the Warren power to move things with her mind, Penny "Grams" Halliwell becomes Prue, Piper, and Phoebe's legal guardian when their mother dies and their father leaves. She binds her granddaughters' powers to protect them as children, but stipulates that their magic will be restored when she dies. Recognizing that their animosity as young adults will endanger them as witches, she plans to strip their powers permanently, but dies before using the potion.

Grams watches over the young women as they cope with their new destiny and learn to use their powers. She doesn't reveal herself, or that she's been invisibly turning the pages in the Book of Shadows, until their first anniversary of becoming the Charmed Ones. As their lives unfold, she makes appearances when circumstances warrant.

A High Priestess of the Craft, Grams presides over Piper and Leo's ill-fated Handfasting and eventually over their wedding. She knew about Paige, but was sworn to secrecy for everyone's protection. Married four times, she cursed her wedding ring, which has humorous consequences for Phoebe. Consumed by anger and bitterness toward the men in her life, Grams overcomes this when Wyatt is born. She gives the blessing at his Wiccaning, then retreats to watch over all, silent and unseen, but always there.

PATRICIA HALLIWELL

Patty Halliwell has the Warren family power to freeze and believes that being a witch defines her. Pregnant with Phoebe and separated from her husband, Victor, she's working as a waitress when her grown daughters journey back to 1975. To save them from Nicholas, who wants the Halliwell powers, she gave the warlock immunity from the Power of Three and let Grams bind their powers as children. She voids the immunity, allowing the sisters to vanquish Nicholas after Grams dies.

Patty is killed by the Demon of the Lake while Phoebe is still a toddler. When she returns for Piper's wedding, a gift from the Elders, she connects with her daughters on a maternal level and accurately observes that Piper is the heart of the family and Prue the protector. Phoebe had the hardest time after Patty was gone because they never got to know each other.

Patty appears to give Prue confidence when Barbas attacks with her own fear of drowning. Responding to Piper's fear that death will take her away from her baby, Patty appears again with a simple message: Piper must have faith that she won't meet her mother's fate. Following Prue's funeral, Piper and Phoebe summon Patty to meet Paige, the secret fourth daughter born of her love with Whitelighter Sam Wilder.

Since he can't fight Grams regarding his daughters' future as witches, Victor Bennett leaves after Patty dies. Unable to protect them, he can't live in constant dread of the threat posed by demonic evil. Although he saved six-year-old Prue from the Nothing, he felt helpless, as a mere mortal, unable to protect his daughter. Knowing their powers were restored when Grams died, he returns to steal the Book of Shadows, hoping to save them from their dangerous magical destiny. Prue is not as understanding as Piper and Phoebe about his misguided but well-meaning interference. It isn't until he saves Prue from the Nothing a second time that she forgives him for leaving them.

Convinced that Sam Wilder broke up his marriage, Victor isn't happy that Leo is a Whitelighter. However, when he realizes how much Piper's new husband loves her and her sisters, he gives him a chance. Although he's devastated when Prue dies, Victor knows that she couldn't deny her heritage or Charmed duty. He stays out of Phoebe's romance with demon Cole and, having returned to the fold after a long absence, accepts Paige as family. He meets and marries Doris on a cruise ship without suspecting she and a sorcerer are using him to get to Piper's baby. Victor throws himself into harm's way to save Piper and his magical grandson.

SAM WILDER

Named New York Teacher of the Year in 1872, Sam Wilder became a Whitelighter when he died, and he was eventually assigned to Patricia Halliwell. Contrary to Victor's belief, Sam and Patty were not lovers until after she and Victor were separated. The daughter born of their forbidden relationship was given to the church for adoption, the hardest thing Sam ever had to do. When he lost Patty to the Demon of the Lake, he gave up on himself. Human again, with clipped wings, he stays near the lake knowing Patty's daughters will eventually return to the scene of her death. He dies again saving Prue from the demon that killed her mom.

Since Sam is last seen ascending to the afterlife with Patty, everyone is surprised when he becomes Paige's first Whitelighter assignment. Although given Whitelighter status again, he errs and loses his wings a second time. Still, he's insulted that the Elders send a newbie to redeem him until he learns that Paige is his daughter. Sam finds the strength and will to face up to his past failures, giving him the ability to heal himself, reclaim his Whitelighter powers, and save the others.

13

ANDY TRUDEAU

Inspector Andy Trudeau has been married and divorced since he and Prue Halliwell dated in high school. He's very open to renewing a romantic relationship when their paths cross during a murder case involving women who practice witchcraft. Although they get along, Andy's suspicions are aroused because Prue is so often mysteriously involved in the crimes he's investigating. The secrecy and lack of trust drive a wedge between them.

When Andy finally finds out that Prue is a witch, he has no problem believing it. He's always suspected that magic was real, but he doesn't want to live in constant danger from demons. He's suspended during an investigation of his numerous unsolved cases when he won't cooperate. All the cases involve the occult and raise questions about Prue. He gives her his files and admits that he loves her—right before he's killed by Rodriguez, a warlock posing as an investigator for internal affairs. Prue encounters Andy's spirit when she's near death. He accepts his destiny and sends Prue back to fulfill hers.

When Dan Gordon moves in next door, the sparks fly between him and Piper. Now in construction, Dan once played second base for the Mariners before he threw out a knee. Honest, good-looking, and experienced with babies, he's ready to settle down—the perfect man. He loves Piper, but resents and mistrusts Leo. When he finds information that proves Leo can't possibly be who he claims, Dan is upset because Piper isn't concerned. Then he realizes his place in Piper's life when he hears her say Leo's name in a fevered delirium.

Wanting only the best for her, Dan bows out graciously when Piper finally faces that she loves Leo. When Piper confesses that she's a witch, Dan isn't able to accept it. His memory is erased by a genie, and he leaves to start a new life with fond, but non-magical memories.

JASON DEAN

The handsome new owner of *The Bay Mirror* made a fortune with an online dating venture during the dot-com boom. A no-nonsense go-getter who expects results, Jason Dean pushes Phoebe to achieve her potential. Jason and Phoebe are attracted to each other. They recognize the professional pitfalls of getting involved yet can't resist the overwhelming emotional and physical chemistry. The blossoming romance seems destined to survive the strains of Jason's demanding enterprises and Phoebe's demanding, but still secret, Charmed family life. Then he moves to Hong Kong for six months. Things might work out when he returns, but Phoebe moves on.

Book of Three

A Chronological Halliwell Family History

After her powers are restored, Phoebe Halliwell refers to the Book of Shadows for guidance and knowledge, especially about the family's history with the Craft. The Halliwells are direct descendants of Melinda Warren, a witch who was burned at the stake during the Salem Witch Trials in 1692. Before she died, Melinda decreed that one day three sisters born of the Warren line would emerge as the Charmed Ones, the most powerful witches the world has ever known.

Paige Matthews's magical soul predates the beginning of the Warren line by several hundred years. In the twelfth century, she existed as the Evil Enchantress, a powerful witch who almost spawned a world where Dark Magic ruled. Returning to the past from the year 2001, Paige, Phoebe, and Piper bind her previous evil incarnation's powers and prevent an ill-fated pregnancy.

Charlotte Warren, Melinda's mother, was kidnapped by an evil witch practitioner in Virginia. Ruth Cobb planned to raise Charlotte's baby as evil to prevent the dominant influence of good magic in the ensuing centuries. Ironically, the Halliwells were sent back from the year 2000 to rescue Melinda, thus securing the Warren line and their own existence. Melinda Warren was born on October 31, 1670.

Melinda was betrayed by her lover, Matthew Tate, a warlock who stole her powers and turned her over to the witch hunters. Although she trapped him in a locket and retrieved her powers, she did not save herself with magic to protect her daughter, Prudence. As she hoped, the girl survived to marry and have a daughter, thus continuing the Warren line.

Summoned by blood to help the Charmed Ones imprison Matthew Tate a second time, Melinda informs the three witches that they all exhibit established family traits: "Short tempers, great cheekbones, strong wills, and powers."

Great-Great-Great-Aunt Brianna disgraced a Lord of War during the Crimean War (1853–1856) when she separated him from his weapon. Her power to move things with her mind was great enough to send a sword hundreds of miles away.

The existing Halliwell Manor was built after the original house was destroyed in the San Francisco earthquake of 1906. Knowing the land was a spiritual nexus in the eternal battle between good and evil, the Charmed Ones' great-grandparents moved into the house to insure that the site remain on the side of good. Phoebe is the only sister who was born in the house. She has a stronger connection to it and, as a consequence, may be more susceptible to the dark side of her nature.

In the 1920s three cousins, who would be reincarnated as Prue, Piper, and Phoebe Halliwell, ran a speakeasy in Halliwell Manor. P. Bowen was a professional photographer, a talent that carried through to Prue, and P. Baxter had relationships with earlier versions of Dan, a piano player, and Leo. P. Russell, who had the power to throw fire, loved a warlock, Anton, and turned evil. Knowing Anton and the bad witch were plotting to steal their powers, the cousins cursed and killed P. Russell on February 17, 1924, to prevent her from ever joining forces with her immortal warlock lover.

P. Baxter married Gordon Johnson. Their daughter, Penelope Johnson, possessed the Warren family power to move things with her mind. According to the family tree, Penny had a brother, Gordon Johnson II. Although married many times, she retained the Halliwell name and demanded that her daughter, Patricia, born in 1950, keep the Halliwell name when she married Victor Bennett (listed on the family tree as Victor Jones).

Patricia Halliwell had three daughters with Victor: Prue, Piper, and Phoebe. Penny's three granddaughters called her Grams.

Strong-willed and powerful, Grams bound her granddaughters' magic in 1975 so Nicholas, a warlock who coveted the three Halliwell powers, couldn't kill the girls to acquire them. To remove the immediate danger to her children, Patty gave in to Nicholas's demand for immunity to the Power of Three. She did not know she would drown before steps were taken to protect her daughters from Nicholas when Grams died in 1997, and the powers were restored on the autumnal equinox of that same year.

Although Patty and her Whitelighter, Sam Wilder, didn't become romantically involved until after she separated from Victor, Victor blames Sam for the separation and believes he's the reason they didn't get back together.

Unknown to everyone except Grams, Patty had a fourth daughter by Sam on August 22, 1977. Since the child was born of a forbidden union, they orbed to a church and left her with Sister Agnes to be adopted. Their only requests were that her name begin with P and that Sister Agnes not tell anyone about her origins until the grown girl returns to ask.

At age six, when Prue was home sick with Victor, she rushed outside to help a boy who was captured by an ice cream truck. Her father saved her from the Nothing, a vortex in the alternate world of a winter playground. Grams's concern about his lack of powers and ability to protect the girls drove him away. On Piper's birthday, a demon struck as she hugged her father. Grams vanquished the demon, but Victor left for good.

On February 28, 1978, Patty Halliwell tried to vanquish the Demon of the Lake at Camp Skylark. As she prepared to electrocute the water creature, Sam warned her away. She turned to freeze him, in order to save him, but was taken over by the demon from behind, and drowned. Unable to protect his most precious charges, Sam became human and stayed near the site to protect Patty's daughters, whom he knew would come eventually.

At seventeen, Prue went through a difficult rebellious phase. She was drawn to trouble, including a boyfriend who attacked her. Since the scoundrel disappeared a short time later, it's assumed

Grams exacted her own brand of justice. In spite of that, Prue was class president and a cheerleader at Baker High.

Cursed with braces in high school, Piper suffered from insecurities. She felt so invisible and inferior that Prue had to finish her speech when she ran for class secretary as a freshman. She graduated from Baker High School in 1992.

Paige was supposed to sing the school song at her eighth-grade graduation, but she froze and ran away. Not only did she miss the ceremony, but Bobby Maynard broke up with her.

Phoebe dated a Peter in high school who wasn't very nice. Prue dated Tom Peters, captain of the football team, in college.

Prue suppressed guilt for a car accident that put Phoebe in the hospital for a week. Even at age twenty, Prue deferred to Grams's judgment and wishes. She was not allowed to go to school to become a photojournalist. Knowing that they would receive their powers someday, Grams cultivated Prue's sense of duty to care for her younger sisters, an obligation she shouldered without fail.

In 1994 at the age of seventeen, Paige was a troubled teenager who skipped class, picked fights, smoked, drank, and partied hard. Her first love was Bobby Maynard and her best friend was Michelle Miglis. She and Glen have been friends since high school. She argued with her adoptive father, a fireman, in the car right before an accident killed both of her parents. On a trip back from 2002, Paige tries to avert the accident, but fails. She survived the original accident because she orbed, but she was not responsible for the tragedy.

When Grams was hospitalized in early 1997, Piper and Prue sublet their North Beach apartment and moved back into Halliwell Manor with Grams and Phoebe. Kit, the Siamese cat, continually haunted their doorstep. Grams's illness did nothing to bring the three sisters closer together, a fact that drove Grams to make a potion to stop them from becoming witches again. She had a heart attack and died before using it. Piper and Prue remained in the Manor but Phoebe moved out. When Phoebe returned from New York in October, she found the Book of Shadows in the trunk where Grams hid it and recited the spell to restore their powers.

Estranged from his daughters since he left when they were children, Victor returned after Grams died, hoping to stop his daughters from using their powers. While their grandmother lived a long life, their mother was the victim of evil. Even so, Phoebe, Piper, and Prue refused to deny who they are, and he finally accepted that they are adults with a right to choose their own destiny.

The last words Prue said to her mother were, "I love you." Since Patty died, she has not been able to say them to her sisters for fear she'll lose them, too. The emotional barrier is broken when the voice and image of her mother helps her conquer her fear of drowning. However, she continues to deal with her fear of dying young until she meets Sam Wilder at Camp Skylark in 1999, twenty-one years after her mother died on the camp dock. Sam sacrifices himself to the demon that killed Patty, saving Prue and allowing her to finish the job her mother started. Sam is seen leaving for the afterlife with Patty, but the Elders make him a Whitelighter again.

Phoebe and Prue get a mortgage on the Manor to finance the purchase of P3 for Piper in the fall of 1999. Prue quits her job at Buckland in February 2000 and becomes a professional photographer for *415* magazine. Phoebe goes back to college.

Leo Wyatt first makes the Halliwells's acquaintance as a handyman in the fall of 1998. He and Piper fall in love and break up; Piper dies; Leo saves her and becomes human, but then he gets his wings and Piper back. They try to marry without permission with a Handfasting ceremony in October 2000. The Elders make Leo leave, then relent to put them on probation when Piper realizes her love for Leo is not as important as protecting Innocents. They finally earn the right to marry, and Grams's spirit presides over the ceremony on February 22, 2001.

Just before the sixtieth anniversary of Guadalcanal, the ghosts of Rick and Nathan Lang, who also died there, haunt Leo. They play on his misguided guilt until Piper vanquishes them. Leo goes to the reunion as his own grandson and meets the families of the men he saved because he didn't die with the Lang brothers.

Prue Halliwell is killed by The Source's assassin, Shax, in mid-May 2001.

Paige Matthews, an assistant social worker at South Bay Social Services, first meets Piper and Phoebe at Prue's funeral in 2001. Her surprise ability to orb leads to the discovery of her origins and status as a half-sister and witch who reconstitutes the Power of Three. Prior to the funeral, she felt drawn to the Halliwells and wondered if their mother was her mother. She has an Aunt Julie and Uncle Dave, relatives of her adoptive parents.

Cole Turner enters the Halliwells' life during a court case in the fall of 2000. At first he's on a mission to kill the Charmed Ones for the Triad. However, he falls in love with Phoebe and can't kill her or do anything to hurt her, which protects her sisters. Although he's a half-demon struggling to suppress his evil nature, Phoebe loves him.

Phoebe graduates from college with a degree in psychology in the spring of 2001, but she has difficulty finding a job because she requires a flexible schedule.

Cole and Phoebe are married by a Dark Priest in the mausoleum chapel on March 14, 2002. Cole assumes his duties as The Source in the weeks following. Phoebe is hired to write an advice column at *The Bay Mirror*. Unaware of Cole's activities, Phoebe becomes pregnant. When his evil identity is revealed, Phoebe chooses to become Cole's Queen at his coronation as The Source on April 25, 2002. The Power of Three is stronger than Cole's hold over Phoebe, and the Charmed Ones vanquish Cole on May 2, 2002.

Phoebe learns the baby she carries was not conceived by her and Cole, but is a creation of the Seer. The unborn Source is vanquished by its own power in May 2002. Piper learns that she's pregnant a week or so later. Ramus, an Elder, tells Leo the baby will be more powerful than he can imagine.

Cole returns from being vanquished again in the fall of 2002, and although he and Phoebe still love each other, it's not enough. Cole returns to work at Jackman, Carter and Kline. Phoebe has billboards and media interviews about her column, *Ask Phoebe*.

Paige is assigned her first Whitelighter charge in November 2002 and meets Sam Wilder, her biological father, a Whitelighter about to lose his wings. Giving her up as a baby was the hardest thing he ever had to do. His reconciliation of his feelings allows him to save Paige from Darklighter poison.

Victor meets Doris on a singles cruise and marries her, unaware that she's a demon. They visit his daughters the night of the Wiccan Festival of Light, February 16, 2003. Doris is killed, and Wyatt

Matthew Halliwell is born. Wyatt's Wiccaning, when he is welcomed into the family with the blessing of all the Warren line matriarchs, takes place May 4, 2003, with Grams presiding.

When Leo becomes an Elder, Piper faces her worst fear: that he'll leave and not come back. She will never forget him, but Leo uses his power to take away the pain.

Now that Paige has done the superwitch thing, she decides it's time to get back to her other, neglected real life with friends and a career.

ALTERNATE HISTORY 1

Unfortunate events are set in motion when Prue, Phoebe, and Piper use magic to teach an inconsiderate neighbor a lesson. As a result Nathaniel Pratt becomes obsessed with finding and prosecuting witches for practicing the Craft. Prue becomes the single-minded, successful owner of Buckland, opening branches in Paris, Tokyo, and London. However, she sacrifices her personal life and has little or no contact with her sisters. Piper marries Leo, has a daughter, Melinda, and divorces Leo. Phoebe uses her powers to kill Cal Greene, a baseball player who escaped a murder charge on a technicality. She's convicted and sentenced to burn at the stake. The time line is erased when earlier versions of the Charmed Ones leap forward in time to prevent Phoebe's death. Since she accepts her guilt and fate, which is a direct result of her act of revenge, the Elders send them back to the present. Having learned their lesson, they wisely refrain from harassing Pratt with magic, and the future is changed.

ALTERNATE BOOK OF SHADOWS

The 2009 version of the Book of Shadows, which existed in an alternate, now nonexistent time line depicted in "Morality Bites," did not contain the Return Spell. Other spells, some of which violated the Wiccan rule of no personal gain, were unique to this volume.

ALTERNATE BOOK OF SHADOWS 2

Following Prue's Black Wedding to the warlock Zile in "Bride and Gloom," the Triquetra on the cover of the Book of Shadows glows red and goes dark as the Charmed Ones turn evil. Black magic spells appear on its pages and evil is no longer barred from touching it. The Book reverts to the power of good when Zile is vanquished and the black bond is broken.

While trying to save Dr. Griffiths, Piper and Prue are hurled through a wall by Shax, The Source's assassin. Leo revives them, but since Phoebe's vanquishing spell only forced the demon to retreat, Prue and Piper vanquish him again without knowing they are on live TV. A media circus ensues, prompting them to send Leo to the Underworld to arrange for Tempus to reset time. Prue is unable to contact Leo down there when a wannabe witch shoots Piper. Although she rushes Piper to the hospital, Piper dies. Prue is about to die from a SWAT team bullet when time reverses. The reset did not affect events in the Underworld.

ALTERNATE HISTORY 3

In a reality where Phoebe did not cast a spell to ask if she should marry Cole, she learns that he's The Source, calls off the wedding, and vanquishes him. Unaware of that reality, in March 2002 the present-day Phoebe does cast the spell, which calls back both a ten-year-old version of herself and the older version from the alternate history to the Manor. Although Old Phoebe resists saying anything that will change the past, she realizes Phoebe of 2002 may be right. Old Phoebe has spent her whole life regretting the decision to kill Cole, wondering if she could have saved him. Perhaps she's been sent back to give herself—and him—another chance. She dies to save Cole, which gives Phoebe the answer she's looking for.

Phoebe's ten-year-old self does not remember being brought into the future. It's assumed Grams magically erased the memory.

21

ALTERNATE HISTORY 4

Having seen her new romantic interest shot in a vision, Phoebe arranges to meet Miles at his office for lunch. A delivery truck blocks Piper's car at the curb. Since Miles left his office, they take off on foot and turn left at an intersection. Piper freezes a shootout just before the bullets hit Miles, and his death is averted. At dinner Phoebe saves Miles from an attacking warlock, and later she keeps him from falling off a balcony. Cole is warned by a warlock from the future that Phoebe will die if she keeps saving Miles, denying Death its due.

Since the warlock came back to prevent a future that's happened in his time frame, another divergence in the time line happens here. The future warlock takes advantage of being in his past. Bacarra plots with himself to steal the Book of Shadows and disempower the Charmed Ones. Phoebe and Paige are turned to dust by fireballs. Leo orbs Piper to the alley where she makes the time ripple back to a few minutes before the shooting incident. She convinces her earlier self who is waiting in the car to stop Phoebe from saving Miles. The permanent time line is set when they turn right instead of left at the intersection and are too late to freeze the bullets before they hit Miles.

ALTERNATE BOOK OF SHADOWS 3

The warlock Bacarra is not recorded because he is from the future and not part of the Charmed experience. In the preexisting time line, Bacarra knows a spell and a potion utilizing Charmed blood that creates a mask of good. This deceives the Book of Shadows, allowing present and future versions of Bacarra to steal it, use Tuatha's Spell to Disempower a Witch to strip the Charmed Ones' powers, and vanquish them.

ALTERNATE HISTORY 5

Elevated to avatar on January 19, 2003, Cole alters history so Paige does not meet her sisters at Prue's funeral. Paige is in the Neutral Plane when the shift takes effect and enters the new reality with her old memories intact.

P3 is abandoned, Piper is on a vendetta to vanquish Shax for killing Prue, and she and Leo are divorced. Phoebe lives in the Manor with Cole, who retains his old memories but has only Belthazor's power. Phoebe hates Cole in this reality, too, and only stays with him to protect Piper. Paige's knowledge of how to successfully vanquish a Lazarus demon convinces Piper and Leo that she really is a sister from a better world. Deducing that history will correct itself if the Power of Three connects and kills Cole, Paige, Piper, and Leo get a slice of his flesh, and Paige makes the vanquishing potion from memory. When they orb into the Manor, Piper is knocked unconscious. However, when Paige and Phoebe join hands with her, the Power of Three returns. Paige orbs the potion away from Cole, and Phoebe throws it, killing him. Cole remains vanquished when reality reverts.

A warlock thrown into the past by Piper's memory-enhancing spell crushes the plastic bride-and-groom cake topper at Piper and Leo's ruined wedding. He also kills the cat, Kit. As a consequence, future witches don't have the protection and services of familiars, and Leo's head fills with cries of pain. Piper replays the pertinent memory, which allows Paige and Phoebe to save the cat and preserve Katrina's human destiny in the present. The cake topper, however, is gone from the present, where it previously existed.

ALTERNATE HISTORY 7

Chris Perry arrives from twenty years in the future. In that time line, Meta turns Paige to stone and steals her orb power. Paige is turned to dust, and the Power of Three is dissolved. As a result, all the Elders are killed, and the Titans rule the world.

BOOK OF
WHITE MAGIC

In the beginning Prue has the ability to move things with her mind. Piper appears to stop time, but she actually slows everything at a molecular level. Phoebe has visions of the future when she touches certain things or people. As the Book of Shadows foretells, the powers and their knowledge of them grow as time passes.

GENERAL TENETS REGARDING THE CHARMED POWERS:

- Powers must not be used for personal gain: "Something Wicca This Way Comes."
- The powers do not work on good witches: "Is There a Woogy in the House?"
- Using a new power effectively takes practice: "Ms. Hellfire."
- A spell cannot backfire if there's no personal gain: "Murphy's Luck."
- *Magic to magic.* The powers, if temporarily possessed by another, will be attracted to the Charmed witch of origin: "Astral Monkey."
- The powers do not exist when traveling to a time that predates the acquisition of powers: "All Halliwell's Eve."
- If the Charmed powers are used against each other, the bond of the Power of Three is severed. The powers are lost until the personal and magical rift between them is repaired: "Power Outage."
- Charmed magic can be used to reverse the effects of evil magic without consequences: "The Importance of Being Phoebe."
- The loss of one sense will cause a Charmed one to develop a sixth sense. This ability has always been inherent in the strength of the Power of Three: "Sense and Sense Ability."

PRUE:

- Develops the ability to channel her power through her hands as well as her eyes in "Blind Sided."
- Pressed by a hectic double life in "Ms. Hellfire," the ability to astral project emerges.
- Astral-projected Prue does not have powers: "Heartbreak City." However, she works on developing this ability in "Primrose Empath."
- Prue's astral self operates independently while she sleeps in "Just Harried."

PIPER:

- The freeze doesn't reach beyond the room she occupies, even when outside a telephone booth as in "The Wendigo."
- Gains the control to unfreeze a single entity while leaving others frozen in "Ms. Hellfire."
- In "Sleuthing with the Enemy" Piper is able to unfreeze only a demon's head, allowing him to talk while immobile.
- In her evil incarnation in "Bride and Gloom," she is able to literally freeze things, turning them to ice, which can then be shattered.

- The power to slow molecules expands to include speeding them up in "Exit Strategy," allowing Piper to blow things apart.
- The freeze power does not work on ghosts, "A Paige of the Past," and many Upper-Level demons.

PHOEBE:

- First flash from the past, as opposed to a premonition, occurs in "The Witch Is Back."
- She temporarily acquires the ability to "think" objects into existence from the Shadow Demon in "Is There a Woogy in the House?"
- Succeeds in deliberately experiencing visions from selected items in "The Power of Two."
- According to Prue in "Déjà Vu All Over Again," the visions are never wrong, but the Charmed Ones manage to affect, and usually prevent, the outcome only half the time.
- Has a knack for writing spells; those composed in a hurry or under pressure do not always work: "Animal Pragmatism."
- Deprived of the stolen Dragon power to fly when the genie's wishes are reversed in "Be Careful What You Witch For."
- The power to levitate is activated under duress in "The Honeymoon's Over."
- In "Primrose Empath" the emanations in a room vacated by a demon assassin are so strong, Phoebe has a vision without touching anything.
- In "The Eyes Have It," Phoebe not only sees, but for the first time goes into the future. When she returns to the present, she returns with the same physical wound inflicted on her future self.
- She foresees an ordinary, destined event in "Witch in Time," perhaps caused by an emotional bond with the subject.

PAIGE:

- NOTE: A forty-eight-hour window exists after magical powers are awakened for the entity to choose whether to use the gifts for good or evil. Despite the direct influence of The Source, Paige chooses good in "Charmed Again, Part One" and "Charmed Again, Part Two."
- Intense fear causes Paige to orb herself out of harm's way in "Charmed Again, Part One."
- The ability to move things by orbing them, either into her hand or from one spot to another, with a wave of her hand while calling them, manifests in "Charmed Again, Part Two."
- Gives Leo a healing assist for Cole with her Whitelighter half: "Charmed Again, Part Two."
- Orbs a knife without calling for it in "Enter the Demon."
- Since Whitelighters can sometimes sense their charges, she believes she can sense evil: "Size Matters."
- Orbs herself out of and back into the same location on purpose, as opposed to on reflex in "Size Matters."
- As the Evil Enchantress in a past life, she had the power to make potent potions and conjure the elements: "A Knight to Remember."

- Writes her first Power of Three spell, a haiku to vanquish Ludlow, in "Lost and Bound."
- She can orb an energy ball and throw it back at the demon who created it.
- Begins orbing herself from one location to another, and taking her sisters with her in "The Three Faces of Phoebe."
- She is able to sense and locate Leo in "Saving Private Leo."
- Succeeds in conjuring doves, a feat Prue never mastered, in "Sympathy for the Demon."
- When given her first Whitelighter assignment in "Sam I Am," Paige senses his location.
- Uses the Whitelighter glamour power to look like someone else in "House Call."

WYATT MATTHEW:

- As prophesized by a wise, ancient apothecary:
  When three planets burn as one
  over a sky of dancing light,
  magic will rest on a holy day
  to welcome a twice-blessed child.
- Healed Piper from within during her pregnancy, making her invincible in "A Witch's Tail, Part Two."
- Born in swaddling orbs in "The Day the Magic Died."
- Protected by a shield of magic that he can turn off if his trust is gained in "Baby's First Demon."
- Power to sense those he loves and to orb to their location, in "Sense and Sense Ability."

Book of White Magic

White Magic Entities

KIT (CAT FAMILIAR): Wearing a collar with the Charmed Triquetra attached, Kit is often present at crucial magical events, such as the murder of a witch in "Something Wicca This Way Comes."

Kit is nearby when Piper and Phoebe cast a spell to attract a lover in "Dream Sorcerer." Consequently every tomcat in the neighborhood is drawn to the Manor.

The cat perceives the invisible, astral-projected presence of Rex Buckland in "Wicca Envy" and reacts with hissing distress. She has a similar reaction to warlocks, as seen with Rodriguez in "Déjà Vu All Over Again" and Malcolm in "The Painted World."

In "Pre Witched" a flashback reveals that Kit showed up while Grams was ill and on the verge of dying.

Prue, as a dog, chases Kit through the house in "Look Who's Barking."

Kit's fate is revealed in "Cat House" two years after she left because the Charmed Ones no longer needed a familiar. The cat was transformed into the human Katrina as a reward for exemplary service. She guides future familiars, which is why a warlock targets her. Phoebe kills him, saving the cat in the past and Katrina in the present.

SUPERSTITIONS

According to Piper in "From Fear to Eternity":
- Cover your mouth when you yawn or you might let the devil in.
- Any relationship started on Friday the Thirteenth is doomed.
- Throw spilled salt over shoulder, or be attacked by evil spirits.
- Two people walking together should walk in line so paths don't cross.

According to Grams as recalled by Phoebe:
- The direction a ladybug flies will lead you to your ideal mate.

Collected by Paige in "Lucky Charmed" for luck:
- rabbit's foot
- wishbone
- horseshoe
- four-leaf clover
- salt
- charm bracelet

TIME RIPPLE

Whenever a destined event is prevented from happening, a ripple occurs in the infinite flow of time. It closes when the event plays out as originally intended, or when anyone traveling through a time ripple returns to their point of embarkation. All events taking place within the visual frame of reference within the ripple portal can be reviewed. Timepieces clock the movement of time outside the ripple.

CHINESE MAGIC

PROTECTION CHARMS: As depicted in "Dead Man Dating," the charms resemble small Chinese dragons, which repel ghosts and evil spirits when hung outside a home or other domain. They have no effect on witches.

FAIRY MAGIC

Used to create a protective shield that prevents the Titans from sensing the Elders inside.

FAIRY-TALE MAGIC

FAIRY TALES: Every copy is a manifestation of the original. Some are fables and others are historical accounts of battles between good and evil. If fairy-tale props are used for evil, the tales will be corrupted forever, as in "Happily Ever After."

 Fairy-Tale Magic: Runs out at midnight ("Happily Ever After").

 Fairy-Tale Fortress: The *Book of Fairy Tales* is a portal to the fortress where all things fairy tale are kept ("Happily Ever After").

 Keeper of Fairy Tales: Curator of the props associated with all the stories, his apprentice becomes Keeper when he dies ("Happily Ever After").

PROPS: Those used in "Happily Ever After" include the poisoned apple, casket, and the Seven Dwarfs from *Snow White*; the prince, glass slippers, gown, carriage, and pumpkin from *Cinderella*; the woodsman, red cape, and wolf from *Little Red Riding Hood*; and the water bucket and red slippers from *The Wizard of Oz*.

GOLDEN GOOSE: Three of these creatures are sent to Baby Halliwell as a gift prior to his birth in "The Day the Magic Died."

MIRROR: The mirror on the wall imprisons the Evil Witch in "Happily Ever After" until the glass breaks. The witch is freed, and she imprisons the Keeper's apprentice. Whoever is in the Mirror sees all things and cannot lie. The apprentice is freed when the Evil Witch is destroyed.

MYTHICAL MAGIC

ETERNAL SPRING: A stream of magical water that endows immortality and invincibility. Concealed in a rock, it's protected and can only be accessed by nymphs, as in "Nymphs Just Wanna Have Fun."

31

FAMILY PROTECTION RING: Victor Bennett is saved from destruction by wearing the seventeenth-century ring in "Thank You for Not Morphing." Twin gold bands twined together are inlaid with two chrysolite gems that symbolize the duality of man and woman. The Egyptians believed the green stones would protect against spells, curses, and evil spirits.

GRAMS'S RING: Cursed by Grams with the inscription, "To gain another is to lose yourself." Intended to remind her not to marry again, the ring causes Phoebe to become her worst married nightmare—Samantha Stephens from *Bewitched*. The spell is broken when the ring is removed from her finger. She drops it down the bathtub drain.

MANOR: The Victorian house was rebuilt at 1329 Prescott Street after the original structure was destroyed in the San Francisco earthquake of 1906. The land is a Wiccan or Spiritual Nexus, which can be good or evil. The Halliwells moved in to claim the Nexus for good and to prevent evil from existing there. Almost one hundred years later, Cole takes legal possession of the Manor to gain access to the Nexus and use it for evil. Phoebe uses the spell from "Is There a Woogy in the House?" to close the rift again and return the land to good magic in "The Importance of Being Phoebe."

MELINDA WARREN'S BLESSING CUP: Melinda drank from the cup on her wedding day, and Piper uses it as something old for her wedding in "Just Harried."

SPIRIT BOARD: First introduced in "Something Wicca This Way Comes," the Halliwell Spirit Board is made from an irregular cross-section of a large tree. The alphabet, Triquetra, and Roman numerals one through ten are etched into the top. An inscription is burned into the underside:

> To my three beautiful girls,
> may this give you the
> light to find the shadows.
> The Power of Three will
> set you free.
> Love,
> Mom

Enchanted to react when Prue, Piper, and Phoebe are reunited after their grandmother's death, the heart-shaped pointer moves of its own accord to direct Phoebe to the attic, where she locates the Book of Shadows.

The inscription on the back of the Spirit Board allows Prue to identify an entry in the Book of Shadows written by her mother in "From Fear to Eternity." With an assist from Leo, Max Franklin sends an SOS via the Spirit Board to the Charmed Ones in "Secrets and Guys."

The identity of Abraxas, the demon who stole the Book of Shadows, is revealed by the Spirit Board in "Witch Trial."

When Prue is trapped in the netherworld between good and evil with War (one of the Four Horsemen of the Apocalypse) in "Apocalypse, Not," she uses the Spirit Board to send her sisters a message.

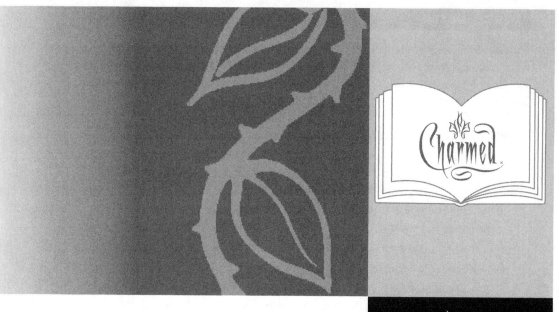

Book of White Magic
White Magic Practitioners

The guardian angels of good witches have the power to heal, hover, and orb from one earthly or mystical location to another by turning into a stream of sparkling light. Their identities and purpose are supposed to be kept secret from their charges. Love relationships between Whitelighters and witches are forbidden, the only exception being Leo Wyatt and Piper Halliwell after rigorous trial and tribulation.

WHITELIGHTER ABILITIES AND LIMITATIONS:

- Whitelighter "dust," a powder that makes people susceptible to suggestions, is sparingly used to erase painful or dangerous memories. First vague reference in "Devil's Music," and is used on a jury in "Trial by Magic."
- Whitelighters cannot heal dead people, animals, themselves, self-inflicted wounds, or non-magical ailments.
- Clipped wings render a Whitelighter mortal and susceptible to sickness, aging, and death.
- Only allowed to heal mortals who are injured by evil.
- Cannot heal demons: attempting to do so causes a recoil, throwing the Whitelighter away from the injured demon, as in "Sleuthing with the Enemy."
- Communicate with each other through a clicking language: "Blinded by the Whitelighter."
- If in the mortal world, Whitelighters cannot sense witches who are in the Underworld; if in the Underworld, they cannot be contacted by witches in the mortal world: "All Hell Breaks Loose."
- Hear the voices of charges all the time: "Siren Song."
- Can speak the language of their charges, whatever it is: "Siren Song."
- Can assume the physical appearance of someone else, as Leo does to help Darryl in "Y Tu Mummy También," and Paige in "House Call."
- They travel through the Neutral Plane when they orb: "Centennial Charmed."

KNOWN WHITELIGHTERS:

LEO WYATT's Whitelighter identity is revealed to the Halliwells in "Secrets and Guys." A World War II medic, he was killed at Guadalcanal and immediately given Whitelighter status. Although he's not destined to become an Elder, his actions in the wake of extraordinary circumstances set him on that path: "Oh, My Goddess, Part Two."

SAM WILDER: The New York Teacher of the Year in 1872, Sam was Patty Halliwell's Whitelighter, "P3 H2O."

NATALIE appears in "Blinded by the Whitelighter" to warn the Charmed Ones that witches are being killed. A by-the-book Whitelighter, she disapproves of Leo's emotional ties to the family, and faults the witches for their lack of discipline and respect for rules. Leo fears she is right. His emotional connection may be clouding his judgment and endangering the Charmed Ones, so he steps aside. A warlock is running rampant and Natalie devises a plan to battle against him with the Charmed Ones as her soldiers. However, when the sisters follow the plan rather than their instincts, Natalie is killed.

CHRIS PERRY orbs into the manor in "Oh, My Goddess, Parts One and Two." Claiming to be from twenty years in the future, he says he has come back so the Charmed Ones can save the world. When Leo becomes an Elder, he assigns Chris as the girls' new Whitelighter. Although Chris is able to handle the Book of Shadows, which suggests he's good, Wyatt raises his force-field against him, raising one of many questions about the Whitelighter. Chris conveniently leaves out details of his knowledge about the future, claiming to be only on the side of good. But why did he come back? And what is his plan for Leo?

FUTURE WHITELIGHTERS:

- Daisy in "Love Hurts."
- Maggie Murphy in "Murphy's Luck"
- Maria in "Saving Private Leo"
- Melissa in "Siren Song"

ELDERS

- The highest level of Whitelighter; the Elders control the ranks of the guardian angels and keep track of the good witches they protect. The abilities and duties of the Elders include:
- The Elders are not the final authority of the forces of good.
- Can listen in at will, but do not unless they catch words or phrases that attract their attention.
- Elders are able to transport witches through time at their discretion.
- They collect information on all types of supernatural beings, good and evil, and dispense the information as necessary or appropriate.
- Are in contact with the Powers of Evil when circumstances warrant; i.e., "Magic Hour," to stop Leo and Piper's Handfasting ceremony.
- Are not all-knowing:
  - In "Apocalypse, Not" Leo had to infiltrate the domain of the Four Horsemen to identify them and their objective.
  - In "Sight Unseen," they know little about the Triad except that it's very high in the Evil Hierarchy.
  - In "Sleuthing with the Enemy," they do not know the Triad has been killed.
  - Certain planes, such as the ether between life and death, are not on their radar, as in "Awakened."
  - Cannot see the mortal realm during an eclipse, as in "Magic Hour."
  - Witches who have passed on are beyond the control of the Elders, as is Grams in "Magic Hour."
  - Will know if a Charmed One dies, but cannot always locate her if she is being concealed by an Upper-Level demon as in "Bride and Gloom."

- Do not know the secret location of the Fairy-tale Fortress in "Happily Ever After."

- In "Blinded by the Whitelighter" they do not know Belthazor survives.

- Must figure out why there's a surge in demonic activity in "Bite Me," and again in "The Importance of Being Phoebe."

They can be any age, such as Kevin in "Witches in Tights."

Know of no demon with powers more potent than Cole's in his third demonic existence.

Many are killed, others dispersed by the Titans, who want revenge for being entombed three thousand years ago: "Oh, My Goddess, Parts One and Two."

Leo, as an Elder, can become invisible when cornered.

RAMUS, RETIRING ELDER: He has the power to foresee the future. In "Witches in Tights," he allows himself to be vanquished by the warlock Arnon, knowing that his power will find the proper host in Kevin.

CECIL: He strongly suggests that Leo should always follow his instincts. When Cecil dies, Leo's grief indicates the Elder was more than a casual adviser, "Oh, My Goddess, Parts One and Two."

GOOD WITCHES

ANDREW: A male witch killed by Belthazor with an athame. Seeking revenge, his mortal fiancée, Emma, uses Phoebe's vanquishing potion, hoping to kill Belthazor in "Black as Cole." Cole's human side survives.

AVIVA: A wannabe Wiccan, she's the first witch the Charmed Ones meet. Given the power of heat by the demon Kali in "The Fourth Sister," the teenager is a pawn in Kali's plot to steal the Halliwell powers.

COLEMAN, SUSAN: A witch of the Triple Crescent Coven targeted by the demon Sykes in "Black as Cole" but saved by the Charmed Ones.

EVA: A Wiccan of 1670 Virginia, she called the Charmed Ones back in time to save Melinda Warren and the influence of good magic through the ages. She instructs the Halliwell sisters in the precepts of natural magic.

FRANKLIN, MAX: A young male witch. Max's power to move things he can't see emerged after his mother died in "Secrets and Guys." Prue helps him and his father come to terms with his magical gift.

JANNA: Bearer of half of a powerful amulet in "Exit Strategy," she helps the Charmed Ones make a power-stripping potion for Cole, but is killed by Raynor's will and Belthazor's hand.

KARI: A witch of the Triple Crescent Coven killed by the demon Sykes in "Black as Cole."

KEVIN: A teenaged artist in "Witches in Tights," Kevin is a witch with the power of thought projection. It's a rare, natural talent that makes his drawings come to life. He becomes an Elder and is given Ramus's power to see the future.

LEEZA: Bearer of half a powerful amulet in "Exit Strategy," she's killed by Raynor, who frames Belthazor for the murder.

NICOLAE, DR. AVA: Although non-practicing, she is a Shuvani High Priestess. She helps the Charmed Ones defeat Orin, the gypsy hunter who stole her family's Evil Eye in "The Eyes Have It."

SELENA: Daughter of a witch, she has never tapped into her powers. That does not stop the witch hunter, Jackman, from trying to burn her at the stake in "Witch Way Now?" She is saved by the Charmed Ones' human skills and courage.

SHADOW'S WITCH: Name unknown, a witch betrayed and killed by her black cat familiar, Shadow, when he transformed into a warlock in "Pre Witched."

SHUVANI: High Priestesses of the gypsies as portrayed in "The Eyes Have It." They include Madam Tereza, Lydia, and Dr. Ava Nicolae. Madam Tereza was a palm reader. Lydia mixed potions with ease, read tea leaves, and was the Keeper of the Evil Eye, which magnifies and channels power. They are all experts with herbal remedies, potions, and spells.

STEADWELL, MARCIE: A perky witch practitioner and target of Barbas in "Ms. Hellfire." She is versed in useless popular culture and Wiccan lore, such as what spell ingredients should not occupy the same shelf.

STEVIE: A Wicca who welcomes Phoebe and Prue into the circle in "Witch Trial." She understands that on the Equinox, the anniversary of the Charmed Ones regaining their magic, the power convergence is stronger, and the potential greater if they make the connection—with each other and the Power of Three.

TANJELLA: The owner of an occult shop in "From Fear to Eternity," she is scared to death by Barbas, who uses her fear of being buried alive in an earthquake.

WARREN, MELINDA: The witch who began the Halliwell family line, she was burned at the stake in Salem, Massachusetts, in 1692. The Charmed Ones summon her from the grave in "The Witch Is Back," and save her from falling into evil hands at birth in "All Halliwell's Eve."

ZOE: A member of the Wiccan Gathering in "From Fear to Eternity," she is killed by Barbas with her fear of fire.

ANGEL OF DESTINY: Robed and benign, he appears in "Witch Way Now" with an offer. As a reward for vanquishing The Source, the Charmed Ones may relinquish their powers and lead normal lives without fear of demonic attack. Although they consider it, they choose to follow their destiny as witches.

APOTHECARIES: Agents of good magic, one of whom prophesied Wyatt Matthew Halliwell's birth: "The Day the Magic Died."

CHOSEN ONE: In "That Old Black Magic," Kyle Gwydion is the seventh son of the seventh son in the seventh generation of those given the power to command the wand that can vanquish the evil witch, Tuatha.

CUPID AGENTS: As presented in "Heartbreak City," these human-form beings are empowered by rings to spread love and bring perfect couples together. They are the potential for love.

ELF: A cranky elf applies for employment as Wyatt's nanny in "Sam I Am." She spreads the word about a Darklighter attack, discouraging other applicants.

FAIRIES: Rulers of the Enchanted Kingdom in "Once upon a Time," they can be seen only by innocent eyes, usually children's.

FIRESTARTERS: Extremely rare and coveted magical creatures, usually mortal. The power is linked to their emotions, and first manifests at the onset of puberty. If subjugated while still impressionable, they can be persuaded to use their powers for evil. Because of this, they are often trained to be bodyguards of The Source.

GARGOYLES: As described by Cole in "Charmed Again, Part Two," these creatures are stone in their resting state but awaken to ward off evil. This is demonstrated when The Source attempts to enter a church.

HUGHES, CHARLEEN: Decapitated by a Libris Demon for proving demons exist in "Ex Libris," she is a ghost who must seek justice for another to be released. She haunts a pawn shop, forcing the owner to confess to the murder of Tyra L. Wilson.

LEPRECHAUNS: Leprechauns spread luck throughout the world. A Gaelic chant with a shillelagh in hand summons the rainbow road. Pots of luck nuggets can be found at the end of it. Although mischievous tricksters, they are not evil.

MARK: Killed by Tony Wong to fake his own death in "Dead Man Dating," Mark is a ghost who needs to be identified and properly buried. If he's not, Yama will capture his soul, and he'll be condemned to eternal hell. After the Charmed Ones prove that Tony is alive, Tony is killed by police gunfire, and Yama takes his soul. Piper intervenes on Mark's behalf and the spirit Gatekeeper leaves him alone.

MERMAIDS: Mermaids are cold-blooded, immortal, and love shiny baubles and sea shanties. Some get lonely. They can become human if they find love, as Mylie did in "A Witch's Tail, Part One." The call of the sea is intense and irresistible, as Phoebe found out when she became a mermaid. She reverted to being human when she acknowledged loving Cole.

MUSES: Invisible light beings that inspire passion and creativity. The Charmed Ones' muse, Melody, appears in "Muse to My Ears." A muse does not linger long, as passions run higher when they are around.

NYMPHS: Tree sprites that protect the forest and the Eternal Spring, as demonstrated in "Nymphs Just Wanna Have Fun." They are usually found in groups of three. They can't hear the call of the satyr's pipe unless three nymphs are dancing. They fade into foliage, cherish and nurture nature, and seek the oasis of water at midnight. They celebrate death as renewal of life. Only certain magical creatures can be changed into nymphs. A relentless pursuit of the Craft with no time for fun made Paige an ideal candidate.

PROPHETS: Also magical seers in "The Demon That Came in from the Cold," these loud street people foresee future events but are usually ignored.

SANDMEN; OR VIRDE INSOMNIO: There are many, like angels, who exist on another plane and visit good beings in their sleep to bring them dreams. Without dreams to vent potent issues, people will give in to anger while awake. Sandmen are made of dream dust, which can be collected when they die as in "Sand Francisco Dreamin'."

SATYR: Plays the pipe for nymphs, who protect and care for him: "Nymphs Just Wanna Have Fun."

SHAMAN: Bo Lightfeather, and his father, Soaring Crow, both had the gift of premonition in "The Good, the Bad, and the Cursed."

SPIRIT OF ANGELA PROVAZOLLI: Angela's spirit was summoned in "Trial by Magic" to clear Angela's husband of her murder by proving to a jury that magic is real.

SEVEN DWARFS: As depicted in "Happily Ever After" they preserve the dead and prefer to be called Little People.

UNICORNS: As shown in "The Day the Magic Died," these gentle, mystical creatures have horns made of pure magic.

ZEN MASTER: Wise and knowledgeable, the Zen Master in "Enter the Demon" is able to use the surface of water to see other planes and open a portal to access them.

AGGRESSOR, THE: A drawing that comes alive if Kevin, a young artist, wills it. The Aggressor is the boy's alter ego in "Witches in Tights." He kills a criminal in self-defense then, feeling guilty and hoping to be destroyed, attacks the Charmed Ones. Kevin survives to become an Elder.

ANGEL OF DEATH: A black, shadowy essence, Death also appears as an imposing figure wearing black. He is neither good nor evil, but inevitable. Since all mortals must die, he always gets whom he comes for. Those who become fixated on Death without grieving and moving on risk meeting him sooner than originally destined.

AVATARS: Although these beings are not restrained by concepts of good and evil, they shape the future to their own designs.

CLYDE: A malevolent spirit who controls journeys through time, he arranges for Leo to take Paige back in "A Paige from the Past." Since he ignores summoning spells, it is necessary to make him angry with threats and insults to get him to appear.

FINN: A Golem created by Gammill in "Size Matters," he develops a conscience and saves Paige from harm before he's destroyed.

FITZPATRICK, SHAMUS: A leprechaun, he appealed to the Charmed Ones in "Lucky Charmed" to save his kind and their realm from a reptile demon named Saleel, who was killing them to steal their luck. Shamus does not live to see his friends unite to defeat the reptile demon by bringing a meteor down upon him with bad luck.

GENIE: A trickster, but not evil by nature, the genie in "Be Careful What You Witch For" makes a deal with the Triad to help a Dragon warlock defeat the Charmed Ones. In return, they will free him from his bottle. When the warlock kills Prue, the genie's remorse compels him to return to his bottle to reverse the results of the wishes. To repay the kindness, the Charmed Ones use one of three more wishes to make him mortal and free. A free genie has no powers. Once human, they cannot be found by evil.

GUARDIAN OF THE URN: Whenever someone steals the blue Egyptian urn, the hieroglyphic persona on the vessel becomes sparkling light and coalesces into the female Guardian. She punishes a thief's greed using a ring that produces lethal creatures, such as spiders, scorpions, or cobras. Only a selfless act can nullify the certainty of death, as in "Feats of Clay."

JESSUP, BANE: Although he worked with Barbas in "Ms. Hellfire" to kill the Charmed Ones, he wants to sever his connections with evil in "Give Me a Sign." He kidnaps then releases Prue so she won't be harmed, and he keeps his word to turn himself in. Trusting Prue's instincts about Bane, the Charmed Ones participate in his plan, causing the mind reader, Litvack, to duel to the death with another demon.

40

PETERS, TOM: After blowing out his knee and ending any hope of a football career, Tom accrued crushing gambling debts. He makes a Faustian deal with his manager, Mr. Kellman: In exchange for having the debts paid, he forsakes his humanity to become a demon. Upon graduating from the Demonic Training Academy, he must kill an innocent to complete the transformation, an act Prue Halliwell prevents. When faced with an order to kill his mother, his humanity wins out over his demonic conditioning.

WILLIAMSON, DR. CURTIS: Specializing in contagious diseases, he treats Piper for Oroya fever in "Awakened." Her miraculous recovery prompts him to look for a universal antibody in the Halliwells' blood samples in "Astral Monkey." When he's accidentally injected with Charmed blood, he gains all the Charmed powers, something his mortal body isn't equipped to handle. Consequently he is driven mad. Although motivated by a desire to save the good, he injures and kills criminals. He dies when the Charmed Ones repel a weapon he unleashed on them.

WITCH DOCTORS: As depicted in "House Call," they've moved past the bone-through-the-nose stereotype to wearing suits, but they still use a skull implement to cleanse places of evil spirits. The Elders discourage working with them. Although they operate on the side of good, they have an arrogant faith in their own wisdom. A decision to eliminate the Charmed Ones with a hex backfires when the witches break the spell and invade their home turf. A truce is called for the benefit of all.

41

BOOK OF SHADOWS

The Halliwell Book of Shadows, an ever-changing collection of spells, magical lore, and family history handed down through many generations, rests in a steamer trunk in the attic of Halliwell Manor until the events in "Something Wicca This Way Comes."

Guided by the Spirit Board, Phoebe finds the large, leather-bound book. The Triquetra embossed on the dusty cover is also found on the first page with the title, Book of Shadows, and the year 1693. Under the auspices of the full moon that same night, Phoebe recites the first incantation.

To Restore the Charmed Ones' Powers
("SOMETHING WICCA THIS WAY COMES")

Hear now the words
of the witches,
the secrets we hid
on this night.

The oldest of Gods
are invoked here,
the great work of
magic is sought.

In this night and
in this hour,
I call upon the
Ancient Power.

Bring your powers
to we sisters three!
We want the power!
Give us the power!

44

THE RULES

More open to the prospect of being a witch than Piper and Prue, Phoebe studied the Book of Shadows, and it still proves to be a source of information vital to their Charmed existence, including the following:

- ✪ There are three essentials of magic: timing, feeling, and the phases of the moon.

- ✪ Melinda Warren, an ancestor of the Halliwell witches, decreed that her descendents would become stronger and stronger with each generation. The process would culminate in the birth of three sisters destined to be the most powerful witches the world has ever known: the Charmed Ones.

- ✪ The Charmed Ones are charged with protecting the innocent.

- ✪ Good witches follow the Wiccan Rede: "And it harm none, do what ye will."

- ✪ Wood carvings that depict terrifying images of three women battling different incarnations of evil ominously foreshadow the future.

- Evil witches or warlocks kill witches to obtain their powers.
- The Charmed Ones' powers will grow.
- The Book is a source of critical information regarding evil entities.
- The spirits of previous witches in the Warren line add information to the Book of Shadows as needed.
- The ability to use an unfamiliar power may require a trigger, such as love, to activate the healing power.
- There are nineteen warlock-specific death spells in the Book of Shadows, but the test for a warlock is well hidden.
- Warlocks do not bleed.
- Since the Enchanted Realm can be seen only through innocent eyes, the Book of Shadows does not contain any references to fairies, elves, or trolls because it was written by adults.
- Because it is the history of the powerful Warren line of witches, the Book of Shadows is the most powerful of all magical tomes. It is coveted by all evil entities. It is an extension of the three sisters and becomes whatever the Charmed Ones are, good or evil.
- The Book of Shadows cannot be photocopied.
- The Book of Shadows cannot be removed from the Manor by anyone except a Charmed One.
- The Book of Shadows often opens to the appropriate passage in order to facilitate the Charmed One's research.
- The Book of Shadows does not provide information about evil mortals.
- To make using the Book of Shadows as a reference more efficient, Paige color-coded the pages:
  RED: demons and warlocks
  WHITE: benevolent beings
  GREEN: nature

Charmed Tenets

- The ritual to call a baby's fairy guards cannot be performed until the child has a name.
- Handfasting, a ceremony of eternal joining for two lovers, lasts a year and a day in Wiccan lore.
- Power is strongest at midnight, under a full moon.
- A circle of protection can be created with apples and sage.
- Summoning only works with spirits.
- Wicca Gatherings: Festivals of the eight Sabbats that mark the seasons, such as the autumnal equinox. Following ancient tradition, some Circles may celebrate in the nude.
- Witches can see ghosts.
- Something that doesn't actually exist, such as film characters in "Chick Flick," can't be killed.
- **NOTE**: Contrary to the beliefs of some Craft hobbyists, ordinary spell ingredients do not have conflicting harmonics.

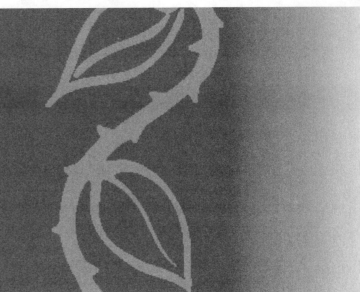

Book of Shadows
Spells and Potions

To Break the Bond of Love
("SOMETHING WICCA THIS WAY COMES")

The newly empowered Charmed Ones consulted the Book of Shadows to find out how to vanquish Piper's warlock boyfriend. They found the following instructions and spell:

Place a basket and a poppet on a table encircled by nine candles anointed with oils and spices. The candles may vary in shape and size. (Piper then added roses from Jeremy to give the spell an extra kick, and held the roses against the poppet.) Say the following incantation:

Your love will wither and depart
from my life and from my heart.
Let me be, Jeremy,
And go away forever.

Repeat Spell until the danger is past.

Piper also pressed thorns into the poppet and placed it in the basket. Upon finishing the incantation, the poppet burst into flames.

RESULT: Jeremy Burns broke out with a severe case of large thorns. The bond was severed, but Piper was not rid of the warlock until the sisters invoked the Power of Three:
The Power of Three will set us free.

To Banish Javna
("I'VE GOT YOU UNDER MY SKIN")

The prophet Muhammad used the Hand of Fatima centuries ago to banish Javna.
Evil Eyes, look onto thee,
may they soon extinguished be.
Bend thy will to the Power of Three,
eye of earth, evil and accursed!

RESULT: Prue's hand magically transformed into "The Hand of Fatima," where each finger becomes a different evil. The power of Javna's Evil Eye attacked Stefan.

To Rid the Manor of Evil
("THANK YOU FOR NOT MORPHING")

When in the circle that is home,
Safety's gone and evils roam,

Rid all beings from these walls,
Save us sisters three,
Now heed our call.

RESULT: Three shape-shifters are vanquished in an agony of molten fire.

To Attract a Lover
("DREAM SORCERER")

Phoebe and Piper set lighted candles around a bowl containing a potion. They made a list of the traits they desired and placed the paper in a black cloth bag. Putting the bag in a bowl, they recited this incantation twice:
I conjure thee, I conjure thee.
I'm the Queen, you're the bee.
As I desire, so shall it be!

RESULT: The wind that rose during the recitation ended abruptly in a puff of pink smoke when the spell was completed. Within a short period of time, men fitting the description written into the spell began showing interest.

WARNING (NOT NOTED IN THE BOOK OF SHADOWS): Undesired consequences are inherent in this "lust spell." Suitors may become obsessed, with an absolute and irrational disregard for faults or rejection. However, the spell is easily reversed, and suitors do not retain memories of their enchanted relationships.

NOTE: Men seeking to attract women must carry a piece of honey cake under their armpit for days.

To Vanquish Kali
("THE FOURTH SISTER")

To vanquish Kali, shatter her reflection.

The Truth Spell
("THE TRUTH IS OUT THERE AND IT HURTS" AND "NECROMANCING THE STONE")

For those who want the truth revealed,
Opened hearts and secrets unsealed.
From now until it's now again,

After which the memory ends.
Those who now are in this house
Will hear the truth from others' mouths.

WARNING: All who are within the house will be affected.

The Curse of Matthew Tate
("THE WITCH IS BACK")

Used by the Charmed Ones to imprison the warlock Matthew Tate in Melinda Warren's locket. After Prue accidentally freed Matthew, they mixed a potion of ordinary herbs and added a feather from a spotted owl. Opening Melinda's locket, they recited:
Outside of time,
Outside of gain,
Know only sorrow,
Know only pain.

To Bring an Ancestor Back
("THE WITCH IS BACK")

To call the family's matriarch, Melinda, they sit in the attic, bathed in the light of many candles. Each sister cuts her finger with a knife, to mingle the blood of the three with Melinda's locket while reciting:
Melinda Warren,
Blood of our blood,
Great-great-great-great-great-great-grand-mother,
We summon thee.

RESULT: The summoned one appears in flesh and blood with her knowledge, memory, and all her powers.

To Return an Ancestor to Their Own Time
("THE WITCH IS BACK")

With Matthew sealed back in Melinda's locket, it is time to return the Halliwell ancestor to her rightful place. Seated in a circle by the light of many candles, Phoebe, Piper, and Prue join hands with Melinda and say:

Melinda Warren,
Blood of our blood,
We release you.

The Relinquishment Spell
("WICCA ENVY")

NOTE: There is no mention of being able to reverse this spell in the Book of Shadows.
From whence they came
Return them now;
Vanish the words,
Vanish the powers.

RESULT: The words from every page in the Book of Shadows and the Charmed powers are captured in a metallic lantern.

Confidence Spell
("FEATS OF CLAY")

Piper casts a Confidence Spell over Doug, a clumsy, lovesick Quake employee who becomes an arrogant show-off under the influence of a magical double dose. He ignores the girl he loves instead of asking her to marry him, forcing Piper to reverse the spell. Apparently, some things are not meant to be manipulated by Charmed magic.

NOTE: There is no entry for the Egyptian Guardian of the Urn in the Book of Shadows. However, a reference to "The Seven Deadly Sins" indicates that a selfless act may neutralize greed and satisfy the Guardian's quest for justice. This is proven true in "Feats of Clay."

Unbecoming a Wendigo
("THE WENDIGO")

To un-become a Wendigo, kill the infecting Wendigo by melting its heart of ice.

Friday the Thirteenth
("FROM FEAR TO ETERNITY")
SPELL BY PATRICIA HALLIWELL

The Demon of Fear appears once every thirteen hundred years on Friday the Thirteenth. He feeds on fears of witches for his survival.

If he can kill thirteen unmarried witches before midnight, he'll be freed from the Underworld to wreak his terror every single day.

He kills by turning a witch's greatest fear against her. In the face of your greatest fear, your powers are paralyzed.

To defeat him, release the fear.

The scent of sandalwood, which Patty often wore, wafts through the attic when the Charmed Ones check the Book of Shadows for a reference to releasing fear. Prue senses her mother's presence. A note has been added to the page:

To let go of your fear, trust in the greatest of all powers.

After the Demon of Fear is sent back to the Underworld, Prue studies the page. As she watches, new words appear in her mother's sparkling handwriting:

Thanks for letting them into your heart.

To Dispel the Effects of Superstitions
("FROM FEAR TO ETERNITY")
SPELL BY PIPER HALLIWELL

When Piper's superstitions get the best of her one Friday the Thirteenth, she recites the following while burning the ends of dried sage over an open flame:

Sage so fair
from far and wide,
take my troubles
and brush them aside.

RESULT: The spell fails.

To Confine the Shadow Demon
("IS THERE A WOOGY IN THE HOUSE?" AND "THE IMPORTANCE OF BEING PHOEBE")

Grams taught this spell to the Halliwell sisters in the form of a story rhyme when they were children.

I am light.
I am one too strong to fight.

Return to dark
where Shadows dwell.
You cannot have
this Halliwell.
So, away and
leave my sight,
and take with you
this endless night.

NOTE: Phoebe uses this spell to send the Shadow, Cole, and the demons in the Manor into the Nexus in "The Importance of Being Phoebe." Cole escapes, too powerful to be confined.

To Defeat the Lords of War
("WHICH PRUE IS IT ANYWAY?")

A clan of supernatural flesh-and-blood warriors, the Lords of War are responsible for all major wars since time began. They move from one conflict to another through reincarnation, but their enchanted weapons protect them from the weapons of men. The rigid Code of Honor demands that when one is disgraced, he or she must steal back their lost abilities, which includes the magic of a firstborn witch, as it is supposed to be the strongest.

NOTE: The strength of three is required to defeat Gabriel Statler. So Prue chants the following to triple the strength of her powers:

Take my powers,
Blessed be,
and multiply their
strength by three.

RESULT: Three Prues—which prompts the question, "Which Prue Is It Anyway?" The Prue clones are identical to the original and have her memories up to the moment the spell was cast. When they are no longer needed, they will simply disappear.

To Unbind a Bond
("THAT '70s EPISODE")

The bond which was not
to be done,
give us the power to

see it undone,
and turn back time
to whence it was begun.

To Return in Time
("THAT '70S EPISODE")

Used to return to the exact moment of temporal departure; requires the Power of Three to succeed.
A time for everything
and to everything in place,
return what has been moved
through time and space.

Nicholas Must Die
("THAT '70S EPISODE")
SPELL BY PENELOPE "GRAMS" HALLIWELL

To vanquish the warlock Nicholas for good, Grams left the following instructions and spell for her granddaughters.

Blend the spell ingredients with a pestle in a bowl and recite as mixture smokes:
Lavender, mimosa, holy thistle,
Cleanse this evil from out midst.
Scatter its cells throughout time.
Let this Nick no more exist.

The Prophesy of the Rowe Coven
("WHEN BAD WARLOCKS GO GOOD")

Since the tenth century, each generation of the Rowe family has grown stronger as the warlock line advances toward the formation of the Rowe Coven. Three brothers will become the most powerful force for evil ever. Nobody has found a spell or a weapon that can stop them.

To Destroy a Grimlock
("BLIND SIDED")

Gather Schisnadra root for a potion. Toss the green liquid onto the Grimlock to blind and dissolve it.

To Lure an Evil Spirit
("THE POWER OF TWO")

Mix equal parts of mercury and acid with the blood of one of the spirit's victims and pour it over his grave.

Killer Cocktail
("THE POWER OF TWO")

Since an evil spirit can only be vanquished by another ghost, Phoebe finds something that—if done right—will create an instant spirit. The Killer Cocktail consists of a little oleander, jimsonweed, and bloodroot. It stops the heart immediately. Whoever takes it can be revived with CPR, but it must be done within four minutes to prevent brain damage.

To Vanquish an Evil Spirit
("THE POWER OF TWO," "SAVING PRIVATE LEO," AND "NECROMANCING THE STONE")

An evil spirit cannot be vanquished on a physical plane, only on an astral plan. Since a spirit must recite the spell, a witch must die to say it.
Ashes to ashes,
spirit to spirit,
take his soul,
banish this evil.

Repeat the incantation until the evil spirit transitions.

To Switch Powers
("LOVE HURTS")
What's mine is yours,
what's yours is mine.
Let our powers
Cross the line.
I offer up
This gift to share.
Switch the powers
Through the air.

RESULT: All magical beings in the vicinity of the spell being cast will switch powers. Repeat to switch back.

The Devil's Sorcerer, also known as Tempus
("DÉJÀ VU ALL OVER AGAIN")

Manipulator of Time,
Serving only his will always,
Always for evil's gain.
Remove him, remove him
From the time he's in.

To Accelerate Time
("DÉJÀ VU ALL OVER AGAIN")

Use to break a time loop and displace Tempus from the time frame he's in. He will not be vanquished with this spell, but merely forced back into the Underworld.

Winds of time, gather round.
Give me wings to speed my way.
Rush me on my journey forward,
Let tomorrow be today.

Rite of Passage
("WITCH TRIAL")

Fight it with the Power of One, or else . . . more powerful Evil awaits that will destroy you.

To Defeat Abraxas
("WITCH TRIAL")

Abraxas is a demon of the astral plane who destroys witches by demonizing their power.

When Abraxas steals the Book of Shadows, he does not take the book from the house, but into a different plane of existence through a portal.

Jeremy, the Woogy Man, and Nicholas return as Abraxas removes the power from the Book of Shadows by reading it backward. The Charmed Ones remember the spells to vanquish them again, but must invoke the Power of Three with the spell that restored their powers and the strength of acting as one.

To Move Ahead in Time
("MORALITY BITES")

To save Phoebe from being burned as a witch in the future, the Charmed Ones write their desired arrival date on paper and then set the paper afire. They then recite:

Hear these words, hear the rhyme.
We send to you this burning sign.
Then our future selves we'll find
in another place and time.

WARNING: The Move Ahead in Time Spell and Return Spell may only be used once. Then they will disappear.

To Create a Door

When you find
your path is blocked,
All you have to do
is knock.

The Smart Spell
("THE PAINTED WORLD")
SPELL BY PHOEBE HALLIWELL

Phoebe tries to increase her odds of getting a job by writing a smart spell. After the spell is written on paper, she folds it and holds it to her temple while reciting:

Spirits send the words
from all across the lands.
Allow me to absorb them
through the touch of either hand.
For twenty-four hours,
from seven to seven,
I will understand all meaning of
the words from here to heaven.
P.S.
And, there will be no personal gain.

Spell to Free a Warlock
("THE PAINTED WORLD")

In the 1920s a witch named Nell tricked a powerful warlock into a painting with a hidden spell that only his power of X-ray vision could see:

Absolvo Amitto Amplus Brevis
Semper Mea.
To free what is lost, say these words:
Mine forever.

These words will free anyone trapped inside the painting:
Verva omnes liberant.
Words free us all.

As flame lights shadow
And truth ends fear,
open the locked box
to my mind's willing ear.
May the smoke from this candle
into everywhere creep,
bringing innermost voices
to my mind in speech.

The Demon Masselin
("DEVIL'S MUSIC")

Vanquish with an ingested antacid potion.

To Attract a Succubus and Destroy with Fire
("SHE'S A MAN, BABY, A MAN!")

To save an Innocent that Phoebe saw in a premonition, the Charmed Ones draw the universal male symbol on the floor and place lighted candles around the circle with six candles concentrated at the point where the base of the arrow connects. They then sit within the circle and Prue recites:

By the forces of Heaven and Hell,
draw to us this woman fell.
Rend from her foul desire
That she may perish as a moth to fire.

RESULT: The candle flames flare and the spell caster turns into a man. The gender effect will reverse when the succubus is vanquished in fire.

Scrying for Something Lost
("THAT OLD BLACK MAGIC")

To find a person or thing, suspend a crystal on thread over a map.

To Hear Secret Thoughts
("THEY'RE EVERYWHERE")

Invoked to determine whether or not Jack Sheridan and Dan Gordon are warlocks, Prue and Piper say the following with lighted candles for protection.

To Vanquish the Collectors
("THEY'RE EVERYWHERE")

Their hunger for knowledge is your ally.

NOTE: There is no reference to the Demon of the Lake or how to vanquish it when needed by the Charmed Ones in "P3 H2O." Patty Halliwell died trying and never returned to make an entry.

To Vanquish Drazi
("HEARTBREAK CITY")

The vanquishing potion is negated if Drazi wears the ring he stole from Cupid, because you can't kill love.

Potion to Send Cupid Home
("HEARTBREAK CITY")

A travel potion with an aphrodisiac kick, the key ingredient is the desire to go home because "home is where the heart is." Phoebe mixes it under Cupid's watchful eye.

Recipe: Mix with 100 slow strokes:
lavender
oysters
rosemary
chocolate
basic Karis root compound

To Stop a Crying Baby
("RECKLESS ABANDON")

Sometimes a baby just has to cry.

52

To Vanquish a Ghost
("RECKLESS ABANDON")

OPTION #1: Boil a mandrake-root potion and pour over the ghost's bone.

OPTION #2: Destroy the object of its obsession.

The Awakening Spell
("AWAKENING")

When it looks like Piper will die of a rare disease, Prue and Phoebe cast a spell to heal her. To be effective they place a poppet on Piper's chest, on which they put drops of her blood and they recite:

Troubled blood with sleep's unease,
remove the cause of this disease.
Sleep eternal nevermore
and shift the source of illness borne
to this poppet whom none shall mourn.

To Reverse the Awakening Spell
("AWAKENING")

What was awakened from its sleep
must once again slumber deep.

To Dehumanize Animal Men
("ANIMAL PRAGMATISM")

WRITTEN BY PHOEBE HALLIWELL TO RIGHT A SPELL CAST BY SOME COLLEGE WOMEN

After she adds margarita salt (a satisfactory substitute for the Salt of Life) to a pouch of feathers and herbs, Phoebe recites:

Something wicked in our midst,
in human form these spirits dwell.
Make them
animals sayeth the spell.

WARNING: This spell affects all humans within the realm of the spell's influence. Animal forms are random and varied.

TO REVERSE THE DEHUMANIZE ANIMALS SPELL
Recite:

Undo the magic acted here,
Reverse the spell so all is clear.

Past Life Spell
("PARDON MY PAST")

SPELL BY PHOEBE HALLIWELL

NOTE: Must be cast by the subject alone, who lapses into a sleeping state while under the influence of the spell but may return at will without an additional incantation.

Remove the chains of time and space
And make my spirit soar.
Let these mortal arms embrace
The life that haunts before.

To Curse P. Russell
("PARDON MY PAST")

Evil witch in my sight
Vanquish thyself.
Vanquish thy might
in this and every future life.

To Shift into a Past Life
("PARDON MY PAST")

In this time and in this place,
Take this spirit I displace,
Bring it forth as I go back
To inhabit a soul so black.

To reverse, switch the pronouns. In the case of P. Russell, Anton's protective amulet prevents a reversal of the spell.

To Invoke a Sign of True Love
("GIVE ME A SIGN")

SPELL BY PHOEBE HALLIWELL

I beseech all powers above
send a sign to free my sister's heart.
One that will lead her to her love.

To Erase Bad Luck
("MURPHY'S LUCK")

SPELL BY PRUE HALLIWELL

From this moment on
your pain is erased,
your bad luck as well.
Enjoy your good luck, Maggie,
you're free from that hell.

To Vanquish Cryto
("HOW TO MAKE A QUILT OUT OF AMERICANS")

What witches have done and then undone,
Return this spirit back within,
And separate him from his skin.

Separate a Witch from Her Powers
("HOW TO MAKE A QUILT OUT OF AMERICANS")

To a boiling crucible of the blackest lead
combine gypsy blood with a mandrake's head.
More of the nightshade will you boil,
the henbane, datura, and from nux an oil.
With hemlock root complete the draught,
foul and dark like the might and craft
of the creator of this brew and her desire
to steal from another for vengeance,
*   power or ire.*

To Call a Witch's Power
("HOW TO MAKE A QUILT OUT OF AMERICANS" AND "CHARMED AND DANGEROUS")

Powers of the witches rise
course unseen across the skies.
Come to us who call you near;
come to us and settle here.

Impromptu Spell to Vanquish the Demon of Illusion
("CHICK FLICK")

Evil that has traveled near,
I call on you to disappear.
Elementals, hear my call,
Remove this creature
from these walls.

To Truly Vanquish the Demon of Illusion

Since beings that don't exist can't be destroyed in reality, the only way the Charmed Ones can vanquish the Demon of Illusion is to make a potion to enter the film he's inhabiting. A second potion is required to vanquish him in his realm.

WARNING: The potion tastes like asphalt.

To Vanquish a Libris Demon
("EX LIBRIS")

Demon, hide your evil face.
Libris die and leave no trace.

WARNING: Resembling a Reaper Demon, the Libris Demon uses a sickle to decapitate victims.

To Strip Charmed Powers from Another
("ASTRAL MONKEY")

Pheobe concocts a potion that combines two separation-of-power spells with one human-form–animal-extraction spell.

To Vanquish the Demon of Anarchy
("APOCALYPSE, NOT")

Sower of discord,
your works now must cease.
I vanquish thee now
With these words of peace.

RESULT: This spell must be recited simultaneously with an evil incantation in a dead language, with all participants forming the points of a pentagon. If the proper potion is also applied, it opens a vortex into a netherworld between good and evil.

Spell to Open the Netherworld Vortex

Sower of discord,
your help we implore.
I summon thee now
with these words of truce.

Guardians
("THE HONEYMOON'S OVER")

To vanquish a Guardian, drive a stake into the triangular rune on his forehead.

Handfasting
("MAGIC HOUR")

Handfasting is the eternal joining
of two people in Love.
It is a sacred ceremony of commitment
presided over by a High Priestess.
Best performed at a time
of sunrise or sunset where both
the Sun and the Moon are present
in the joining of the two lovers.

To See Beings of the Enchanted Realm
("ONCE UPON A TIME")

To facilitate the rescue of a fairy princess from trolls, Prue combined the spells To See What Can't Be Seen, To Cultivate Innocence, and The Power of Three spell.

In this 'Tween time, this darkest hour,
we call upon the sacred power.
Three together stand alone,
command the unseen to be shown.
In innocence we search the skies,
enchanted are our newfound eyes.

RESULT: A delay in the working of the spell may have been caused by Piper's reluctance to participate following the loss of Leo. The anomaly was corrected when she realized this.

To Defeat Troxa
("SIGHT UNSEEN")

Troxa is an invisible demon whose weakness is that his ectoplasmic biochemistry is sensitive to cold; he may become partially visible when exposed to freezing temperatures.

The Crystal Cage
("SIGHT UNSEEN," "CHARMED AND DANGEROUS," "SAND FRANCISCO DREAMIN'," "BABY'S FIRST DEMON," AND "SENSE AND SENSE ABILITY")

Cast a spell over siderite crystals and place on the floor around the object chosen as bait—the Book of Shadows, for Troxa. When an entity—for it may also affect humans—enters the area of influence, the remote warning crystal will glow. The crystals forming the trap will emit highly charged energies that grab the captive and render him, her, or it helpless.

VARIATION: An attacking demon can also be trapped by completing the five-point pattern with the crystals when it is within the pattern.

To Vanquish Belthazor
("POWER OUTAGE," "SLEUTHING WITH THE ENEMY," "LOOK WHO'S BARKING," AND "CENTENNIAL CHARMED")

THE VANQUISHING POTION: Boil cockleshells, pig's foot, crickets, elm bark, and mandrake root together. Add the demon's flesh and recite the following to activate:

Spirits of air, forest, and sea,
Set us of this demon free.
Beast of hoof, beast of shell,
Drive this evil back to hell.

A brief, smoking explosion signifies the potion is potent.

WARNING: Cole/Belthazor has had an alchemist transmute his blood, making him immune to any potion made of the old Belthazor flesh.

NOTE: This potion works to vanquish all Upper-Level demons using flesh specific to the particular demon, such as Sykes in "Black as Cole."

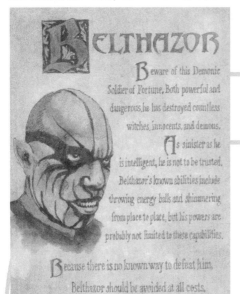

BELTHAZOR

Beware of this Demonic Soldier of Fortune. Both powerful and dangerous, he has destroyed countless witches, innocents, and demons.

As sinister as he is intelligent, he is not to be trusted. Belthazor's known abilities include throwing energy balls and shimmering from place to place, but his powers are probably not limited to these capabilities.

Because there is no known way to defeat him, Belthazor should be avoided at all costs.

To Summon Belthazor and Krell
("SLEUTHING WITH THE ENEMY," AND "LOOK WHO'S BARKING")

Magic forces black and white,
reaching out through space and light.
Be he far or be he near,
bring us the demon Belthazor here.

This is a derivative of the spell to summon Melinda. The principle of "magic to magic" will attract a demon to its own flesh in the potion.

NOTE: Introduced in "Sleuthing with the Enemy," the spell to summon Belthazor is also used to summon Krell, the demonic bounty hunter who was after Belthazor.

To Release an Empath's Power
("PRIMROSE EMPATH")
SPELL BY PRUE HALLIWELL

Free the empath,
release his gift.
Let his pain
be cast adrift.

RESULT: The spell causes the empath's gift to transfer when he touches Prue during the incantation.

To Defeat Vinceres
("PRIMROSE EMPATH")

Vinceres is a demonic assassin—timeless, unstoppable, and immune to witches' magic.

Although strong enough to survive having the Power of Empathy, the demon is destroyed by an internal infection of human emotion delivered via Astral Prue.

To Vanquish an Alchemist
("COYOTE PIPER")

Let flesh be flesh and bone be bone.
The Alchemist shall transform none.
Cruel scientist of evil born,
With these words face the fire's scorn.

To Dispossess a Life Essence
("COYOTE PIPER")

NOTE: This spell requires the Power of Three.
Host soul, reject the poison Essence.
Let love's light end this cruel
possession.

The Ice-Cream Truck
("WE ALL SCREAM FOR ICE CREAM")

The Ice-Cream Man plays the "Devil's Chord," which is a series of notes that, when sounded together, specifically attract demon children like moths to a flame.

Only the Nothing can vanquish them.

Deflection
("BLINDED BY THE WHITELIGHTER")

The power of deflection is a witch's best shield against the forces of darkness.

To Vanquish Eames
("BLINDED BY THE WHITELIGHTER")

Time for amends and a victim's revenge.
Cloning power, turn sour;
Power to change, turn strange.
I'm rejectin' your deflection.

Lost-and-Found Spell
("WRESTLING WITH DEMONS")
SPELL BY PHOEBE HALLIWELL

To find Cole, recite while holding a candle and crystal:
Guiding Spirits, I ask your charity,
lend me your focus and clarity.
Lead me to the one I cannot find.
Restore that and my peace of mind.

To find Tom Peters:
Show me the path
That I cannot find
To save Tom and restore
Prue's peace of mind.

To Reverse the Lost-and-Found Spell

I return what I didn't want to find.
Let it be out of sight, out of mind.

To Kill a Female Warlock
("BRIDE AND GLOOM")

Powers of light,
Magic of right,
Cast this blight
Into forever's night.

High Priestess Wedding Ceremony
("JUST HARRIED")

We are gathered here today
to unite two souls as one.
Do you, Leo Wyatt and Piper Halliwell, join
us here of your own free will, to acknowl-
edge the eternal bond shared between you?

At this point the bride and groom exchange personal vows. Then the High Priestess continues:
Here before witnesses Leo and Piper
have sworn their vows to each other.
With this cord I bind them to those vows.
However, this binding is not tied, so that
neither partner is restricted by the other.
Because the only true enforcement of love
is the will to love.

The bride and groom recite:
Heart to thee, body to thee.
Forever and so mote it be.

The entire wedding party repeats:
So mote it be.

To Vanquish Seekers
("DEATH TAKES A HALLIWELL")

Knowledge gained by murd'rous means
is wisdom's bitter enemy.
The mind that burns with stolen fire
Will now become your funeral pyre.

To Call Death
("DEATH TAKES A HALLIWELL")

Spirits of air, sand, and sea,
Converge to set the Angel free,
on the wind, I send this rhyme,
Bring death before me, before my time.

How to Perform a Séance— a Ceremony to Contact the Dead
("PRE WITCHED" AND "TRIAL BY MAGIC")

When a pesky Warlock wouldn't stay vanquished, Grams opened the Book to this page. The séance requires six candles, white and purple in color, and a white cloth. Sweeten the air by burning cinnamon, frankincense, and sandalwood. As the candles and incense burn, the Book says to concentrate on contact with the spirit and chant the spell that follows. If the mortal name of the deceased is known, adjust the chant accordingly.
Beloved unknown spirit,
we seek your guidance.

We ask that you commune
with us and move among us.

NOTE: This spell was added to the spell To Summon the Dead in "Trial by Magic," and a variation of the ritual tools and ceremony was performed.

To Inflict the Pain of Nine Deaths
("PRE WITCHED")

Nine times this evil's cheated death,
felt no pain and kept its breath.
This warlock standing in our midst,
Let him feel what he has missed.

To Strip Cole's Powers
("EXIT STRATEGY")

Ginger root (billings root; archaic); shake water vigorously for two hundred heartbeats then add a pinch of dandelion and a dash of chickweed. Cool until the potion turns bloodred.

To Track a Banshee
("LOOK WHO'S BARKING")

The piercing cry
that feeds on pain
and leaves more
sorrow than it gains.
Shall now be heard
by one who seeks
to stop the havoc
that it wreaks.

RESULT: Prue is turned into a dog until the Banshee is banished from Phoebe by Cole's declaration of love.

To Vanquish Shax
("ALL HELL BREAKS LOOSE")

NOTE: This spell requires The Power of Three.
Evil wind that blows
That which forms below,
No longer may you dwell:
Death takes you with this spell.

Summoning Spell
("CHARMED AGAIN, PART ONE")

VARIATION: To Restore the Charmed Ones' Powers

Hear now the words of the witches,
The secrets we hid in the night.
The oldest of Gods are invoked here;
The greatest work of magic is sought.
In this night, in this hour,
I call upon the ancient power,
Bring back my sister,
Bring back the Power of Three.

To Call a Lost Witch
("CHARMED AGAIN, PART ONE"
BUT VARIATION IN "HELL HATH NO FURY")

Put the following ingredients in a silver mortar:
A pinch of rosemary
A sprig of cypress
A yarrow root
Grind with a pestle while chanting:
Power of the witches rise,
Course unseen across the skies,
Come to us who call you near,
Come to us and settle here.

Spill the blood of the caller into the mortar, and continue chanting:

Blood to blood, I summon thee,
Blood to blood, return to me.

RESULT: Although used to recall Prue, this spell reached out to Paige Matthews, the lost Charmed One, and drew her into the Halliwell circle with an extinguished candle and a newspaper.

To Summon the Dead
("CHARMED AGAIN, PARTS ONE AND TWO" AND "NECROMANCING THE STONE")

The following is chanted with a sage stick, five white candles, and incense. It is a variation of the séance ritual.

Hear these words, hear my cry,
Spirit from the other side,
Come to me, I summon thee,
Cross now the Great Divide.

RESULT: Again intended to call Prue, this spell drew Grams into the space within the points of a pentagram marked by five lighted candles. It was used again to summon Patty to meet Paige, and later to call Grams to Wyatt's Wiccaning.

The basic spell to Summon the Dead was expanded in "Trial by Magic" to include the following lines from the Séance Ceremony to Contact the Dead:

Beloved Spirit, Angela,
we seek your guidance.
We ask that you commune with us
and move among us.

To Send Inspector Cortez Away
("CHARMED AGAIN, PART ONE")
STARTED BY THE GHOST OF GRAMS AND FINISHED BY PHOEBE UNDER DURESS

We call the Spirits to help undo
And send him off to Timbuktu.

Enchantment Spell
("CHARMED AGAIN, PART TWO")

Magic forces far and wide
enchant these so those can't hide.

Allow this witch to use therein,
so she can reveal the evil within.

RESULT: Enchanted sunglasses reveal any evil lurking within an individual, including Belthazor within Cole and a black aura around Paige when she considers using her powers for evil.

Instant Karma Spell
("HELL HATH NO FURY")

To make a demon feel the pain he or she inflicts, recite:

Let crucify pain
and evil ways,
follow this villain
through all his days.
Reverse the torment
he creates
to turn on him
a crueler Fate.

RESULT: Paige chants to teach a coworker guilty of sexual harassment a lesson. It backfires, endowing her with a very large chest.

Vanishing Spell
("HELL HATH NO FURY," "CHARMED AND DANGEROUS")

Let the object of objection
Become but a dream,
As I cause the seen
To be unseen.

RESULT: Cures Billy's acne.

NOTE: Paige tries to cure Phoebe's mysterious acne with the Vanishing Spell the morning of her wedding in "Marry-Go-Round." Due to the interference of Cole's black magic, the spell makes Phoebe invisible and cannot be reversed. However, Paige is able to transfer the invisibility effect to herself. The dark spell plays out when the wedding is called off.

NOTE: This spell satisfies Piper's fastidious obsessions by making the house disappear in "House Call." Phoebe is inside at the time.

To Reverse the Vanishing Spell

Let the object of objection return
So that its existence may be reaffirmed.

To Promote Compromise
("HELL HATH NO FURY")

These words will travel
through the minds
of stubborn parties
and unbind
the thoughts too rigid
to be kind.
A compromise they'll
disentwine.

To Reverse a Karma Spell Used for Revenge

Write the original spell and burn the paper while chanting:
Guided spirits, hear our plea,
annul this magic.
Let it be.
Please, let it be.

60

Paige's Accidental Spell to Switch Bodies
("ENTER THE DEMON")

Just once I'd like to know
What it's like to be Phoebe
And kick some serious ass. Bam!

IN ALL VARIATIONS: Throw a dash of powdered toadstool into the bubbling potion; the spirits of the subjects will be exchanged.

Variation of the Switch Bodies Spell

I want to be [insert name].

To Reverse the Switch Bodies Spell

I want to be [insert name] again.

To Vanquish Gammill

NOTE: Gammill is also known as The Collector
("SIZE MATTERS")

Small of mind,
but big of woe,
the pain you caused
you now will know.

To Call a Lover to Oneself
("A KNIGHT TO REMEMBER")

Bring together my prince and me,
let him fall on bended knee.
I summon him to my side,
that he may take me to be his destined bride.

This spell was first cast by the Evil Enchantress in the Middle Ages. When it's cast again by Paige Matthews in 2001, a portal opens between the two time periods.

To Open a Portal to the Prince's Past
("A KNIGHT TO REMEMBER")

Bring together my prince and me,
His kingdom now I wish to see.
Crossing history to his side,
From myself I will not hide.

To Vanquish the Shocker Demon
("A KNIGHT TO REMEMBER")

Vanquish, we three witches cry.
One final shock and then you die!

An All-Purpose Vanquishing Spell
("BRAIN DRAIN")

Evil hiding in plain sight,
I use this spell with all my might.
Stop your changing form and shape,
this vanquish now seals your fate.

RESULT: Piper uses without effect while existing in an illusion created by The Source.

Mind Link
("BRAIN DRAIN")

Life to life,
mind to mind,
our spirits now
will intertwine.
We meld our souls
and journey to
the one whose thoughts
we wish we knew.

To See a Muse
("MUSE TO MY EARS")
INSPIRED SPELL BY PHOEBE HALLIWELL

Being of creativity,
show yourself now to me.
Your light which shines upon our face,
let your vision now embrace.

To Reverse the Spell to See a Muse

Being of creativity,
Hide yourself now from me.
Your light that shines upon our face
From our vision now erase.

To Vanquish a Warlock
("MUSE TO MY EARS")

Evil is a faithful foe,
but good does battle best.
We witches will with these words
waste the warlock's evil zest.

To Find a Muse
UNINSPIRED SPELL BY PHOEBE HALLIWELL
To locate the warlock Devlin through the Ring of Inspiration he wears that holds the essences of the muses.
Being of creativity,
we call ourselves now to thee.
Your light, now darkened in a ring,
shall feel the Power
of Three we bring.

To Summon Clyde, the Ghost of the Past
("A PAIGE FROM THE PAST")

The malevolent spirit that controls journeys in time ignores all summoning spells. To make Clyde appear, it's necessary to make him angry. Strings of colorful insults peppered with threats usually works.

EXAMPLE: "Get down here, Clyde, you fetid worm from the bog of eternal stench. Your mother was a chunky substance from a Jinn cesspool. And she smelled bad, too." (Spoken by Leo Wyatt)

To Stretch the Imagination
("TRIAL BY MAGIC")

Let mind and body soar
to heights not reached before.
Let limits stretch
that you may catch
a new truth to explore.

RESULT: Unfortunately, Glen is turned into a man with elastic limbs rather than someone able to embrace the fantastic on faith. The spell is reversed before he leaves the Manor.

To Break Force-Field at the Ludlow Academy Gate
("LOST AND BOUND")

Door unlock.
No magic block.

Spell failed when Phoebe attempted it; however, Phoebe was recovering from being Samantha Stephens for a day.

To Vanquish Ludlow

The brittle winter
gives way to flowers of spring.
Ludlow is vanquished.

This was Paige Matthews's first attempt at a Power of Three spell. The haiku form, although unusual, achieves the desired result.

To Contain the Hollow
("CHARMED AND DANGEROUS")

Representatives of good and evil must read the inscription on the ancient box that contains the Hollow. The box will then be returned to the vault and all the powers it consumed will be restored to their rightful owners.

Aboleo extium cavium
Du eternias.

To Vanquish the Source
("CHARMED AND DANGEROUS," "LONG LIVE THE QUEEN," AND "SYMPATHY FOR THE DEMON")

Prudence, Patricia, Penelope, Melinda,
Astrid, Helen, Laura, and Grace,
Halliwell witches, stand strong beside us,
Vanquish this evil from time and space.

NOTE: Used to vanquish Cole. This spell did not work to vanquish Barbas when he had Cole's enormous powers.

Should I Marry Cole?
("THREE FACES OF PHOEBE")
SPELL BY PHOEBE HALLIWELL

The question above is written and burned while reciting:

My love is strong, my spirit weak,
it is an answer that I seek.
A question burns within this fire,
so I may hear my heart's desire.

RESULT: Younger and older versions of Phoebe appear to help her find the answer.

To Vanquish Kurzon
("THREE FACES OF PHOEBE")

NOTE: Spell requires the Power of Three
Hell threw you from its inner core,
but earth won't hold you anymore.
Since heaven cannot be your place,
your flesh and blood we now erase.

To Vanquish a Harpy
("BITE ME")

NOTE: Spell requires the Power of Three
Claws of pain, we have to sever.
Demon, you are gone forever.

To Vanquish Vampires
("BITE ME")

Vampires are immune to a witch's powers, but can be vanquished with a Power of Three spell.

The usual weapons may fend off or kill an individual vampire, but killing the Queen eradicates the entire line.

Piper's Anti-Phoebe Potions
("LONG LIVE THE QUEEN")

Potions are mixed for every contingency:
1. One duplicates Piper's power and scalds flesh
2. Magical Mace slows an attacker without doing serious harm
3. Various explosives, paralytics, and poisons

The Tall Man
("WOMB RAIDER")

Oral tradition tells of a giant whose body served as a portal to other dimensions.

Because he was imprisoned centuries ago, nobody knows what this demon's name is or if he even exists.

There's no known vanquishing spell for him. The Source felt so threatened, he condemned the giant to spend eternity in a cage.

To Find a Lost Love
("WITCH WAY NOW")

Place five lighted white candles to form the five points of the pentagram, sit within, and chant:

Whither my love
wherever you be,
through time and space
take your heart
nearer to me.

RESULT: Phoebe's astral self finds Cole's human half in demon purgatory. The effects of a Beast attack on Astral Phoebe seem real. When Piper and Paige find Host Phoebe screaming in the attic, they pull her out with the Reversal Spell:

Return thy love
wherever she be,
through time and space
bring her
back to me.

Consecrated Scry
("WITCH WAY NOW")

NOTE: This spell is to find someone specific.

Light a candle. Before the flame subsides, let the wax from the candle drip onto the crystal. Once consecrated, scry with the crystal for the one who is sought.

To Find the Sea Hag
("A WITCH'S TAIL, PART ONE")

SPELL BY PAIGE MATTHEWS
Spell combines Eastern thinking with Western Wicca:

Powers of the witches rise,
Find the Hag who speaks in lies.
Balance chakra, focus chi,
and lead us through the cruel, cruel sea.

RESULT: Phoebe, whose heart denies her love for Cole, is turned into a cold-blooded mermaid. She decides she likes it that way, and there is no reversal spell for her sisters to force her to change. Coming to terms with her love restores Phoebe's humanity.

Fearless Spell
("A WITCH'S TAIL, PART TWO")

SPELL BY PIPER HALLIWELL
Locked in, boxed in,
full of fear,
my panic grows manic
till I can't hear.
In need of reprieve

so that I can breathe.
Remove my fear,
please, make it leave.

To Vanquish Necron
("A WITCH'S TAIL, PART TWO")

NOTE: Spell requires the Power of Three

Necron is a skeletal being who hovers between life and death. He has the power to incinerate any living creature to feed on its life force.

WARNING: The previous two witches who vanquished skeletal beings died in the process.
Tide of evil, washed ashore
to bring this darkness ever more.
With all our strength we fight this fate,
Make this evil obliterate!

The blast from Necron's vanquish is so explosive, all present are knocked unconscious, but survive.

To Reveal Phoebe's Heart
("A WITCH'S TAIL, PART TWO")

SPELL BY PAIGE MATTHEWS
Open Phoebe's heart to Cole.
Reveal the secret that it holds.
Bring forth the passion of love's fire
That he may feel her true desire.

RESULT: A glowing ring of light penetrates Cole's heart.

Potion Tip from Grams
("HAPPILY EVER AFTER")

NOTE: Be sure to cut mandrake root to expose the meat for it to work properly.

Poison Antidote Spell
("HAPPILY EVER AFTER")

Hear our call
for those who fall.
Purge her to awaken
from this toxin taken.

Variation of the Spell to Vanquish The Source
("EYES HAVE IT")

Combines gypsy magic with the power of the Charmed Ones to vanquish Orin, the gypsy hunter:

Marina, Teresa, Lydia.
Nicolae gypsies,
stand strong beside us.
Vanquish this evil
from time and space.

Grams's General Demon Vanquish
("SYMPATHY FOR THE DEMON")

Heard in one of Piper's suppressed memories, called forth by Barbas.

Hell's fiend, creature of death,
fire shall take your very breath.

To Trace a Previous Scry
("Y TU MUMMY TAMBIÉN")

Scrying secrets, come to me.
Drop again so I may see.

Paige uses a scrying crystal found at a crime scene to identify Jeric's next victim, Phoebe.

To Expel the Soul of Isis
("Y TU MUMMY TAMBIÉN")

Two warring souls now burn inside
where only one soul can reside.
I call upon the Power of Three
to save her body and set Paige free.

To Strip Phoebe's Powers
("THE IMPORTANCE OF BEING PHOEBE")

This witch's powers cannot fight
the lure of evil magic's might.
Before misuse lands her in hell
remove the powers of Phoebe Halliwell.

This spells works, but it's instigated by the shape-shifter posing as Phoebe to make Phoebe defenseless.

To Summon a Witch Doctor
("HOUSE CALL")

Combine liverwort, pinch of dragon root, and snakeskin while chanting:

Free us from the ties that bind
of evil magic intertwined.
We call upon the One who cures
he who's to the dark inured.

To break a hex cast by a Witch Doctor, the victim must reach deep down within themselves to realize they are behaving strangely. An emotional shock will also end the spell.

Sleep Spell
("SAND FRANCISCO DREAMIN'")

Let we who waken from our sleep
return at once to slumber deep.

Prophesy and Birth
("THE DAY THE MAGIC DIED")

According to an ancient apothecary's prophesy, on the night when three planets burn as one over a sky of dancing lights, magic will rest on a holy day to welcome the birth of a twice-blessed child.

During this period, the pages in the Book of Shadows are erased. All magic and the Book are restored when Wyatt Matthew Halliwell is born.

To Return a Unicorn
("THE DAY THE MAGIC DIED")

Take this beast before I end her.
Ship her back, return to sender.

RESULT: Due to the absence of magic in the universe, this spell did not work when first tried.

To Vanquish Cronyn and Company
("THE DAY THE MAGIC DIED")

Beast of legend, myth, and lore,
Give my words the power to soar
And kill this evil evermore.

RESULT: Since all magic was suspended pending Wyatt's birth, dust shaved from a unicorn's horn of pure magic enabled this spell to annihilate Cronyn, Doris, and Stanley's body.

To Find Luck
("LUCKY CHARMED")
SPELL BY PAIGE MATTHEWS

Finances have run amok,
creditors I soon must duck.
I cast this spell to find good luck
and hope my life will cease to suck.

To Enhance Memory Recall
("CAT HOUSE")
SPELL BY PIPER HALLIWELL

Let the truth be told,
let our lives unfold
so we can relive our memories
and stop being enemies.

This spell was chanted to hasten a psychologist's analysis of Piper's marriage to Leo.

RESULT: The spell casts Phoebe and Paige into the past where they experience events as Piper and Leo recall them. Piper returns everything to normal with a reversal spell.

To Locate Wood Nymphs
("NYMPHS JUST WANNA HAVE FUN")

As suggested by Paige, the spell is written and empowered with items that are representative of the four elements:

WIND: a novelty fan
FIRE: matches
WATER: bottled
EARTH: dirt

To Turn Tull into a Tree aka How to Neutralize an Invincible Foe
("NYMPHS JUST WANNA HAVE FUN")

Paige chants:
Changing seasons
changes all.
Life renews
as creation calls.

Piper chants:
Nothing's immune,
everything transmutes.
So take this demon
and give him roots.

To Summon the Creeper
("NECROMANCING THE STONE")

Demons who dwell
In slivers of night,
Uncloak your shadows,
To witches' sight.

To Vanquish the Necromancer
("NECROMANCING THE STONE")

The potion contains dragon root, eel skin, and blood wort.

To Summon the Matriarchs
("NECROMANCING THE STONE")

I call forth from time and space
matriarchs from the Halliwell line,
mothers, daughters, sisters, friends,
our family's spirit without end,
to gather now in this sacred place
to help us bring this child to grace.

Spells Listed in the 2009 Book of Shadows

Once in the future, Prue and Piper find these spells in the 2009 Book of Shadows. They know they must have marked them for a reason, and set out to determine what it is.

To Induce Slumber
To Change One's Appearance
To Create Money
To Bend Someone's Will
To Erase a Memory
Binding Spell

Book of Shadows

Spells from Non-Charmed Sources

A Protection Spell
("MS. HELLFIRE")
**ORIGINALLY CAST BY WICCA WANNABE
MARCIE STEADWELL**

Sung while flitting through the house with an incense stick:
Favor us, Sister Moon,
with your protective beams.
Give all who dwell
within this spell
safe days and sweet dreams.
For those who dwell
underneath this roof.

Valentine Love Spell
("ANIMAL PRAGMATISM")

NOTE: Spell was found in a novelty book and rewritten by Phoebe Halliwell
From strike of twelve, count twenty-four,
that's how long this spell is for.
If to abate my lonely heart,
enchant these gifts I thee impart.

Phoebe rewrites the novelty Valentine spell to correct the order. A spell must first state whatever is lacking and then what is needed or desired, not the reverse. Three students successfully cast the rewritten version to turn animals into men for Valentine dates.

Wiccan Benediction
("EXIT STRATEGY")

Recited by Janna at the close of a Wiccan Circle:
The birth and rebirth of all Nature,
the passing of Winter and Spring,
we share with the life universal,
Rejoice in the Magical Ring.

Funeral Ceremony
("CHARMED AGAIN, PART ONE")

First used at Prue's funeral.
That which belongs to fellowship and love,
that which belongs to the Circle,
remains with us.

The wheel turns.
As life is a day so our sister
has passed into night.
Nothing is final,
and we who remain behind
know that one day we will once again
share
the bread and wine with our sister.
Oh, Blessed Spirit, we bid you farewell,
for you await a new destiny.

At this point the cord that was lying on the altar is placed in silver chalice and covered, and the candles extinguished.

Tarot Reading
("MARRY-GO-ROUND")

Simplified, cards are dealt by Paige in regard to Phoebe and Cole's wedding: the Lovers for the past, Despair for the present, and Death for the future.

To Summon a Siren
("SIREN SONG")
PARTIAL SPELL BY LEO WYATT
Oh, singing lady of the dusk,
who preys on men, turns love to lust,
we harken ye . . .

To Give Good Luck
("LUCKY CHARMED")

A Leprechaun blessing:
Sláinte is táinte.
Luck to you!

To Call the Rainbow Road
("LUCKY CHARMED")

Raise a shillelagh and chant:
Go n-éirian bóthar leat.

The Wiccaning Ceremony:
A Blessing for Infants
("NECROMANCING THE STONE")

"The next generation has been born into our family, our legacy."

SPELL BY PENELOPE "GRAMS" HALLIWELL

We pledge to be with this child,
this beautiful boy, always.
Apart but never separate,
free but never alone.
He is one of us, and because of that
we will bless him
with all the goodness that we are.
Welcome to our family,
Wyatt Matthew Halliwell.
Blessed be.

To Bestow the Powers of the
Ancient Mortals

Eccere, oh, see ac mando ma mento.
Behold, oh, bring forth and command my will.

BOOK OF BLACK MAGIC

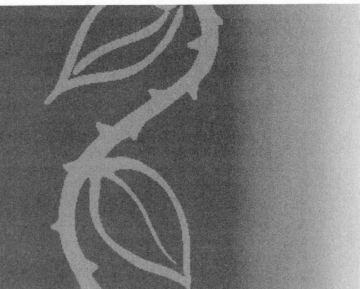

Black Magic Practitioners

AVATARS: A force of power that isn't restrained by concepts of good and evil, avatars nonetheless shape the future to their own design. They exist outside of time and space, and possess enormous power. Cole is elevated to avatar just prior to his death. ("Centennial Charmed")

BEAST: In the demon equivalent of purgatory, a Beast feeds on the powers that are stripped from vanquished demons as they enter. Cole learns to absorb the powers and kills the Beast. ("Witch Way Now")

BLOODY MARY AND THE SLASHER: Movie monsters sent into reality by the Demon of Illusion to kill the Charmed Ones. Bloody Mary kills with a knife, and the Slasher attacks with an ax. They can be destroyed in real life the same way they die in their respective films. Bloody Mary falls out a window, and the Slasher is electrocuted with a space heater. ("Chick Flick")

CHARON: Seen in Alcatraz, a female spirit shrouded in flames that is that ferries souls to hell. ("The Power of Two")

FAMILIARS: See Warlocks, Shadow

HOLLOW, THE: A force with the power to consume all magic, all life, and the world, it was contained thirty-five hundred years ago with the cooperation of good and evil. The Source releases the Hollow to strip the Charmed Ones' powers. The Source is victimized when Cole becomes the Hollow, absorbs its powers, and weakens it for the Charmed Ones to vanquish with a spell. The Seer and Phoebe chant the inscription on the Hollow's box to contain it again. ("Charmed and Dangerous")

KIERKIN: An Underworld Alchemist, Kierkin creates the Life Essence, Terra, from his own blood. He has the ability to transform one thing into another, such as energy into matter, and can bring the dead back to life. ("Coyote Piper")

UNNAMED ALCHEMIST: He transmutes Cole's blood to make Cole immune from potions using Belthazor's flesh. This is accomplished with an infusion of energy through a cut on Cole's arm. ("Look Who's Barking")

WENDIGO: The first Wendigo was a mortal who removed and ate his lover's heart when she betrayed him. His heart turned to ice, and he became a monster. Appearing as a normal person by day, it stalks people in love or people with good hearts during the three phases of the full moon, and it subsists on human hearts. They can have a preference for a specific blood type. If wounded by a Wendigo, the victim turns into one. The only cure is to kill the infecting beast by melting its frozen heart. Consequently the Wendigo is afraid of fire. ("The Wendigo")

DARKLIGHTERS

Darklighters exist to kill Whitelighters and future Whitelighters using a crossbow with arrows dipped in a poison for which there is no cure. While Darklighters may have individual powers and agendas, they all dress in black, mimic voices, and travel as streams of black ash.

There are no Darklighter vanquishing spells or potions listed in the Book of Shadows. Whitelighters can overpower and orb Darklighters to an unknown fate, as in "Murphy's Luck." Darklighter poison is fatal to Darklighters as well as Whitelighters. ("Siren Song")

In "Love Hurts," the Darklighter Alec uses the power of a burning touch to kill humans who are destined to become Whitelighters. Prue uses a spell to switch powers, and turns his deadly touch against him.

The Darklighter in "Murphy's Luck" drives good souls to suicide with the power of suggestion, preventing them from becoming Whitelighters.

Renegade Darklighters like Ronan in "Sam I Am" are stronger and more powerful than normal Darklighters. They track and target fallen Whitelighters, usually those who are one step from losing their wings.

DEMONS

ABRAXAS: A demon that exists on the astral plane, he tries to destroy the Charmed Ones by reading the Book of Shadows backward to bring back the evil they vanquished and eventually strip them of their powers. ("Witch Trial")

ANDRAS, SPIRIT OF RAGE: Escalates existing anger into acts of violence in hopes of ascending to full demon status. ("Power Outage")

AXEL: To earn rewards and respect from the leaders of the Underworld, this Upper-Level demon hires Tracers to eliminate Sandmen. Without dreams, people will give in to anger and evil by acting out their issues in the waking world. An ambitious Tracer decides that killing the Charmed Ones is a faster career path, and that Axel is in his way, so he kills him. ("Sand Francisco Dreamin'")

BARBAS, DEMON OF FEAR: The Demon of Fear appears in human form once every thirteen hundred years on Friday the Thirteenth to feed on the fear of witches for survival. If he kills thirteen unmarried witches by midnight, he can escape the Underworld to terrorize witches every day. His victims are paralyzed and scared literally to death when he turns their greatest fears against them. He often employs his ability to mimic voices. Releasing the fear will defeat him. ("From Fear to Eternity," "Ms. Hellfire," and "Sympathy for the Demon")

BELTHAZOR: Cole Turner's demon alter ego, Belthazor is a monster of red and black visage. In human form Cole possesses the powers of an Upper-Level demon such as opening time portals. His shadow acts as a Triad spy and messenger. According to the Elders, this infamous, demonic soldier of fortune is most evil and vile.

He was sent by the Triad to kill the Charmed Ones. He tries driving Prue insane with an empathic gift, and uses anger to sever the Power of Three. However, loving Phoebe awakens his dormant humanity.

Belthazor destroys a bounty hunter to save Phoebe, and she fakes vanquishing him. When Cole goes undercover to spy on the Brotherhood of the Thorn, Belthazor is forced to emerge. Cole is tricked into becoming Belthazor and killing a witch. Belthazor/Cole becomes immune to potions of Belthazor flesh after an Alchemist transmutes his blood.

When Cole helps Phoebe escape from the Underworld, demon hunters pursue him relentlessly. If Cole uses his senses to locate an evil, the demon hunters can hone in on him. Cole calls on Belthazor to emerge to save Phoebe from a Sykes demon that's emulating him. Belthazor destroys Sykes with his Brotherhood athame, but before Cole regains control, he's struck by a power-stripping potion. Belthazor is gone, but the human, Cole, survives. ("Once upon a Time," "All Halliwell's Eve," "Sight Unseen," "Primrose Empath," "Power Outage," "Sleuthing with the Enemy," "The Demon Who Came in from the Cold," "Exit Strategy," "Look Who's Barking," "Charmed Again, Part One," "Hell Hath No Fury," and "Black as Cole")

BROTHERHOOD OF THE THORN: An organization of Upper-Level demons chosen by and loyal to The Source. Bound by a lifelong blood oath, they spread evil by more sophisticated means than mere killing, such as corporate takeovers and mergers. (See Demonic Hierarchy for specific agents.) ("The Demon Who Came in from the Cold" and "Exit Strategy")

CHILDREN (appearance only): Vicious killers, these unnamed demons appear as trapped children. An ice-cream truck that's driven by a mortal plays a song composed of the "Devil's Chord," which attracts them. The ice-cream truck is a portal into the "playground," a holding area where they are confined until the Nothing consumes them. ("We All Scream for Ice Cream")

CREE: Son of Orin the gypsy hunter, he emits energy that sears his victims' eyes and then kills them. He then removes their eyes. ("The Eyes Have It")

CRYTO, DEMON OF VANITY: Before he was condemned to the spirit world in the sixteenth century, Cryto gave people youth in exchange for their souls. He becomes corporeal when summoned into a shell of corpse skins and preys on the town until he's sent back into the ether. ("How to Make a Quilt out of Americans")

DANE: A henchman of Cole when Cole becomes The Source, Dane incites others in the High Council to challenge Cole's authority. After the Charmed Ones vanquish Cole, Dane is chosen as the next Source by the High Council. Since he is not linked by lineage or magic to The Source, he must step aside when the Seer becomes the surrogate mother for the next Source. He is killed when the fetus Source's overpowering magic consumes the Seer at her coronation. ("Long Live the Queen" and "Womb Raider")

DEMON OF ILLUSION: Traveling in a print of the classic film *Kill It Before It Dies*, this demon creates and spreads violence. The Charmed Ones enter the movie to vanquish it. He's destroyed when Prue burns the actual film frames he occupies. ("Chick Flick")

73

DEMON OF THE LAKE: A water being that dwells in a lake, this creature drowns people from the inside. Patty Halliwell died trying to kill it with electricity, which separates water particles. The demon sneaks up on its prey and sometimes appears as its last victim to lure the unsuspecting. Prue electrocutes the demon after Sam Wilder lets it take him over. ("P3 H2O")

DEMONIC BOUNTY HUNTERS: Unstoppable Lower-Level demons who are driven by greed. ("Lost and Bound")

DEX: An adviser to Cole when he becomes The Source and assumes leadership of the Underworld. ("The Importance of Being Phoebe")

DORIS: A partner of Cronyn the Sorcerer who cons Victor into marrying her in order to kidnap Piper's Charmed baby. She is vanquished with a spell and a generous dusting of unicorn horn. ("The Day the Magic Died")

DRAZI: A human-form demon, Drazi fell in love with a mortal woman, and now wants revenge on Cupid, who turned her affections to a mortal man. Cupid's ring, which he steals to spread hate, protects him from the Charmed Ones' vanquishing potion. Once Cupid's ring is removed, the potion turns him into a black puddle. ("Heartbreak City")

GAMMILL, A.K.A. THE COLLECTOR: Disfigured by a witch to make him as hideous outside as in, he shrinks women to five inches tall with a wand, then turns them into ceramic figurines. He is shrunk and vanquished by a spell. ("Size Matters")

GRIMLOCKS: Underground demons, they are human-form albinos with glowing red eyes. Grimlocks gain the ability to see auras of goodness by stealing the sight of kidnapped children. They kill generous, benevolent people by remote strangulation with a single hand closing into a fist. The aura-sight lasts for twenty-four hours as long as the source-child is alive. A potion of Schisnadra root kills it. ("Blind Sided")

HAWKER: Merchants at the Demonic Market, Hawker demons will obtain desired magical merchandise. ("Baby's First Demon")

JAVNA, A.K.A STEFAN: Several centuries old, Javna adopted the contemporary alias of Stefan, a New York photographer. His young human form attracts women, who are subjected to the Evil Eye that transfers their youth into his aging body. The rejuvenation process requires a week of ritual feeding once a year, and changes the victims into senile, elderly women. This premature aging is reversed when the Charmed Ones use the Hand of Fatima to turn the magic of the Evil Eye back on Javna, causing him to wither to dust. ("I've Got You Under My Skin")

JAYDA AND JENNA: Two female demons who are indebted to Saleel and agree to kill the Charmed Ones when he guarantees luck will be on their side. ("Lucky Charmed")

JERIC: An Egyptian demon who killed witches. Unable to vanquish him, the ancients mummified him instead. He was freed by the evil witch, Isis, and has spent millennia finding witch bodies for her spirit to inhabit. He was blown up by Piper. ("Y Tu Mummy También")

JUDGE, THE, AKA WILLIAM "FREE WILLY" HAMILTON: Posing as a human judge, this Upper-Level demon uses mortal criminals to spread evil. It assigns Guardians to protect the human host. Beastly in its natural form, the Judge is vanquished in fire by Cole Turner. ("The Honeymoon's Over")

JULIE: Assistant to Cole, The Source, her qualifications include the ability to shimmer two miles in thirty seconds, shape-shift, throw fire, and mimic voices. A seductress, she works with the Seer to turn Cole against Phoebe. Drawing on the power of The Source within, Phoebe kills her with fire. ("Saving Private Leo" and "We're Off to See the Wizard")

KAZI KING (AND HIS MINIONS): A base-level demon, the Kazi King makes his warriors from his own flesh and feels whatever they feel. When the King is vanquished by the Crone, his minions are vanquished as well. ("Sense and Sense Ability")

KEATS: An Upper-Level demon, he forms an alliance with the Queen of the Vampires to challenge the new Source. Cole reminds Keats that there are worse things than death and sets him afire to make the point. ("Bite Me")

KELLMAN: Operating as a business manager, this Upper-Level, human-form demon preys on athletes in need. In exchange for having their troubles erased, humans agree to undergo demonic training that destroys their humanity. The act of killing an innocent completes the transformation. ("Wrestling with Demons")

KRELL, A ZOTAR: A demonic bounty hunter, Krell tracks fugitive demons. Krell can't detect a demon in human form and has trouble tracking scent in a cemetery. Cole vanquishes him with an energy ball. ("Sleuthing with the Enemy")

KURZON: An Upper-Level demon, Kurzon was banished from the Underworld for leading a failed coup against The Source. He emerges as a contender for The Source's power, but makes the mistake of trusting the Seer. He is vanquished by a Power of Three spell. ("The Three Faces of Phoebe")

LAZARUS DEMON: This High-Level demon has the power to resurrect itself, and it attacks with telekinesis. It stays dead only if it's buried in a cemetery and, if exhumed, grows stronger the longer it's away from one. It appears in Cole's alternate reality. ("Marry-Go-Round" and "Centennial Charmed")

LIBRIS DEMONS: These demons are an integral component of evil's system to prevent demonic existence from being proven in the mortal realm. A reaper-type demon, the Libris lurk in places where humans are likely to produce unequivocal evidence that demons are real. In that event, the Libris beheads the too-curious human with a sickle. When the Charmed Ones vanquish a Libris, the demon's body disappears, a system safeguard so no physical evidence is ever found or preserved, but the sickle remains. ("Ex Libris")

LITVACK: A Level-Two demon with the power to see into minds and kill with fire. Because he is an Upper-Level Demon, he can issue magical energy weapons to his minions. Litvack has no tolerance for incompetence. He is immune to witches' powers and has gained favor with The Source by feeding him witches. ("Give Me a Sign")

LUDLOW: An Upper-Level demon, Ludlow defies the Firestarter and Piper's powers. He runs an academy surrounded by a formidable force-field and has the power to literally freeze with a snap of his fingers. Ludlow is vanquished by a Power of Three haiku. ("Lost and Bound")

LUKAS: He implants sin balls in paragons of good with a predisposition to one of the Seven Deadly Sins. The infected victims self-destruct within hours, condemning them to the Bottomless Pit of Everlasting Torment and consigning their souls to Lukas, who needs to collect seven souls to escape his private hell. Lukas is vanquished when the Charmed Ones infect him with multiple sin balls, and he is cast into the pit. ("Sin Francisco")

MALLICK: Assigned to kill a probation officer who rehabilitates juvenile offenders. ("Long Live the Queen")

MASSELIN: A reaper-type demon who feeds off terrified souls, he gives a band manager success in exchange for a steady supply of trusting young women. He dissolves when Prue forces a poison potion down his throat. ("Devil's Music")

MINION OF BARBAS: Bribed to join Barbas on the ledge above the fiery pit, he teaches the Demon of Fear to project illusions and suggestions. Once they are free, he urges Barbas to use the powers Cole acquired in demonic purgatory to take over the Underworld. Barbas destroys him with one of his own fireballs. ("Sympathy for the Demon")

MISCELLANEOUS DEMONS THAT THREATEN SPIRITS—RIGORS, ZOMBIES, AND CREEPERS: Vanquishing the leader of the reaper-type Creepers kills the entire clan; potion required. ("Necromancing the Stone")

MORDOCK: With aspirations to rule the Underworld, Mordock spends decades learning how to free the Titans. He believes he can use their power to bring himself to glory. Meta incinerates him. ("Oh, My Goddess, Part One")

NECRON: He exists between life and death and uses electrical energy to feed off the life forces of others. The Sea Hag tries to collect a mermaid's immortal essence to pay her debt to him. He is vanquished by a Power of Three spell, and the Charmed Ones survive the explosive force of this skeletal being's demise. ("A Witch's Tail, Part Two")

ORIN: A gypsy hunter, Orin was blinded by the combined powers of several gypsy High Priestesses decades ago. The gypsy spirits that Ava and the Charmed Ones conjure with a vanquishing spell repel the magic of the Evil Eye, killing Orin. ("The Eyes Have It")

PARASITES: Cursed by a witch, this pair of white-haired demons lost their powers. They now feed on the magic of others to survive, and hire a Hawker to kidnap Wyatt, whose protective force-field is a self-sustaining source of endless magic. ("Baby's First Demon")

POWER BROKERS: Identical in every respect, these demons collect, trade, buy, and sell demonic powers. They store these disembodied powers in human hosts to prevent them from being stolen. If the powers are left too long, the human becomes disoriented, paranoid, violent, and dies. ("The Fifth Halliwheel")

RAT PACK: Demons who blend into human establishments disguised as rats, they enlist greedy humans to help with illegal fund-raising schemes. Evil needs money to operate in the mortal world, which makes the rats willing to deal with the Charmed Ones in exchange for an innocent's life. They kill and devour anyone who crosses them, including their own. ("Trial by Magic")

SALEEL: A lowly reptile demon, Saleel kills leprechauns and uses their shillelaghs to summon the rainbow highway. An aspiring leader of the Underworld, he buys grassroots support with luck. He is easily vanquished with a potion if he can be found. The Charmed Ones unite with the leprechauns to overdose Saleel with bad luck, which brings a meteor crashing down on him. ("Lucky Charmed")

SCAVENGER: A silvery Lower-Level demon that shoots lengths of cord from its wrists to snare victims; it feeds on the kills of other demons. ("Black as Cole")

SEA HAG: A witch of the sea, she exerts control over the water environment, such as calling hurricanes, rain, and tidal waves. She gives Mylie, a mermaid, legs, with the understanding that if Mylie doesn't find love, she'll give up her immortal life essence, which the Hag owes to the demon Necron. Phoebe kills her with an auger shell, which absorbs her life force and leaves only salt. ("A Witch's Tail, Part One")

SEEKERS: Vampire-like demons that feed on information extracted by piercing a victim's brain stem. They have the ability to float and levitate others. Sent by The Source to track down Belthazor, they are vanquished by a Power of Three spell. ("Death Takes a Halliwell")

SHADOW: A spy for the Triad, the Shadow disconnects from its host to carry messages back to the Underworld. Initially associated with Cole Turner, it later partners with Sykes. ("All Halliwell's Eve" and "Black as Cole")

SHAX: The Source's assassin, this black-and-white demon arrives as a tornado wind. The vanquishing spell from the Book of Shadows finally works against him when the Power of Three is reconstituted with Paige to chant it. ("All Hell Breaks Loose" and "Charmed Again, Part One")

STANLEY: A minion of Cronyn's, he's duped into believing that his name will become legend if he dies trying to kill the Charmed Ones on the night of the twice-blessed child's birth. ("The Day the Magic Died")

SYKES: Black with red striations, Sykes emulates Belthazor. Posing as an assistant district attorney, he is partnered with Cole's old Shadow messenger, uses energy balls, and kills witches with Cole's athame. Belthazor uses the same knife to vanquish him. ("Black as Cole")

TALL MAN, THE: Confined for centuries in the Seer's unbreakable cage, he is a portal to other dimensions. The power of The Source growing within Phoebe destroys him. ("Womb Raider")

TRACER DEMONS: Lower-Level demons, they track magical beings through different dimensions for bounty. One is blown up by Piper. ("Sand Francisco Dreamin'")

TROXA: Only visible in the cold, he's tricked by Cole to steal the Book of Shadows. When he's caught in Prue's crystal, the Triad vanquishes him in fire. ("Sight Unseen")

TULL, SON OF NAIDES: To avenge his father and cure his brother, Tull uses a dead satyr's pipe to trick wood nymphs into opening the Eternal Spring. He drinks of the forbidden water and becomes immortal and invincible. Since the Charmed Ones can't vanquish him, they turn Tull into another immortal but harmless entity—a tree. ("Nymphs Just Wanna Have Fun")

TURNER, COLE: Third demonic incarnation; See Belthazor and The Source for information on his first and second demonic lives.

Vanquished by the Charmed Ones as The Source, Cole is sent to demonic purgatory, where he absorbs the powers of the fallen demons and kills the Beast. He returns to the mortal world with invincible powers. The only thing greater than his love for Phoebe is his determination to do good things, but he can't always control the evil within. When Paige gives Cole another chance at humanity, he drinks a potion that transfers his powers to

Barbas, but takes them back to save the sisters. He eventually must accept that Phoebe no longer loves him. Not wanting to live without Phoebe, he tries everything he can to destroy himself, but he will not be vanquished—even by the Power of Three. Out of options, he becomes an avatar and alters history with his new power. He is aware of the changed reality, but now he has only Belthazor's limited power and protection. Phoebe vanquishes him with a potion, and Cole is truly gone. ("Witch Way Now," "A Witch's Tail, Parts One and Two," "Siren Song," "Witch in Time," "Sam I Am," and "Centennial Charmed")

VINCERES: This demonic assassin is timeless, immune to witches' magic, and thought to be unstoppable. Afflicted with an empathic gift, he passes the ability on to Prue. Confident of his invincibility, Vinceres is unprepared when Prue's astral self invades his body and kills him with overwhelming human emotion. ("Primrose Empath")

WOOGY MAN: A shadow demon of pure evil, it exists in the Spiritual Nexus in the land under the Manor. Released by an earthquake when Phoebe was five, the Woogy Man was trapped by a rhyme Grams taught her granddaughters in a story. When another earthquake unleashes the evil essence again, it tries taking over the Manor and turning Phoebe to the dark side. Finding the strength to fight back, she recites the rhyming spell to trap the demon below. ("Is There a Woogy in the House?")

XAVIER, SON OF NAIDES: Xavier rejects his younger brother Tull's plan to use the satyr's pipe to trick the wood nymphs into revealing the Eternal Spring. Xavier loses an arm to Piper's power, and is vanquished by a potion before his brother finds the lifesaving spring. ("Nymphs Just Wanna Have Fun")

79

DIGNITARIES

DANTALIAN, DARK PRIESTESS: To gain the power in the Charmed Ones' Book of Shadows, Dantalian conspires with the warlock Zile to turn the Halliwell witches evil. After Zile's Black Wedding to Prue, Dantalian betrays him and steals the Book, but underestimates the Power of Three. Love enables the sisters to break the evil spell and vanquish the Priestess with their restored Book of Shadows and powers of good. ("Bride and Gloom")

DARK PRIEST: One performs a Black Wedding that unites Phoebe and Cole to each other and evil. Another officiates at Cole's coronation as The Source, and another when the Seer ascends as the surrogate Source. ("Marry-Go-Round," "We're Off to See the Wizard," and "Womb Raider")

GHOSTS

FRANKIE AND LULU: Gangster lovers who robbed jewelry stores in the 1950s, their ghosts enter the present when Clyde opens a time portal for Leo and Paige. They possess Phoebe and Cole, rob a jewelry store and bridal shop, and go to a church to get married. Clyde captures both spirits and sends them back. ("A Paige from the Past")

LANG, RICK, AND NATHAN: Boyhood friends of Leo Wyatt, they enlisted to fight in World War II together and were in the same unit at Guadalcanal. The Langs blame Leo for leaving them in a medical tent that blew up. To get revenge sixty years later, they start killing people close to Leo. Piper is dead just long enough to chant the spell to vanquish the ghosts. ("Saving Private Leo")

LUNDY, ELIAS: The Van Lewen family chauffeur was obsessed with Martha Van Lewen, who shot and killed him. To make her suffer, Elias lingered as a ghost with a lightning-like power to inflict pain and death. He kills her husband and two sons, but the Charmed Ones save her grandson, Matthew. Although Elias hides his bones so the witches can't destroy him with a potion, Martha removes the object of his wrath—herself. The ghost is vanquished when Martha commits suicide. ("Reckless Abandon")

WARD, JACKSON: Born in 1928, this convicted murderer was the last inmate executed at Alcatraz in 1963. Out for revenge, he haunts his cell until a spirit from hell helps him escape in the body of a dead tour guide. Having acquired the ability to wield physical things, Ward kills Judge Renault and a former D.A.'s son by stabbing them thirteen times. His ghost is vanquished when Prue dies to cast the spell on the astral plane. The fiery spirit takes his soul to hell. ("The Power of Two")

INANIMATE OBJECTS

AUGER SHELL: The auger shell drains the life force of a being when placed over its heart. ("A Witch's Tail, Part One")

DRAGONBLADE: A magical knife with the power to trap human souls. ("Enter the Demon")

GRIMOIRE: The evil version of the Book of Shadows, needed in The Source's coronation ceremony. It contains the rituals and spells of black magic, including a spell to resurrect and to transfer The Source's powers. The pages are black, the script white. It protects itself from good and cannot be destroyed. Leo buries the *Grimoire* deep in a West Andes mountain so that its evil powers may never be used again. ("We're Off to See the Wizard")

MONKEY TOTEM: Centuries ago a sorcerer created a monkey to steal his enemies' senses, but the sorcerer mistreated the little fella, so the monkey stole his master's voice and was turned into a wooden totem as punishment. ("Sense and Sense Ability")

NINJA: Used as a poppet to cure Piper, the action-figure doll is animated by an awakening spell. It spreads Piper's deadly disease with the tip of its sword until the reversal spell turns it back into a harmless toy. ("Awakened")

NOTHING, THE: A vortex within the magical playground that consumes the childlike demons, it does not distinguish between good and evil when it feeds. ("We All Scream for Ice Cream")

SEER'S CAGE, THE: Made of unbreakable magic by the Seer, the cage imprisoned the Tall Man for centuries. The Seer uses it to hold the Charmed Ones when she becomes the surrogate Source. While no magic can escape the cage, it allows magic to enter. Once the Seer is vanquished, the cage loses its power. ("Womb Raider")

MORTALS

ALTMAN, GAIL: A lifelong friend of Penelope Halliwell and member of her coven, she was called Aunt Gail by the Halliwell sisters. Old age and cancer drove her to steal the Charmed Ones' powers so she could entice Cryto from the spirit world into a shell of corpse skins. Restored in physical form, the Demon of Vanity makes Gail young, ages her friends to death, and trades youth for souls in town. When she tries to protect Piper, Prue, and Phoebe, Gail becomes Cryto's last victim. ("How to Make a Quilt out of Americans")

ANIMAL-MEN: Animals that were turned into men with a novelty spell, but retained their animal instincts. Rabbit and Snake murder Pig and go on a crime spree, get their wish to stay human, but are caged in jail for their crimes. ("Animal Pragmatism")

BERMAN, WHITAKER: A jilted, paralyzed dream researcher uses his lab's dream-inducement system to violate women's sleep. Proving the old adage that one who dies in a dream dies in real life, Berman throws women who reject him off a tall building in their dreams. Although they die in bed, they sustain massive internal injuries similar to those of suicidal jumpers. When Prue becomes a target, she uses her powers to hurl Berman off the building. He is crushed in his sleep. ("The Dream Sorcerer")

CARLTON, JEFF: The band manager for Dishwalla, he made a pact with Masselin. In exchange for success, he supplies the demon with women's souls to consume. After the Charmed Ones vanquish Masselin, Carlton is arrested for kidnapping. ("Devil's Music")

DAVID AND MICKEY: Two thugs who kidnap Max Franklin, a young witch with the power of psychokinesis. They plan to exploit Max's powers to open locks and disable alarms for them. Prue foils their plan when she uses her power to lock them in the bank vault they planned to rob. ("Secrets and Guys")

GIBBS: The owner of a pawn shop, he murdered Tyra L. Wilson when she witnessed his illegal business dealings. Tyra's father, Cleavant, diligently hunts for someone to testify against him. When it's obvious no one ever will, the ghost of Charleen Hughes haunts the pawn shop, scaring Gibbs into confessing. ("Ex Libris")

HELLFIRE, MS.: A human hit woman hired by Bane Jessup to kill the Charmed Ones, she dies when Prue repels her bullets. ("Ms. Hellfire")

JACKMAN: An FBI agent with a genealogy going back to the colonial witch hunters, he blackmails the Charmed Ones with a dossier of their activities. The Halliwells capture Selena, who is a witch hunter, according to Jackman. They learn that she is really a witch, and that Jackman intends to burn Selena at the stake. Amulets, buried by Jackman, prevent the sisters' magic from working, forcing them to use human skills to save the dormant witch. Jackman shoots at Phoebe, but Cole reverses their positions so the bullet kills Jackman instead. ("Witch Way Now")

JESSUP, BANE: Working with Barbas, he hires the hit woman, Ms. Hellfire, to kill thirteen witches, including the Charmed Ones. Although the plan fails and he goes to jail, he admires Prue. ("Ms. Hellfire")

LOHMAN, ERIC: A reporter for *The Bay Weekly*, Lohman sees Prue levitate a kidnapped boy. He threatens to publish stories depicting her and Andy in the worst possible light if they don't tell what they know. Since time is critical to saving her Innocent, Prue plays along. When Eric's neck is broken, she recovers the video evidence he took of the sisters' powers. ("Blind Sided")

MILLER, EDWARD: A slumlord who took city money without improving his properties, he evicts his tenants. Angry after superhero Phoebe dangles him off the roof, he videotapes her and her masked sisters in action. When he threatens to blackmail the Halliwells for $50,000 a month, Cole incinerates him. ("Witches in Tights")

SUTTER: In 1873 Sutter terrorizes a western town to acquire interests in property so he can cash in when the railroad comes through. However, when he murders Bo Lightfeather, and nobody tries to stop him, the town is thrown into a time loop by a Native American curse. The loop is broken when Cole and Prue convince the townspeople to stand up for Bo. Sutter ends up in jail. ("The Good, the Bad, and the Cursed")

WESLEY AND PALMER: Thieves who steal an Egyptian urn. The Guardian of the Urn kills Wesley with a spider, and Palmer with a scorpion. ("Feats of Clay")

WIKE, ANDREW: Wike provides a front for the Rat Pack demons' money-laundering scheme. When he confesses on tape to killing Angela Provazolli, the demons kill and devour him for exposing them to danger. ("Trial by Magic")

82

MYTHOLOGICAL MANIFESTATIONS

BANSHEE: Banshees were once witches and feed on souls in great emotional pain. With long white hair and fangs, they are drawn to cries of misery. Their piercing scream kills mortals, who drown in their own blood due to burst blood vessels. If a Banshee calls a witch, she is turned into one of the screaming demons. The transformation becomes permanent once the new Banshee makes its first kill. There is no reversal spell. Accepting the cause of the pain before the first kill releases the witch from the Banshee curse. ("Look Who's Barking")

FOUR HORSEMEN OF THE APOCALYPSE: Chosen by The Source, personifications of War, Death, Famine, and Strife are set upon the world in times of rising hatred and anger to promote the end of the world. Failure, such as the loss of World War II and the absence of nuclear conflict during the Cuban Missile Crisis, ends with the destruction of the inadequate team until another opportunity arrives. A new team is appointed to foster chaos when the true new millennium begins. When War becomes trapped on another plane with Prue, he is not retrieved in time to meet the team's deadline. The Source vanquishes the Horsemen and postpones the apocalypse due to the prevalence of good in the world. ("Apocalypse, Not")

FURIES: Drawn to anger, these female entities with talons and dark-lined flesh punish and kill evildoers by making them hear the cries of their victims. They do not differentiate the gravity of evil deeds and handle petty crime as harshly as murder. ("Hell Hath No Fury")

HECATE: The Queen of the Underworld comes to earth every two hundred years to put an Innocent under a spell to marry her. She will then bear a child that appears human but is completely demonic. Known as Jade D'mon, Hecate is thwarted when Elliot Spencer's human bride, Allison, declares her love. Unmarried and childless, Hecate is sent back to the Underworld by the power of a fourteenth-century Italian knife called a poignard that bears the inscription "I shall not rest until the demon is vanquished." ("The Wedding from Hell")

MULO: A gypsy designation for a dead person who appears in the body of another dead person to warn someone living. Lydia uses a dead patient to warn her niece, Dr. Ava Nicolae, that Orin the gypsy hunter is after her. ("The Eyes Have It")

SIREN: As a mortal, she loved married men who were held blameless for their infidelities. The women of the village burned her to death and her rage turned her into a Siren. The Siren mesmerizes married men and calls their wives with her haunting song, then destroys the couples with the very flames that once consumed her. ("Siren's Song")

TROLLS: Beings of the Enchanted Kingdom along with fairies and elves, trolls desire to take command from the fairy king and queen. They haunt the 'tween places hoping to capture the fairy princess, Thistle, who is being protected by Kate, a human child. The trolls' coup is thwarted when the Charmed Ones, seeing through innocent eyes, trick them into running through a bonfire, which consumes them. ("Once Upon a Time")

SEERS

CRONE, THE: Old and wise, the Crone foresees that Wyatt Matthew Halliwell has the power to end evil. She hopes to prevent or postpone that outcome by removing threats to the Charmed baby and convinces the leaders of the Underworld to forbid attacks on him. ("Baby's First Demon" and "Sense and Sense Ability")

ORACLE: Seer to The Source, she needs permission to solidify and gets impressions of the future in a crystal ball that swirls with dark smoke and radiates energy bolts. Cole kills her with an energy ball. ("Charmed Again, Parts One and Two")

SEER, THE: Seer for The Source for thousands of years, she foresees the latest Source's destruction by the Charmed Ones. When The Source releases the Hollow, she uses Cole as a vessel for the Hollow to vanquish The Source. The Hollow is contained again, but she tricks Cole into becoming The Source and works to sever the bond between him and Phoebe. She convinces Cole to marry Phoebe in a dark ceremony, then plots to eliminate Phoebe after their son, the most evil of beings, is conceived, transferring the baby from Phoebe's womb to her womb. She is vanquished by The Source within her when his power is repelled by the Power of Three. She still exists in Cole's alternate Avatar reality. ("Charmed and Dangerous," "The Three Faces of Phoebe," "Marry-Go-Round," "Womb Raider," and "Centennial Charmed")

SHAPE-SHIFTERS

"DR." ALASTER, A CHAMELEON: Sent by The Source to spy on the Halliwells, his cover as a lamp is blown by Cole. He has the powers of regeneration and telekinesis. ("Brain Drain")

KIERAN DEMONS: Manipulative vixens with personal agendas who can morph to look like anyone. (Kaia and an unnamed dancer in "The Importance of Being Phoebe")

MARSHAL, FRITZ, AND CYNDA: The Halliwells' new neighbors possess the ability to alter their human appearances as well as adopt animal forms. They plot to steal the Book of Shadows to weaken the witches and gain the Book's power. The evil trio is destroyed by a Power of Three protection spell. ("Thank You for Not Morphing")

WEBSTER, HANNAH: Subservient to Rex Buckland, Hannah works with the warlock to acquire the Charmed Ones' powers. She lights fires with her breath and shape-shifts into a panther. Foiled by the witches' powers, she inadvertently kills Rex and is vanquished by The Source in flames. ("The Truth Is out There . . . And It Hurts" and "Wicca Envy")

SORCERERS

CRONYN: Forced to use taxis and cell phones during a universal failure of magic, this sorcerer plots to kidnap Piper's baby. ("The Day the Magic Died")

TEMPUS: Human in form, the Devil's sorcerer manipulates time at will, always for evil gain. He moves back into the Underworld when the Charmed Ones accelerate time, forcing him from the time frame he was in. Tempus's temporal power is also required to undo widespread mortal knowledge that demons and witches exist. The Source orders this done. ("Déjà Vu All Over Again" and "All Hell Breaks Loose")

UNNAMED SORCERER: An evil Suit who uses magic to manipulate the financial markets. When a young employee named Brooke rejects him, he curses her and her true love to live as a wolf and an owl respectively, each for twelve hours a day. They are never human at the same time. The Suit is vanquished when Christopher, freed from his owl form by an eclipse, and Brooke kiss. ("Magic Hour")

SOURCE, THE

THE ORIGINAL: The supreme evil being is The Source of All Evil. He sent Rex Buckland and Hannah Webster to identify and destroy the Charmed Ones. Normally lying low, he surfaces when evil has been exposed in the mortal world. To stop the Charmed Ones from reconstituting, he possesses people close to Paige to turn her evil. Determined to destroy the Power of Three, The Source uses mental illusion to convince Piper to relinquish all the Charmed powers. Weakened by the effort, he is injured by Cole's energy balls. He resurfaces again when he tries to acquire the Firestarter's power. Fearing the Charmed Ones, he tries to strip them of and acquire their powers. He does not anticipate the Seer's betrayal. At her instigation, Cole becomes the Hollow and uses The Source's energy balls to weaken him. The Source is vanquished with a Power of Three spell that calls on the power of the entire Warren line. ("Give Me a Sign," "Apocalypse Not," "All Hell Breaks Loose," "Charmed Again, Part Two," "Brain Drain," "Lost and Bound," and "Charmed and Dangerous")

85

TURNER, COLE: Cole becomes the new Source after he temporarily consumes the Hollow. The power of the Hollow is returned to its sacred box, but the power of The Source is transferred to Cole in the process. Although he tries, he cannot overcome the power of the evil that emerges within him. However, Cole's love for Phoebe is so strong that The Source, his evil side, incorporates it and warns the Seer not to target Phoebe again. Cole's human identity recedes, becoming a mere whisper in his head. Without revealing the nature of the ceremony, Cole marries Phoebe in a Dark Wedding. Cole cements his position as the new Source, manipulates Phoebe with love, convinces her to leave the Manor, and impregnates her. He proposes a merger of Underworld factions to fight the forces of good from a position of strength. Phoebe discovers Cole's identity as The Source just before his coronation. He tries to transfer The Source's powers to the wizard, but Phoebe unwittingly stops the process. Phoebe chooses to become his queen, but her inherent goodness does not allow her to live a life of evil. She helps vanquish Cole with the Power of Three. ("Charmed and Dangerous," "The Three Faces of Phoebe," "Marry-Go-Round," "The Fifth Halliwheel," "Saving Private Leo," "Bite Me," "We're Off to See the Wizard," and "Long Live the Queen")

HEIR: Conceived under conditions dictated by the Seer, The Source's heir asserts himself from Phoebe's womb. Phoebe taps into his fire power to kill an Underworld guard and Julie, Cole's demon assistant. After Cole is vanquished, the demon seed takes a dim view of anyone who criticizes Cole, particularly Paige. He completely takes over Phoebe when she uses his power to kill the Tall Man. Too powerful for the Seer to handle when transferred to her womb, he annihilates everyone at the Seer's coronation, as well as destroying himself when his killing power is repelled by the Power of Three spell. ("The Fifth Halliwheel," "We're Off to See the Wizard," and "Womb Raider")

SPIRITS

ARMOND, THE NECROMANCER: A century ago this spirit with dominion over the dead was a living demon ruler. He absorbs the spirits of magical beings to experience being alive for brief periods of time. ("Necromancing the Stone")

BIG MAMA: An evil entity formed from the residual energy of all the demons killed in the Manor. The Charmed Ones call a witch doctor to cleanse the house of this manifestation. ("House Call")

GUARDIANS, THE: Assigned by an Upper-Level demon, these spirits inhabit criminal mortals. They protect the host in exchange for souls, which are removed through an inverted, triangular rune carved in the victim's forehead. They can be killed by thrusting a stake through the rune on their forehead. The mortal host is unharmed when a Guardian vacates. ("The Honeymoon Is Over")

86

KALI: The spirit of this evil sorceress appears in reflective surfaces, such as mirrors. Surrounded by flames with green catlike eyes, she covets witches' powers. When Aviva, a witch wannabe, objects to harming anyone, Kali possesses the teenager's body to steal the Halliwells' magic. Piper's freeze separates the spirit from the human girl, and Prue hurls Kali into a mirror. Phoebe shatters the spirit's reflection, extinguishing her existence. ("The Fourth Sister")

TERRA, CREATED LIFE ESSENCE: Made from the alchemist Kierkan's blood, this artificially created soul escapes. She possesses human bodies, displacing their souls, and vacates the vessels with a knife to the heart. After Terra inhabits and kills Piper, she's tricked into using her alchemist's ability to bring Piper back. She does it in the form of Leo, whose body she now inhabits. Back in form, the Charmed Ones use a Power of Three spell to dispossess Leo and vanquish Terra. ("Coyote Piper")

YAMA: The Chinese Gatekeeper of Hell appears as a mounted warrior. Helmeted with glowing eyes, he carries a spear, which impales ghosts who have not been properly buried, to capture their souls. The good or evil nature of his victims is irrelevant. ("Dead Man Dating")

SUPERNATURAL BEINGS

LORDS OF WAR: Helena and Gabriel Statler belong to a clan of warriors who have incited all wars since time began. Their weapons are the symbols of their power and make them immune to the weapons of mortal men. During the Crimean War, Brianna, a witch in the Warren line, separated Gabriel from his crystal sword causing him to lose his powers. The sword is recovered, but to end his disgrace, Gabriel must steal back his abilities using the sword, which absorbs the power of anyone it impales. Prue, a firstborn witch and therefore the strongest, becomes a target. However, when the sword impales Gabriel, the weapon absorbs him and dissipates. ("Which Prue Is It Anyway?")

TITANS: Three Greek gods, Cronus, Demetrius, and Meta, were entombed in ice on a mountaintop by empowered mortals three thousand years ago. Vowing vengeance on the Elders for this affront, they kidnap Whitelighters and take their orbing powers after they are freed by a demon named Mordock. Meta, the female, turns the guardian angels to stone with her glowing eyes. As soon as the Titans absorb the power to orb, the stones crumble to dust, killing the victims. Titans also have the power of fire. Cronus incinerates Meta rather than deal with Demetrius's loyalty to her. In an original time line, the Titans gained dominion over the world, which they ruled with absolute power and cruelty. However, because Chris Perry comes back in time to assist the Charmed Ones, Cronus and Demetrius are vanquished by Piper's wrath. As the Goddess of the Earth, she can't be harmed by the Titans' powers and opens a rift that sends them straight to hell. ("Oh, My Goddess, Parts One and Two")

TRIAD: Very high in the evil hierarchy, this council of three hooded human-form demons with black eyes has spent the first two years of the Charmed Ones' existence sending demons out to kill them, including Belthazor. Cole vanquishes them. ("Be Careful What You Witch For," "Magic Hour," and "Power Outage")

YENLO: A student of Zen, Yenlo is angry when he is not chosen as the Zen Master's successor. He is stabbed while trying to kill the master and escapes into Limbo with the injured old man. He can access the mortal realm for brief periods through water surfaces, and he resists the portal to reincarnation for fear of appropriate judgment. He is defeated when the Charmed Ones infiltrate Limbo and trap his soul in a knife called the Dragonblade. ("Enter the Demon")

VAMPIRES

QUEEN: Vampires were banished from the Underworld by the old Source when the Queen sold him out to his enemies. Holy water, a wooden stake, garlic, or a cross may help fight a Queen, but they will not eliminate her. A Power of Three spell is needed. Her minions constantly add to their numbers by turning humans. They are immune to witch magic, they travel as bats, and a Queen's entire line dies when she does. ("Bite Me")

ROWAN: Loyal servant to the Queen of the Vampires, he is responsible for drawing the Queen's attention to the Charmed Ones as possible converts. Phoebe kills him with a stake to the heart. ("Bite Me")

ANTON: An immortal who empowers a protective amulet, he turns the Halliwells' ancestor witch, P. Russell, from good to evil. When they fail to steal her cousins' powers in 1924, he waits until she's reborn as Phoebe Halliwell. His attempt to install P. Russell in Phoebe's body and steal the Charmed powers fails because, unlike the three cousins in the past, the three sisters are bound by love and magic. Anton is destroyed when Prue deflects one of P. Russell's fireballs. ("Pardon My Past")

ARNON: He senses great powers but he only has the power to strangle someone with a thought. To acquire more power, he latches on to a teenage artist named Kevin who has the power to make his drawings come alive. Kevin turns Arnon into a super edition of his own alter ego, The Aggressor. Arnon kills an Elder and steals his powers, but he is still vulnerable and Piper blows him up. The powers he stole live on and find their rightful heir. ("Witches in Tights")

BACARRA, FROM THE FUTURE: Cole from the future sends Bacarra back in time to warn present-day Cole that Phoebe will die if she keeps interfering with Death's efforts to claim her latest boyfriend. Bacarra plots with his present-day self to rule the Underworld in Cole's place, which will be possible with knowledge he now has from the future. They steal the Book of Shadows, strip the Charmed Ones' power, and vanquish Paige and Phoebe with fireballs. ("Witch in Time")

BACARRA, IN THE PRESENT: Scruffy-looking and desperate, Bacarra is stalking an invisible witch when his future self proposes they work together to take over the Underworld. ("Witch in Time")

BUCKLAND, REX: Prue's new boss at Buckland Auction House is close to Hannah Webster, another employee. Their evil natures are revealed when Rex sends Hecate a fertility icon as a wedding present and suggests watching football players get injured for fun. He tricks Prue into releasing the warlock Matthew Tate to help them steal the Charmed Ones' powers. When Matthew fails and it becomes obvious the Charmed Ones' magic is too powerful to defeat, Rex frames Prue, Piper, and Phoebe for theft, murder, and jailbreak. Faced with prison, the Charmed Ones give Rex their powers. Unknown to all, Leo reverses the spell, returning the magic. Rex is killed by Hannah's panther form. His remains are sent to hell in flames. ("I've Got You under My Skin," "The Wedding from Hell," "The Witch Is Back," and "Wicca Envy")

BURNS, JEREMY: Jeremy works as a reporter for the *San Francisco Chronicle* and begins dating Piper shortly after Grams dies. Although Piper is unaware of her magical destiny, Jeremy has been courting her, waiting until the Charmed Ones' suppressed magic is restored. Armed with an athame, Jeremy corners Piper in an elevator. He intends to kill Piper for her powers as well as those of her sisters. Piper freezes him and returns to the Manor for help. Although a spell from the Book of Shadows breaks her romantic bond with Jeremy and impales him with thorns, the warlock is not vanquished until the Charmed Ones repeat the words inscribed on the back of the Spirit Board: "The Power of Three will set us free." This is the first vanquish the Charmed Ones perform. ("Something Wicca This Way Comes")

CAT KILLER, UNNAMED: He attacks Katrina, the Halliwells' familiar-turned-human, to stop her from guiding future familiars. Without the enchanted creatures to guide them, witches are vulnerable. The warlock is thrown into Piper's and Leo's memories with Paige and Phoebe, who replay his murder of the cat, Kit, to prevent it. Phoebe kills him with his own athame. ("Cat House")

COLLECTORS, THE: Not to be confused with Gammill the Collector, each of these demons is equipped with a needlelike finger that drains information from human minds. Two collectors seek the key to translating the *Akashic Records*, a complete history of everything always. Their insatiable hunger for knowledge is their downfall. The Charmed Ones stop the magical download of Eric Bragg, the only human who will ever know the key, and arrange for the warlocks to drain each other to death. ("They're Everywhere")

DEVLIN: Planning to take over the Underworld, Devlin uses the Ring of Inspiration to capture the world's muses. To build up his minions, he kills and steals powers from other evil entities, then sends his empowered followers to distract the Charmed Ones, giving Devlin an opening to capture their muses. Convinced that many warlocks will succeed where one or two have failed, and depriving the sisters of inspiration, Devlin's faction infiltrates P3. Most are killed when they are too blinded by strobelights to blink, and others flee. Devlin is defeated by Cole's human tackle, Piper's potion, and a Power of Three spell. ("Muse to My Ears")

DRAGON: A powerful line of warlocks who breathe fire from their mouths, have the power to fly, and have supernatural strength. One Dragon warlock has a stronger than usual hatred for witches because they vanquished his father. Working with the Triad, he recruits a genie to destroy the Charmed Ones. Although Prue is killed in the ensuing events, the evil deed is undone and the Dragon is vanquished when the remorseful genie cooperates with the Charmed Ones. ("Be Careful What You Witch For")

EAMES: This warlock acquired several powers from murdered witches to implement a plan to destroy all Whitelighters. When he acquires the power to orb Up There, the Charmed Ones are waiting. Acquiring Whitelighter powers includes acquiring their vulnerabilities. Eames is destroyed by Darklighter poison. The witches use a spell to hasten his certain demise. ("Blinded by the Whitelighter")

GAVIN: A warlock from the future, Gavin shoots a lethal beam of light from a third eye in his forehead. He has been sent back to kill everyone connected with making a vaccine against his kind, including the unborn baby of the Charmed Ones' Innocent. There is no reference to him in the Book of Shadows because he doesn't exist yet. However, jamming a crowbar in his third eye puts an end to him. His remains are swept into a cloudlike, blue funnel that opens in midair. ("The Truth Is out There . . . And It Hurts")

JANE: The warlock girlfriend of Malcolm, she has fire at her fingertips. On the pretext of wanting to sell an heirloom, she brings the painting that imprisons Malcolm to Prue. Outsmarted by Phoebe, she sets the painting on fire and burns with her warlock lover. ("The Painted World")

KANE: Adviser to warlocks, he's a coconspirator of Cronyn in the plot to steal Piper's baby. Phoebe and Paige beat him in a physical fight during a magical power outage. ("The Day the Magic Died")

MALCOLM: He's imprisoned in an old painting after using his X-ray vision to read a Latin phrase under the paint. He spends seventy years ducking fireballs and swords. When Phoebe sends the cat into the painting with the escape phrase for Prue and Piper, Malcolm reveals his power to blink from one spot to another. He frees himself but wants the Charmed Ones' powers. He underestimates Phoebe, who drags him and his warlock lover back into the burning painting, where they die. ("The Painted World")

NICHOLAS: He kills by heating his victims from within and hopes to acquire the powers of all three Halliwell witches after Phoebe is born. Nicholas agrees to postpone killing young Prue and Piper in exchange for a blessing from Patty that makes a ring immune to the Power of Three. Thwarted when Grams binds the Charmed Ones' magic, he returns to the Manor every year on the same day at the same time to see if the powers have been restored. To save themselves in 1999, the sisters go back to March 24, 1975, and convince their mother to neutralize the immunity blessing. Nicholas is vanquished with a spell Grams added to the Book of Shadows following their sojourn in the past. ("That '70s Episode")

RODRIGUEZ: Posing as a cop from internal affairs, the warlock investigates Andy Trudeau. When he finds out that Prue Halliwell is the witch Andy is protecting, he kills his human partner. Determined to defeat the Charmed Ones, he accepts the help of Tempus. The Time Demon repeatedly resets the day, allowing the warlock to learn from his mistakes. After Rodriguez kills Andy, Prue repels his lethal fireball, vanquishing him. ("The Power of Two" and "Déjà Vu All Over Again")

ROWE, GREG AND PAUL: Anxious to fulfill the Prophesy of the Rowe Coven, the two brothers must turn their half brother, Brendan, away from the priesthood to evil. Together the three will become the most powerful force for evil ever known. Brendan believes they all must die to prevent the evil triangle, but Prue has faith in his goodness. Brendan prevails to become a priest after his brothers kill each other. ("When Bad Warlocks Go Good")

SHADOW: A black cat familiar who mixed a lethal potion by dropping vials off a mantel, subsequently killing his witch and becoming a warlock. He has until the new moon to purge all vestiges of his previous existence to become immortal. For Shadow, this means completing nine feline lives. When he attacks and kills Innocents, the Charmed Ones have no choice but to kill him—over and over. He is vanquished by the combined pain of his nine deaths brought on by a Charmed potion and spell. ("Pre Witched")

TATE, MATTHEW: In 1692, Melinda Warren imprisons Matthew in a locket in retaliation for his betrayal. Prue inadvertently sets him free. When she uses her power against him, he copies it and becomes immune to its effect. Intent on killing all three Halliwell witches and taking their powers, he underestimates the Charmed Ones' ability to overcome difficulties. With Melinda's help, he's returned to the locket with the original spell. ("The Witch Is Back")

ZILE: An Upper-Level warlock, Zile enlists the services of the Dark Priestess, Dantalian, to capture and marry Prue Halliwell. As a result of the dark union, Prue, her sisters, and the Book of Shadows turn evil. When evil Piper and Phoebe track Prue to Dantalian's lair, Zile shape-shifts into Prue. Warlocks can't express love, so the sisters are able to trap him and destroy the fake Prue. With the black marriage bond broken, the Charmed Ones and the Book are restored. ("Bride and Gloom")

WITCHES

COBB, RUTH: A witch with a basic understanding of natural magic, she resided in Virginia in 1670 and conspired with Cole to keep Charlotte Warren's baby, Melinda, to raise as evil. They hoped to promote black magic and preclude the rise of the Charmed Ones, who were sent back by the Elders to prevent any alteration of the established future. ("All Halliwell's Eve")

EVIL ENCHANTRESS: A twelfth-century incarnation of Paige Matthews's soul, she wishes to bring about the reign of Dark Magic by bearing the Prince's child. Going back in time and calling on her previous power, Paige and her sisters prevent the pregnancy and bind the evil witch's powers. ("A Knight to Remember")

EVIL WITCH: Trapped in the mirror on the wall, she is freed when the glass breaks. She kills the Keeper, imprisons the apprentice, and tries to kill the Charmed Ones with fairy-tale magic and props so that she will reign as the most powerful witch. Piper enters the witch's fortress through *The Book of Fairy Tales* and vanquishes her with a potion that melts her. ("Happily Ever After")

ISIS: An evil witch from ancient Egypt, she saved Jeric from spending eternity as a mummy. They fell in love, but she was killed by Jeric's enemies. Since her death, her spirit has been stored in mummified bodies with a scarab until Jeric can transfer it into a witch's body. Because there are two spirits inside them, the bodies burn out quickly. Her spirit is sent into the afterlife when Piper expels her from Paige's body with a spell. ("Y Tu Mummy También")

RUSSELL, P.: Born in the 1890s as a good witch of the Warren line, P. Russell plotted with her warlock lover, Anton, to kill her two cousins and steal their powers. Instead the cousins separate her from Anton's protective amulet, and curse and kill her. Before she dies she is temporarily transferred into Phoebe Halliwell's body in the year 2000. Her reincarnated cousins, Prue and Piper Halliwell, separate her from the amulet again, saving Phoebe and sending the evil, fire-throwing witch back to February 17, 1924, to die. ("Pardon My Past")

SUCCUBUS: A witch becomes a sexual predator when she renounces emotion and makes a pact with darkness to guard against heartbreak. Men cannot resist her, and she feeds on their testosterone with a razor-sharp tongue. Prue, undercover in a man's body, falls prey to the evil witch's power until Phoebe, psychically linked to the succubus, breaks the daze. The succubus and her egg sacks are destroyed with fire. ("She's a Man, Baby, a Man")

TUATHA: Once good, this wicked witch used magic against Innocents and was entombed two hundred years ago. When she is accidentally freed, she sends a snake to find the wand that is her power and, in the hands of the Chosen One, the instrument of her destruction. Although she strips the Charmed Ones' powers, Prue's quick thinking makes Kyle Gwydion, a.k.a. the Chosen One, believe in himself. Tuatha is vanquished when he wins the wand and wishes her gone forever. ("That Old Black Magic")

WIZARDS

MERRILL: Mentor of Cronyn, he unearthed the prophesy of the Charmed baby's birth from an apothecary's tomb several hundred years before. He is part of Cronyn's plan to kidnap and raise Wyatt for evil. ("The Day the Magic Died")

WIZARD, THE: He seeks revenge for the slaughter of his kind centuries ago by The Source. He convinces the Charmed Ones to steal the Grimoire, which stops Cole's coronation as The Source. With Cole's permission, he casts the black magic spell to transfer The Source's powers to himself and would have succeeded if Phoebe had not intervened and killed him. ("We're Off to See the Wizard")

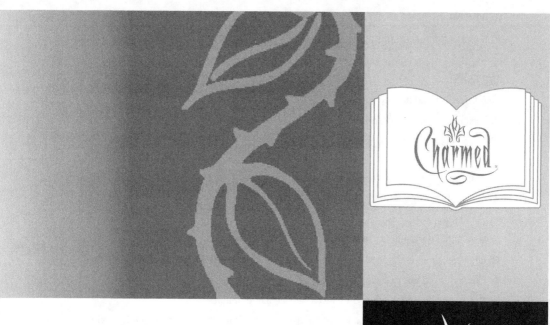

Book of Black Magic
The Demonic Hierarchy

HOLLOW:

- Contained for all eternity, guarded by good and evil to prevent it from consuming all magic

AVATARS:

- A force unrestricted by good and evil
- Exist outside time and space
- Shape the future as they desire

THE SOURCE OF ALL EVIL:

- Reigns over Underworld and evil
- As with the Elders, The Source is not all knowing. He remains unaware that Cole/Belthazor lives until Cole's actions reveal his continued existence.
- Emerges as a hands-on player when the Charmed Ones are renewed after Prue's death
- Flames in and out to travel
- Can be injured when weakened by excessive use of magic
- Releases the Hollow to weaken the Charmed Ones. The Seer unleashes the Hollow on him through Cole Turner, which allows the Charmed Ones to vanquish him, and makes Cole The Source.
- Five hundred years after the last Source came to power, Cole becomes The Source
- The first half-human Source, Cole Turner, incorporates human love into his persona for strength
- Proposes a merger of Underworld factions; consolidates power to fight the forces of good
- His coronation goes forward with Phoebe as his queen

SUPERIOR BEINGS

- Several species of evil beings are greater and more ferocious than demons and may be impossible to vanquish except by The Source.
- The Four Horsemen of the Apocalypse; destroyed by The Source
- The Triad—a powerful Council of Three plotting to overthrow The Source; vanquished by Cole
- Dignitaries: Have the power to conceal their activities, such as rituals
  Demonic Judges
  Dark Priests
  Dark Priestesses: i.e., Dantalian, who was vanquished by the Charmed Ones
- Shax, The Source's Assassin; vanquished by the Charmed Ones
- The Oracle, Seer to The Source; destroyed by Cole
- The Seer: Upper-Level demon who betrayed The Source to contain the Hollow and elevate Cole. Plotted the conception of a new Source, and was destroyed by the unborn Source within her.

TITANS

- Greek gods; entombed by empowered mortals three thousand years ago
- Freed by Mordock with an incantation
- Powers: fire; can turn beings to stone; absorb power of others
- Cronus: vanquished by Piper, the Goddess
- Demetrius: vanquished by Piper, the Goddess
- Meta: vanquished by Cronus

BROTHERHOOD OF THE THORN

- Trigg: killed prophet, vanquished by Phoebe
- Tarkin: sympathetic to Belthazor, vanquished by Piper
- Klea: spying eyes for Vornac and Raynor
- Vornac: image-altering power, vanquished by Phoebe while posing as Cole
- Raynor: leader of the Brotherhood, killed by Cole for turning Phoebe against him

HIGH COUNCIL

- Leaders of the factions, Council has the power to choose a new Source if none survives by lineage or magic.

FACTIONS

- Formed to challenge The Source
- Devlin's Warlocks; Ring of Inspiration to capture muses; prevented from blinking out of P3; Devlin vanquished with a potion
- Kurzon: banished for mounting a failed coup against The Source; vanquished by the Power of Three
- Grimlocks
- Harpies
- Furies
- Warlocks
- Alliances—Against The Source: Queen of the Vampires and Keats; Queen vanquished and line eradicated

WARLOCKS

- Main motivation is to kill witches and steal their powers
- Move by blinking
- Do not bleed
- Ordinary warlocks do not have the power to hide their actions from Upper-Level beings
- Upper-Level warlocks desire the powers of all three Charmed witches
- Blinding or strobe light prevents them from blinking

DEMONS

 All demons strive to improve their positions by destroying good and promoting evil

 Upper-Level demons:
- Have human form and bleed red
- Can sense The Source's aura, a reminder of his power and reach
- Can only be vanquished with a potion using their flesh
- Move up in hierarchy by killing witches
- Throwing fire is an Upper-Level power

 Lower-Level demons bleed green

 Demons don't dream

NOTE: A rivalry exists between demons and warlocks.

BLACK MAGIC SPELLS AND RITUALS

To Summon Kali
("THE FOURTH SISTER")

Anoint a mirror lying face up on the floor and chant from within a circle of lighted black candles:
Come to me, Kali, I conjure thee.

WARNING: Powers given by the spirit of this sorceress can only be used as Kali directs. Touching the mirror containing Kali's image creates a conduit to possession.

The Prophesy of the Rowe Coven
("WHEN BAD WARLOCKS GO GOOD")

To become evil, a half-warlock must kill an Innocent by driving a knife through a circled pentagram drawn over her heart.

To Disempower a Witch
("THAT OLD BLACK MAGIC")

The freed evil witch Tuatha zaps the power of the Charmed Ones with this spell, found in both the *Grimoire* and Book of Shadows. Instructions say to recite the spell over a fresh human heart.
Before the passing of this hour
Take away all their powers.

NOTE: In an erased time line, future and present versions of the warlock Bacarra used this spell to strip the Charmed Ones of their powers.

To Summon Cryto
("HOW TO MAKE A QUILT OUT OF AMERICANS")

This spell, cast by Gail Altman and two friends, is used to call for a demon who will return their youth to them.
We call on the demon Cryto,
reach back throughout the ages.
Humbled by his power,
we invite him into our circle.

Alchemist's Chant to Raise the Dead
("COYOTE PIPER")

Caducus exanimus vita aetus anima.
Fallen, be free, again rise.

Dark Priestess Potion to Paralyze Prue
("BRIDE AND GLOOM")

Placed into a bowl: black magic holy water, an item that touched Prue's lips, hemlock root, a dove feather, and a black scorpion.

Dark Priestess
(A BLACK MAGIC SPELL IN AN ALTERNATE BOOK OF SHADOWS) ("BRIDE AND GLOOM")

Through this book
Weave this spell,
Create this pain
From heaven to hell.
May she suffer . . .

Black Wedding
("BRIDE AND GLOOM")

Performed by the Dark Priestess with a hand on each to be joined and an anointed black cord to bind the union.
In the beginning we were damned,
and through damnation we found
freedom, power, and purpose.
As I unite you today,
I remind you of those gifts,
and in your union may these gifts increase
so your powers may grow
in the service of evil.
So be it.

To Awaken
("BRIDE AND GLOOM") DARK PRIESTESS

Eximo dempres anamatum.
Awaken and rise.

The Seven Deadly Sins
("SIN FRANCISCO")

Demonic Infectors keep crystal boxes that contain balls of each of the Seven Deadly Sins, bottled at The Source and by The Source. These demons, who were once human and consumed by sin in life, use sin balls to corrupt paragons of good. Infectors target a victim's predisposition to sin, and magnify it with a sin ball, leading to the victim's self-destruction within hours. The sin balls can only be disempowered by destroying the Infector.

The Seven Deadly Sins:

PRIDE: *an excessive belief in oneself*
ENVY: *the desire for what others have*
GLUTTONY: *the desire to overindulge*
LUST: *a craving for pleasures of the flesh*
ANGER: *uncontrollable fury*
GREED: *a craving for material wealth*
SLOTH: *an avoidance of work*

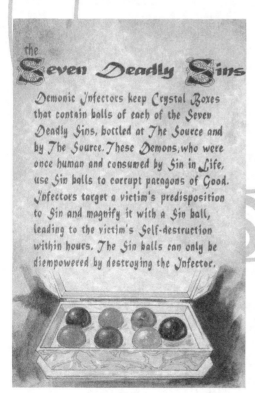

the Seven Deadly Sins

Demonic Infectors keep Crystal Boxes that contain balls of each of the Seven Deadly Sins, bottled at The Source and by The Source. These Demons, who were once human and consumed by Sin in Life, use Sin balls to corrupt paragons of Good. Infectors target a victim's predisposition to Sin and magnify it with a Sin ball, leading to the victim's Self-destruction within hours. The Sin balls can only be disempowered by destroying the Infector.

Cole's Chant to Purge His Love for Phoebe
("LOOK WHO'S BARKING")

Valeo discedo prosum ferocitas,
Malum, diluo eradico.
Command that this must end and die.
Evil, wash it away.

Cole's Chant to Corrupt the White Wedding
("MARRY-GO-ROUND")

Summum supplicium diabolus infernum,
Invocatio paganus sacrificium.
To ask that this temple be
forever invoked for evil

Phoebe and Cole's Dark Wedding Ritual
("MARRY-GO-ROUND")

Conducted by the Dark Priest, the ceremony was performed at night in a cemetery, and the groom "drank" the bride's blood. After concluding the ceremony, the dark priest intones:

Not two but one
till life be gone.

To Sire The Source's Heir
("THE FIFTH HALLIWHEEL")

NOTE: Tonic prepared by the Seer.

Conception must take place on the night of the harvest moon after the woman ingests a tonic containing The Source's blood. The tonic will counteract contraceptive precautions and make her receptive to the demon seed.

To Transfer The Source's Power
(FROM THE *GRIMOIRE* IN "WE'RE OFF TO SEE THE WIZARD")

Malus into exitus omne.
Evil, leave and be in him!

Coronation of The Source
("WOMB RAIDER")

Requires the *Grimoire* and two sacrifices; this ritual is performed by a Dark Priest:

May the world's evil flow through your soul tonight,
and grant you eternal dark.
Are you prepared to take the power and position of The Source
before these leaders of the Underworld?

Occidit una domus.
Omnes quas meruere pati poenas.
Oh, this one the sect installs.
Deem and bring forth all the power!

To Move a Demon Baby from One Womb to Another
("WOMB RAIDER")
SPELL PERFORMED BY THE SEER

The Seer speaks:
Come to me, child.
Let the little children come to me,
for the kingdom belongs
to such as these.
The rose circle represents nature, desire, and fertility.
Kneel.

The spell begins:
Give me strength
and give me might
to steal a child
in still of night.
Darkest forces,
let it be.
Hear my plea.
Bring life to me!

Sea Hag's Spell to Control Weather
("A WITCH'S TAIL, PART ONE")

Water rise up from the sea,
find the one who fled from me.
Gather where the winds are cold,
Then fall tenfold like days of old.

To Imprison Osgood the Apprentice to the Keeper of Fairy Tales in the Mirror
("HAPPILY EVER AFTER")

NOTE: Spell performed by the Evil Witch.
Freedom's loss must be unwitting,
into the glass to do my bidding.

NOTE: The Mirror cannot lie.

Incantations Cast by Present and Future Versions of the Warlock Bacarra
("A WITCH IN TIME")
To Make the Invisible Visible
Aspectus invisus!
Observe!
To Convey a Weapon from Paige
Teleportatio!
Bring me the knife!

Ascension to Avatar
("CENTENNIAL CHARMED")

NOTE: Recited by an Avatar to elevate Cole
Ribus vero fecitorum,
Bitis danae arca convenio hospito Fortis mundus.
Ruler come forth, created and granted,
Blessed gift, agreed as one to be,
Mighty of means.

To Open the Nexus
("THE IMPORTANCE OF BEING PHOEBE")

SPELL WAS CAST BY COLE TURNER
Natum adai necral daya intaylayok

To Give Bad Luck
(A LEPRECHAUN CURSE)
("LUCKY CHARMED")

Marbhfháisec ort!

For life all joy denied you.

To Reconstitute a Vanquished Spirit
("NECROMANCING THE STONE")

Evocum a letiterum abdigo.

Manes ascendo!

Call the spirit from the grave.

Leave this earth.

I command you to rise.

To Free the Titans
("OH, MY GODDESS, PART ONE")

Emergo dormio.

Libertas caelus dicio.

Arise from sleep.

Quickly free the Powers.

EPISODE GUIDE

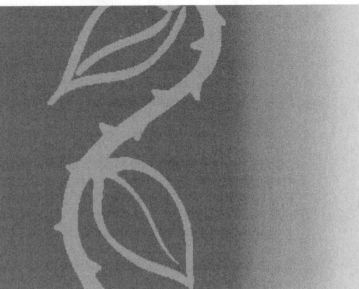

Episode Guide

Season One

"Something Wicca This Way Comes"

(OCTOBER 7, 1998)
Written by Constance M. Burge
Directed by John T. Kretchmer

Prue Halliwell is not pleased when her sister Piper announces that Phoebe, the youngest Halliwell, is returning from New York to live with them in the Victorian house they inherited from their grandmother. Despite Phoebe's denials, Prue believes she had an affair with Roger, her ex-fiancé and coworker at the museum. The awkward tension between them is set aside when the Spirit Board pointer moves to spell "attic." Intrigued when the locked attic door opens of its own accord, Phoebe finds a dusty, leather-bound tome called the Book of Shadows in an old trunk. She recites an incantation that indicates she and her sisters will receive magical powers, but nothing seems to change.

Phoebe is convinced that the Book's story about their ancestor Melinda Warren being a witch is true, and that together Phoebe and her sisters will be the most powerful witches the world has ever known. Prue and Piper are not so easily persuaded. As their powers begin to manifest themselves, though, they start to accept Phoebe's theories. Piper discovers her magical power when she inadvertently freezes the chef during a cooking audition. Prue "thinks" cream into her coffee, which makes her aware of her ability to move things with her mind. Phoebe is thrilled when she prevents an accident she foresees in a vision.

Dealing with powers in the real world will take some practice, but the girls are quickly put to the test when a series of crimes seem to have supernatural overtones. Andy Trudeau, a police inspector and Prue's high school flame, investigates the murders of three women who practiced witchcraft and were all stabbed with a ceremonial knife. He has an interest in the occult, but has no idea how interesting his life is about to become.

Beyond traditional crime fighting, the Halliwell sisters' new abilities pit them against previously unknown challenges and reward them with newfound empowerment. Prue quits her museum job because Roger takes credit for her work.

Piper has no idea that the reporter she's dating is a warlock until Jeremy Burns tries to kill her to steal her power. She instinctively freezes him to escape. When he attacks the sisters at the Manor, Prue slows his advance by mentally flinging him back. A spell Phoebe finds in the Book of Shadows makes Jeremy break out in thorns, but the warlock isn't vanquished until they chant an inscription on the Spirit Board: "The Power of Three will set us free." Together, the three Charmed Ones command more power than any witches ever.

"We're the protectors of the innocent. We're known as the Charmed Ones."

PHOEBE HALLIWELL

"I've Got You Under My Skin"

(OCTOBER 14, 1998)
Written by Brad Kern
Directed by John T. Kretchmer

The Halliwells make significant professional strides when Piper becomes the manager of Quake, a popular restaurant, and Prue is hired at Buckland's Auction House. Piper would much rather return to being normal than accept her fate as a witch. She doesn't share Phoebe's certainty that the Charmed Ones are good. After seeing a documentary about witches, Piper is afraid to enter a church, fearing she will be struck by lightning because she is an evil being.

On the other end of the spectrum, Phoebe's cavalier attitude toward their powers worries Prue. The Book of Shadows emphatically states that they must not use their abilities for personal gain, yet the youngest Halliwell can't resist tapping into her premonitions to see which guys will be most receptive to her advances.

While Piper is fretting and Phoebe is flirting, Andy warns Prue about someone who has been abducting young women in and around Quake. Phoebe is excited when she meets Stefan, a handsome and famous photographer, unaware that he is the man for whom Andy and the police are searching. Phoebe agrees to model for him, but when she arrives at his studio, she gets a premonition about his true intentions. Piper then makes the connection that something is wrong when she recognizes a unique tattoo that identifies an old woman as her young friend, Brittany. Piper and Prue discover that Stefan is the demon Javna, who uses the Evil Eye to steal youth. They rush to Stefan's studio and free Phoebe. The three sisters then recite an incantation to invoke the Hand of Fatima that vanquishes Javna. The effects of the black magic are annulled, and the rejuvenated victims have no memory of their ordeal. Piper begins to realize that she has been given her powers to fight evil, not to make her evil, and verifies it by finally safely entering the church.

"Our powers are not toys."

PRUE HALLIWELL

"Thank You for Not Morphing"

(OCTOBER 21, 1998)
Written by Chris Levinson & Zack Estrin
Directed by Ellen Pressman

When Victor Bennett, the Charmed Ones' long-lost father, shows up at Buckland's, Prue identifies a family heirloom as a protection ring, but she rejects his attempt to make amends. Piper and Phoebe opt to give their father a chance. But when Phoebe hugs him, she gets a premonition of Victor stealing the Book of Shadows. At the same time, a shape-shifting neighbor is breaking into the Manor to steal the Book—but the Book won't leave the house. Prue confronts Victor, who admits he wanted to steal the Book of Shadows to protect his daughters from the evil that it attracts—the evil that killed their mother. Victor never wanted his girls to have their powers, and he objected when Grams arranged to restore them—but Grams was too strong for Victor to fight her.

When another vision shows Marshal, a neighbor, shape-shifting into Victor, Phoebe knows who's *really* after the Book, and locates a spell to vanquish the shape-shifters. Trying to throw off the Charmed Ones, one of the neighbors shape-shifts into Victor, but he doesn't count on Victor being willing to die along with the demons if it means saving his daughters. As one of the Victors instructs Phoebe to say the spell, Prue determines which is her real father. She uses her power to give him the family protection ring, and although he is momentarily stunned when the demons are vanquished, the ring saves him. Victor finally understands that his little girls have grown up and can handle their powers. It is their duty, he realizes, to fulfill their destiny.

A warm and fuzzy family reunion is still not meant to be. Victor leaves town again. The sting of his unexpected departure is softened by a family video of Christmas past, found on the doorstep by the attractive new handyman, Leo Wyatt.

"Some of us have a job." **PRUE HALLIWELL**

"Some of us have fun." **PHOEBE HALLIWELL**

"Some of us have a really bad hair day." **PIPER HALLIWELL**

"Dead Man Dating"

(OCTOBER 28, 1998)
Written by Javier Grillo-Marxuach
Directed by Richard Compton

The ghost of a Chinese-American man, Mark, asks for help, sidelining Piper's dilemma of whether or not to throw Prue a surprise birthday party. Tony Wong, the head of a Chinatown triad, killed Mark. To fake his own death, Wong then put his ring on Mark's finger and burned the body. Mark isn't sure how or why he died, and he tells Piper that if he isn't properly buried soon, Chinese legend says Yama, the Gatekeeper of Hell, will take his soul. But no one can make arrangements because neither his mother nor the police know he's dead. Piper and Mark visit the scene of his murder and run into Yama, who is ready to collect another soul. Piper freezes him so that she and Mark can escape and bring the killer to justice.

Piper and Mark see Mark's death reported on television, but the victim is identified as Tony Wong. They now know who they're after, and Phoebe gets a premonition about Wong's whereabouts. Piper and Mark seek him out, and she photographs Wong with the newspaper headline about his death. She then leaves the picture for Andy. Wong kidnaps Piper, but is killed when the police follow up on the anonymous tip. Yama captures Wong's soul, but Piper intercedes with the Gatekeeper on Mark's behalf. Mark is finally identified and buried, and escorted to what lies beyond by his deceased father. Before he leaves, Mark convinces Prue to embrace every birthday, because nobody ever knows how many they'll have left. Piper mourns Mark and what might have been if they had met before he became a ghost, but takes his advice to heart when she goes ahead with Prue's surprise birthday party.

In the meantime, to make money for a proper birthday present for Prue, Phoebe gets a job as a hotel psychic. She gets a real premonition, but she may not be able to save the victim of a future accident because he thinks she's a crazy stalker. Determined not to lose her Innocent, Phoebe intervenes anyway and saves the man from death by pink Cadillac. Her efforts make her more appreciative of the Charmed Ones' duty to protect the innocent.

"Leave it to me to fall for a dead guy."   **PIPER HALLIWELL**

"It's an improvement. At least he wasn't a warlock."   **PHOEBE HALLIWELL**

"Dream Sorcerer"	(NOVEMBER 4, 1998) Written by Constance M. Burge Directed by Nick Marck

Looking for some casual romance, Phoebe finds a spell to attract a lover in the Book of Shadows. Piper justifies using it as a way of testing their powers. Prue opts out. Aside from fretting about Andy and her secret, she has a busy work schedule, and a disturbing encounter with a man in her dreams. Stress may have caused the nightmare, but that doesn't explain the scratches on Prue's back. Why, Piper wonders, didn't Prue use her powers against her dream attacker?

While Piper and Phoebe deal with enamored men, Prue deals with her sleep intruder's deadly intentions. Andy hasn't told her he's investigating a woman who died in her sleep of internal injuries. The owner of a dream-research lab, Whitaker Berman, is the likely suspect, but Andy doesn't know that Berman is invading Prue's dreams. Taking Piper's advice, Prue, while in her dream, uses her powers in self-defense to hurl Berman off a high-rise, crushing him in his sleep. Piper and Phoebe realize that magically induced romance is meaningless and reverse the love spell.

"There must be more to our powers than warlock-wasting."   **PHOEBE HALLIWELL**

"The Wedding from Hell"	(NOVEMBER 11, 1998) Written by Greg Elliot & Michael Perricone Directed by R. W. Ginty

When the sisters all become involved with Elliot Spencer's wedding, they realize it's not coincidence. Whatever guides their destiny will make sure they find those who need them. Piper and Phoebe handle the catering. Prue is drawn in by an inscribed knife Andy found on a murdered priest. The poignard is needed to kill Hecate, the Queen of the Underworld. Known as Jade D'Mon, she plans to collect on a deal made with Mrs. Spencer years before. Jade needs to marry the Innocent Elliott Spencer, and bear a demon child. Rex Buckland and Hannah Webster from the auction house reveal their evil inclinations by sending a wedding gift to Hecate.

To thwart Hecate, and reunite Elliot with his proper bride, Allison Michaels, the Charmed Ones convince Allison to crash the wedding. Allison's declaration of love breaks Hecate's spell, and in

Elliot's hand, the power of the knife sends her and her demon bridesmaids back to the Underworld. Given their Charmed nature and existence, the Halliwell sisters wonder if they will ever find love and live happily ever after.

"Welcome to the lifestyles of the rich and shameless."   **DARRYL MORRIS**

"My sisters and I, we have special gifts, ones you can't return." **PRUE HALLIWELL**

"The Fourth Sister"

(NOVEMBER 18, 1998)
Written by Edithe Swensen
Directed by Gil Adler

Only Prue is suspicious when Aviva, a teenage girl, returns the Halliwells' missing cat, Kit, and wants to discuss Wicca. Living with her aunt yet feeling alone, Aviva called on Kali, the sorceress in her mirror, to make her part of the Halliwell family. Kali plans to use the naïve girl to acquire the Charmed Ones' magic. However, Aviva is shocked by the force of her powers when she accidentally injures her aunt and almost kills Phoebe with a fireball.

Aided by the Book of Shadows, the Charmed Ones are prepared when Kali possesses Aviva. Piper freezes Aviva/Kali, which drives the spirit from the girl's body. Prue hurls Kali into a mirror, and Phoebe shatters the glass, extinguishing Kali's existence and saving Aviva. Piper and Phoebe compete for Leo Wyatt's affections. Distractions and a lack of privacy drive a wedge between Prue and Andy.

"I like mirrors; they never lie to you. They always tell the truth whether you like it or not."
AVIVA

"The Truth Is out There ... And It Hurts"

(NOVEMBER 25, 1998)
Written by Zack Estrin & Chris Levinson
Directed by James A. Contner

The Charmed Ones' attempt to have a normal girls' night out at the movies is cut short when Piper is called back to Quake. As they're leaving the theater, Phoebe is jostled by a man and gets a premonition of a murdered woman with a hole bored into her forehead. When police cars arrive, the witches assume they're too late to save the woman, but the victim this time was a man—who had the same fatal wound as the woman in Phoebe's vision.

The killer strikes again at a biotech lab. He has a third eye in his forehead from which he shoots a laserlike beam into his victims. All the police know is that they have two seemingly unrelated murders with the same bizarre cause of death. Phoebe goes to the police stations to get some information from Andy that might help save the Innocent she saw in her vision. When she later visits Prue at the office to fill her in, Phoebe bumps into Tanya, the sandwich girl. She gets the vision again and realizes that the killer is after Tanya. But why? What is the pattern to these seemingly random victims? Phoebe puts it all together when she realizes that the demon, who's not in the Book of Shadows, and who's wearing a substance not yet known to man, is after Tanya's unborn baby. He's obviously from the future, and is clearly trying to prevent something from happening. With no known potion or spell, Prue and Piper are forced to fight the demon with their powers and their wits.

He tells them he was sent back to kill all those involved in creating a vaccine that will destroy him and all other warlocks like him. When he attacks Prue, she grabs a nearby crowbar and drives it into his third eye. The warlock is sucked into a swirling vortex and is gone.

As usual, demon fighting isn't the only thing occupying the Charmed Ones' time. Prue is still conflicted about Andy. She wants to be with him, but doesn't know if he can handle her being a witch. When the Book of Shadows magically opens to a truth spell, Prue takes it as a sign. She recites the spell, which lasts for twenty-four hours. Causing everyone to speak the truth, Prue finds out a little more than she bargained for—including the fact that Andy can't cope with her Charmed destiny.

Meanwhile, Phoebe and Piper still vie for Leo, but Phoebe throws in the towel when, under the truth spell, she admits she only wants him because Piper does. And Piper finds out the truth: that Leo likes her as much as she likes him.

"Look who's talking, Little Miss Spell-of-the-Week."　　　**PRUE HALLIWELL**

"The Witch Is Back"

(DECEMBER 16, 1998)
Written by Sheryl J. Anderson
Directed by Richard Denault

Rex Buckland tricks Prue into opening a locket that releases the warlock Matthew Tate. Tate had seduced and betrayed the original Halliwell matriarch, Melinda Warren. Before she was burned at the stake for being a witch, Melinda reclaimed the powers Tate had stolen from her and imprisoned him in the locket, leaving only Warren witches able to free him. Once released, Matthew seeks revenge. He provokes Prue and duplicates her power, which makes him immune to it. He then notes the family name and goes in search of all the Halliwells to find the rest of Melinda's descendants and reclaim Melinda's powers.

Prue heads home to alert her sisters. When Phoebe touches the antique jewelry, she gets a vision of Melinda sending Matthew into the locket. The girls consult the Book of Shadows, which warns that "The warlock must never be freed or he will destroy the Warren line." They decide the best person to stop Matthew is the one who did it before, and together summon Melinda. To everyone's surprise, the spell works. As the Charmed Ones work with Melinda to create the potion to trap Matthew, they enjoy getting to know their ancestor. In turn, she helps them to appreciate their powers. Matthew has one more power to possess, but the combined power of the witches of the Warren line defeats him before he reaches his goal. Melinda holds open her locket, the spell is chanted, and Matthew is imprisoned again. The sisters reluctantly send Melinda back to her time, wearing her locket to ensure that Matthew will not escape again.

Throughout this ordeal, Matthew had left a trail of dead Halliwells in his wake and used his powers to make miraculous escapes. Needless to say, Andy and Morris become involved in the all-too-human aspects of Matthew's crime spree. When the trail once again leads back to Prue and her sisters, Andy isn't surprised, but he's hurt and annoyed that Prue is again keeping secrets.

And why was Rex so keen for Prue to open that locket? He and Hannah are working for some mysterious source of evil to whom he's promised to deliver the Charmed Ones. Matthew proved that Prue and her sisters are indeed his suspected quarry; unfortunately for Rex, Matthew failed to complete Rex's plan.

"Great. So I'm being hunted by a warlock and the San Francisco P.D."
PRUE HALLIWELL

> "We're fresh out of eye of newt."
>
> **PIPER HALLIWELL**

> "You're new in town. You're new in time. Let us smooth your way."
>
> **REX BUCKLAND TO MATTHEW TATE**

> "Magic can't change what isn't meant to be."
>
> **MELINDA WARREN**

"Wicca Envy"

(JANUARY 13, 1999)
Teleplay by Brad Kern & Sheryl J. Anderson
Story by Brad Kern
Directed by Mel Damski

Since the Charmed Ones are too powerful to be defeated with magic, Rex Buckland and Hannah Webster try blackmail to acquire their powers. Invisible when he astral projects, Rex manipulates minds with suggestion. Neither the guard nor Prue realizes she left the Buckland vault with a priceless tiara. When the guard is killed, all evidence points to Prue, and Andy arrests her for murder. Following another Astral Rex directive, Phoebe and Piper break Prue out of jail. Rex takes a picture of them escaping and gives them two options: Go to prison on the basis of his evidence or relinquish their powers to him and go free.

The Charmed Ones reluctantly relinquish their powers, and everything in the Book of Shadows disappears. Rex and Hannah wait for their bounty at Buckland's. They have no intention of letting the former Charmed Ones live, with or without their powers. Hannah shape-shifts into a panther, ready for the kill. Just as the girls face Hannah the panther, Leo enters the attic and restores the magic to the Book of Shadows with a glow that emanates from his hands. This also restores the witches' magic, enabling them to evade the attacking panther. Prue telekinetically throws Rex in the big cat's path and she kills him. Hannah morphs back into human form, and the two warlocks are consumed in flames.

Prue is cleared when Andy's background checks of all Buckland's employees show that the real Rex and Hannah died months before. Since the imposters have disappeared, Andy assumes Rex and Hannah framed Prue in a scheme to steal the tiara. Leo doesn't reveal that he returned the Charmed Ones' powers, and they still have no idea about his true identity, as no one sees him orb on his way to the front door.

> "We just have to take the leap of faith and believe it's going to work out somehow."
>
> **PIPER HALLIWELL**

PHOEBE: "Between you and Leo, and Prue the new-hot-Wicca woman, and me, soon to be employed, things are looking up."
PIPER: "Don't say that! The moment somebody says that everything always goes south."

III

"Feats of Clay"

(JANUARY 20, 1999)
Teleplay by Zach Estrin & Chris Levin &
Greg Elliot & Michael Perricone
Story by Javier Grillo-Marxuach
Directed by Kevin Inch

A young man named Clay is unaware of the death curse attached to an Egyptian urn he helps steal. Separated from his partners, Clay contacts Phoebe, whom he dated in New York, hoping Prue can sell the artifact. Prue learns the urn is stolen and cursed, but Phoebe doesn't believe Clay would knowingly do anything to hurt them. After learning that Clay's partners were killed—Wesley by a spider and Palmer by a scorpion—Prue and Phoebe help Clay escape the Guardian of the Urn, who is immune to their powers.

Piper's magical attempt to help two Quake employees get back together backfires, which suggests that the Charmed Ones are not meant to help everyone. Prue thinks this may include Clay. However Clay sincerely wishes to set things right with the Guardian of the Urn. When the Guardian's cobra strikes at Phoebe, Clay uses his arm to block the snake without concern for his own safety. Clay's life is spared because of his selfless act. The urn vanishes and reappears on its original pedestal in Cairo. Because she has a purpose, Phoebe rejects Clay's offer to go back to her aimless life with him in New York.

"They hired you at the Rainbow Room?"   **PRUE HALLIWELL**

"I'm getting a little freeze frazzled."   **PIPER HALLIWELL**

II2

"The Wendigo"

(FEBRUARY 3, 1999)
Written by Edithe Swensen
Directed by James L. Conway

Piper, stranded with a flat tire, is chased by some sort of monster as she tries to phone for help. The creature is chased off by Billy Waters, but not before Piper's arm is raked by its talons. Billy knows how to destroy the beast because after it killed his girlfriend two months earlier, it showed a fear of fire.

Andy investigates the recent death along with Special Agent Ashley Fallon of the FBI. Fallon has been tracking a series of similar murders for a number of months. Although both detectives are open to the possibility of supernatural occurrences, Andy believes that the pattern is indicative of human behavior.

Piper is convinced that something demonic is behind all of this and finds the creature, called a Wendigo, in the Book of Shadows. The original Wendigo was a human man who, after he was betrayed by his lover, killed her, cut out her heart, and ate it, turning his own heart to ice. Wendigos look like normal people during the day but transform at night. They survive on human hearts, and go hunting for them during the three phases of the full moon. Piper shares this information with Billy, who takes it to Agent Fallon. Billy realizes that Fallon is the Wendigo when he lights a cigarette and Fallon recoils from the fire of Billy's lighter. Fallon kills Billy before he can tell anyone. Later, finding that Andy has a blood type her inner Wendigo craves, Fallon suggests they stake out an open area where the creature is likely to strike that night. Andy agrees.

Infected by her wound, Piper begins to turn into a Wendigo. To save her, Prue and Phoebe must melt the icy heart of the Wendigo that slashed Piper. Their search leads them to a wounded—but breathing—Andy, whose heart is still in his chest. The sisters fire flares at the Wendigo, but miss. Then

The Power of Three

The Power of Three

Charming Men

Pheobe Halliwell

Piper Halliwell

Prue Halliwell

Paige Matthews

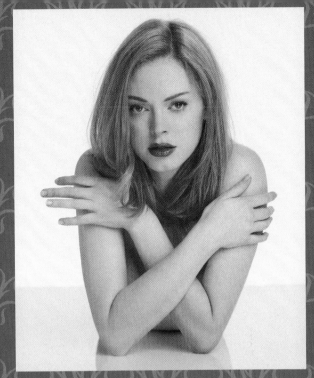

Behind
the Scenes

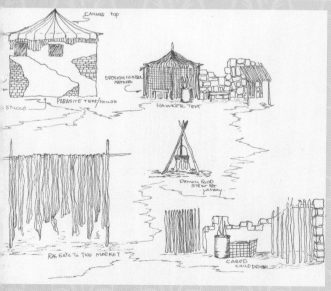

HERE IS AN EXAMPLE OF A POSSIBLE
WATER DEMON FOR THE END OF THE
EPISODE.

Hair Today...

Hair Today...

Special Effects

Special Effects

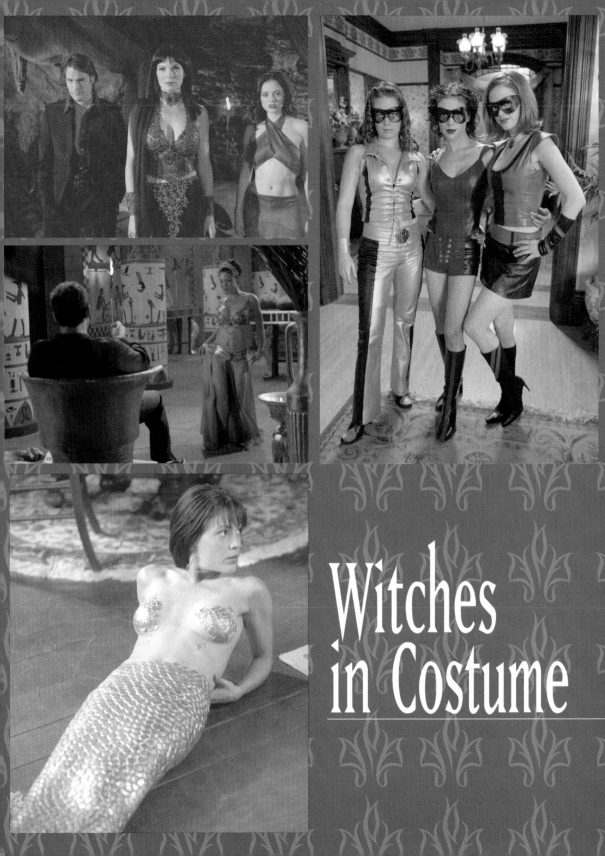

Witches in Costume

The Vanquish

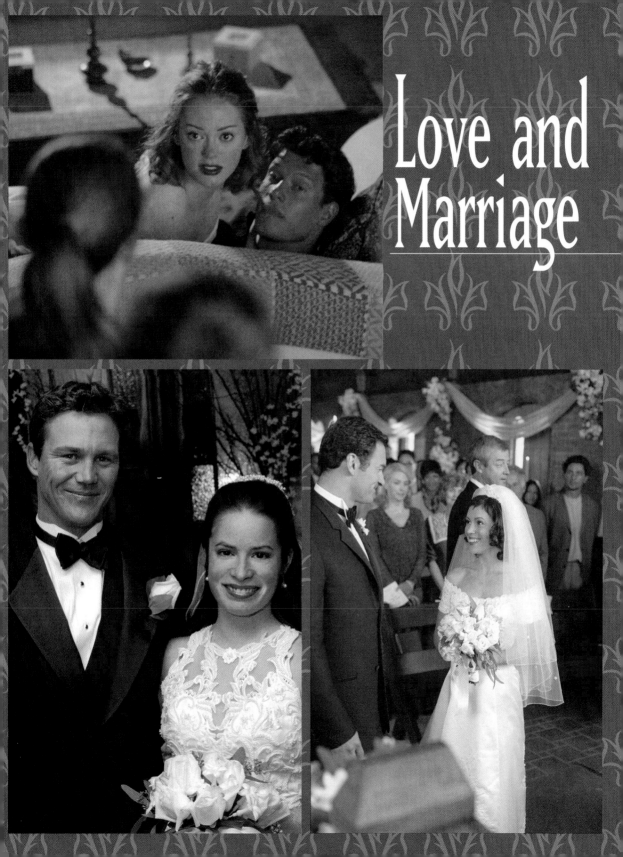

Love and Marriage

a second Wendigo appears. They realize one of their prey must be Piper, but which one? Phoebe shoots the final flare. When one Wendigo instinctively freezes it before the flare strikes, they have their answer. Prue mentally hurls the flare into the other Wendigo's chest and Fallon dies. Piper reverts to human form and Andy recovers from his wound. Unable to come up with a reasonable fabrication, Prue tells Andy the truth about what happened. She tells her sisters he was either too stunned to care or he must have believed it on some level, because he didn't question her story.

During the Wendigo ordeal, Phoebe is also helping with an auction at Buckland. She touches a bracelet and gets a vision of a 1989 car accident. Phoebe finds that the bracelet belonged to a five-year-old girl who had been kidnapped by her father. It was thrown from the car in the accident, but is proof that the P.I. had found the girl. No one ever knew, though, because the bracelet was lost and the investigator died before making any report. Phoebe traces the child through the bracelet, and reunites the now-teenage girl with her mother.

"Every time I touch something at Buckland's I risk having a premonition, and it's too emotional for me."
PHOEBE HALLIWELL

"Big, scary, strong. Kind of like a cross between a werewolf and Charles Manson."
PIPER HALLIWELL ON THE WENDIGO

"From Fear to Eternity"
(FEBRUARY 10, 1999)
Written by Tony Blake & Paul Jackson
Directed by Les Sheldon

Prue is stalked by Barbas, the Demon of Fear, who appears every 1,300 years on Friday the Thirteenth to feed on the fears of witches. He must kill thirteen unmarried witches by midnight to free himself of being doomed to the Underworld. Powerless and paralyzed by their greatest fear, his victims are literally scared to death. Knowing her daughters will have to fight Barbas in their lifetimes, Patty leaves a note in the Book of Shadows: "To let go of your fear, trust in the greatest of all powers." The girls don't initially understand their mother's message. Prue and Phoebe dismiss their fears, while Piper amasses a quantity of talismans to ward off her superstitions of bad luck.

Barbas determines that Prue's greatest fear is drowning (as her mother did). He also learns something Phoebe doesn't even know about herself—her greatest fear is losing a sister. He sets up a two-for-one kill by luring Phoebe to a vacant house being sold by her new boss. Barbas ties her up and imitates her in a phone call to Prue. When the oldest Halliwell arrives, the demon shoves her into a swimming pool as a helpless Phoebe watches. As Prue is about to repeat her mother's fate, Patty appears to her. She implores her daughter to face her fears, and repeats her message from the book—to trust in the greatest of all powers: love. Patty tells Prue to save herself and her sister. Empowered by her mother's encouragement, Prue releases her fear, regains her power and repels Barbas. She is also finally able to say "I love you" to Piper and Phoebe—words she could never repeat before because they were the last thing she ever said to her mother.

Friday the Thirteenth turns out to be less successful for Piper and Phoebe. Piper's obsessive preoccupation with superstition culminates in meeting and losing the perfect man. And although initially it looked like good luck for Phoebe when she got a new job, things don't work out so well in the end. She winds up quitting before the day is out because she won't lie to her new boss's husband about the woman's affair.

"Does a positive superstition cancel out a negative one?"
PRUE HALLIWELL

"Secrets and Guys"

(FEBRUARY 17, 1999)
Teleplay by Constance M. Burge &
Sheryl J. Anderson
Story by Brad Kern & Constance M. Burge
Directed by James A. Contner

When Max Franklin, a young male witch, is kidnapped, he contacts the Charmed Ones through the Spirit Board. Prue seeks Andy's help to locate the mysterious magical Innocent. Using Andy's leads, Prue visits Max's father, who helps her to find the boy. Max tells Prue that his powers emerged when his mother died. He is able to move things he can't see, which is how he sent the message on the Spirit Board. It's also how he turned off alarms at an arcade so that he and his friends could go in and play. The kidnappers want Max to open locks and shut off alarms at a bank so they can rob it. He won't try to escape, because the kidnappers said they would kill his father if he does. Prue tries to free him anyway, but is knocked out by the bad guys. When she wakes up, she finds they've wired Max with explosives to keep him from going anywhere. To stay with Max, Prue allows herself to remain captured and is taken to the bank. Max unlocks the door and disables the alarm, but Prue also tells him to disable the explosive device strapped to him. Free to work their magic, Max and Prue lock the robbers in the vault and escape. Prue tries to make Max and his father understand that the powers are a gift, and assures Max that he will be able to handle them.

Piper has her own problems with Harry, the insufferable new chef at Quake. Luckily, he quits after his first day on the job.

And when Phoebe sees Leo hanging in midair to fix the chandelier, she learns that he is a Whitelighter, a guardian angel for witches. He explains that the rules say Whitelighters aren't allowed to fall in love with witches, so even though he loves Piper, he can't stay with her, and he's got to find some way to tell her. Since the witches aren't supposed to know the angel assigned to protect them, Leo swears Phoebe to secrecy. After several false starts, Leo finally tells Piper that he can't see her anymore. Or, more accurately, Piper figures out what Leo's trying to say, and says it for him. He's taken aback when she's totally fine with the idea. Phoebe tells her sisters the truth about Leo, but they think she's making it up!

"You want me to keep a secret? Wrong Halliwell."   **PHOEBE HALLIWELL**

"Is There a Woogy in the House?"

(FEBRUARY 24, 1999)
Written by Chris Levinson & Zack Estrin
Directed by John T. Kretchmer

When Phoebe was a little girl, she thought she saw a monster in the basement, whom she called the Woogyman (because she couldn't say Bogeyman). Grams taught Phoebe a rhyme to end her fears of the beast, but she still couldn't bring herself to go into the basement. Phoebe was never able to shake her fears about the Woogyman, and after an earthquake causes what the girls think is a gas leak, it turns out Phoebe's fears may have been well founded.

When the gas man comes to make repairs, a shadow emerges from the crevice the earthquake opened in the basement wall. Its evil influence possesses the gas man and makes him lure Phoebe down to the basement, and gets her, too.

Phoebe being possessed is just one of the many tribulations at the dinner party Prue throws for Professor Whittlesey, a wealthy patron of Buckland's. The professor is tenured at Berkeley and her specialty is San Francisco history. She's particularly interested in the Manor because it is said to be built on a spiritual Nexus—meaning that it sits equidistant from the five elements and is a place of great power, either good or evil. By the time the dinner guests arrive, the Woogy's influence has Halliwell Manor literally falling apart. While Piper quickly arranges for the party to move to Quake, Phoebe volunteers to give the professor a tour of the house, including the basement. Professor Whittlesey becomes the Woogy's next victim. The dinner guests leave for Quake, but Prue has a few last words to say to Phoebe about her strange behavior. After they walk their guests out, Phoebe won't let either Piper or Prue back into the house. She magically seals the entryway and, laughing rather maniacally, tells her sisters that they don't live here anymore—he does.

As a place of evil, the Manor begins to fall apart, and Phoebe continues to lure Innocents for the Woogyman. The possessed professor attacks one of her students, and Prue and Piper realize the stories about the Nexus are true, noting that their family moved in after the big earthquake in 1906 to keep the land good. Something must have escaped during this last earthquake to change things. And since everyone who has gone to the basement has come out possessed, could Phoebe's story about the Woogyman be true? Prue and Piper find a way to get back into the house and check the Book of Shadows, but there's nothing in it about the Woogyman. They realize that the way to get rid of the Woogyman is in Grams' rhyme . . . which neither of them can remember. Finally, after trapping her sisters and preparing to kill them, Phoebe has a vision of Grams battling the Woogyman, which is enough to jolt her out of her possessed state. She remembers the rhyme and says it, sending the Woogy back into his fissure. The Manor, and all those who were possessed by the Woogyman, returns to normal. The sisters decide it's time they started making entries into the Book of Shadows, to warn future generations that there really is a Woogyman in the basement.

"Our powers are supposed to progress, not grow at random." **PRUE HALLIWELL**

"Which Prue Is It, Anyway?"

(MARCH 3, 1999)
Written by Javier Grillo-Marxuach
Directed by John Behring

Phoebe has a premonition of a man killing Prue with a ceremonial sword. The Book of Shadows says that the sword is a symbol of the Lords of War, a clan of supernatural war-starting warriors who have existed since time began. As long as the Lords have their swords, they are invulnerable. The Book also says they have a code of honor: If a Lord of War is disgraced, he must steal back his abilities, as well as the magic of a firstborn witch, because their powers are the strongest. Gabriel Statler comes after Prue because he was disgraced by her Halliwell ancestor Brianna.

To help her fight the invulnerable warrior, Prue casts a spell to multiply her powers, but it multiplies Prue and turns her into triplets. To differentiate among the Prues, Phoebe color-codes them with sweaters. The real Prue wears black. The temporary Prues wear pink and blue. Pink Prue and Blue Prue are extremes of Prue's personality, but they all share her confidence. The extra Prues share all of Prue's memories until the time that they split and they say they will be around only as long as they are needed. The original Prue feels all of her clones' pain, as evidenced when Gabriel kills Pink Prue. The clone's body is not absorbed by Gabriel's crystal sword, however, because Pink Prue has no power of her own. Pink Prue's body is brought to the morgue and identified by Andy. He is devastated, then stunned when he goes to the Manor to tell Piper and Phoebe, and finds Prue still alive.

When the second clone strikes out on her own and is killed, Prue must rely on her wits, her power, and her sisters to defeat Gabriel. Rather than relieving Gabriel of his powers by separating him from his sword as Brianna did, the Charmed Ones opt to bring their flesh-and-blood adversary closer to his weapon. Gabriel attacks the sisters at the Manor, and they manage to impale him on his sword, which absorbs his soul and power and then dissipates into nothing. With Gabriel gone, the bodies of the clones vanish without a trace, leaving Andy even more mystified and extremely suspicious.

During all of this, Phoebe has taken up martial arts. She is tired of being the only one without an active power.

"It could be the upstairs-bathroom-hogging Prue or the downstairs-bathroom-hogging Prue or the sitting-in-the-kitchen-drinking-all-the-coffee Prue."
PHOEBE HALLIWELL

"That '70s Episode"

(APRIL 7, 1999)
Written by Sheryl J. Anderson
Directed by Richard Compton

As the sisters look through family pictures, Phoebe laments that these pictures are all the memory she really has of her mother, Patty. Before she can continue, the doorbell rings. It is the same man who brings flowers for Grams every year. Same day, same time, same accident, as he drops the vase again. This year, though, Piper can freeze everything and grab the flowers before the vase hits the floor and shatters. When she unfreezes him, the man notes that he only heard five of the twelve chimes of the clock—which means time was frozen, and the girls have their powers. The man is a warlock named Nicholas, and twenty-four years ago he made a pact with Patty, agreeing to spare her life if she would transfer her daughters' future powers to him. He slips on a ring that instantly makes him younger and immune to the Charmed Ones' powers. They don't understand how their mother could have given away their powers, but Nicholas says he didn't give her much choice.

Nicholas tries to kill them and Phoebe temporarily defeats him with the only power that will work—her martial arts training. The girls run to the Book of Shadows to search for a solution with Nicholas on their heels. They find a spell called To Unbind a Bond that causes them to disappear in a swirl of white orbs and reappear in the same spot twenty-four years earlier so they can stop Patty from giving away their powers and giving Nicholas immunity. The trick is to convince Grams and Patty who they are and why they're there, and to stay out of sight so as not to make any unwanted changes in history. Things would be easier if they had their powers, but since their younger selves still have them (Grams hasn't bound them yet), both of their "selves" can't possess the same powers. Having no powers isn't as hard to handle as not telling Grams and their mother what their futures hold.

Once all the Halliwells accept each other, they get down to the business of vanquishing Nicholas. The Charmed Ones steal Nicholas's ring so that Patty can unbless it. The family bids each other farewell and Grams and Patty recite Grams's spell to send the girls back to their own time, but it doesn't work. They determine that the spell needs the Power of Three, which means the younger versions of Prue and Piper need to say it while holding hands with Patty, who is carrying baby Phoebe. Nicholas bursts in, having discovered his ring missing, and Phoebe holds him off again with another roundhouse kick as Patty gets the little girls to repeat the spell. The older sisters are sent back to the exact time they left, finding a "Nicholas Must Die" spell that Grams added to the Book after their time travel. With the ring unblessed, the spell works and Nicholas is vanquished. Phoebe shows her sisters a note she had written to warn her mother about her death. She was grateful for the chance to finally spend time with Patty but didn't leave the note, because Phoebe knew it was time to let her go.

"Can't you just bake cookies with them like all the other grandmothers?"

PATTY HALLIWELL

"When Bad Warlocks Go Good"	(APRIL 28, 1999) Written by Edithe Swensen Directed by Kevin Inch

Ignoring her sisters' objections, Prue befriends a young man who is attacked by warlocks in a church. Desperate to overcome his half-warlock heritage, Brendan Rowe is joining the priesthood. However, in order to fulfill the Prophesy of the Rowe Coven and become the evil equivalent of the Charmed Ones, his warlock brothers try to tempt him to take the life of a mortal and join the dark side. Prue believes Brendan is good, even when she finds his warlock persona hovering over the injured Father Austin.

Acting on faith and instinct, Prue agrees to a dangerous plan to keep the Rowe Coven from forming. Brendan says he will kill his brothers, and then Prue and her sisters will have to kill him. The warlocks realize that attempting the crime will cause Brendan's evil nature to take over, at which point he'll be willing to commit another evil act, cementing the Coven. They order Brendan to kill Prue, but she uses her power and her faith in his inherent goodness to shock Brendan out of his evil state. When the three brothers confront each other in the church, Greg throws a dagger at Brendan, but Paul jumps in front of him and is mortally wounded. As he dies, Paul pulls the dagger from his own chest and hurls it at Greg, killing him as well. Brendan is free to be ordained a priest and become truly liberated from his evil origins. Although she's happy for Brendan, Prue regrets not being able to pursue a romantic relationship with a great guy.

Meanwhile, Piper has been avoiding Josh, another great guy, because she's afraid of falling for the wrong man again—human or supernatural.

"I'm just following my instincts, and they've never led me wrong before, at least not when I was really listening to them."

PRUE HALLIWELL

"If you're ever going to lose a guy, it might as well be to the Big Guy."

PHOEBE HALLIWELL

<table>
<tr><td>"Blind Sided"</td><td>(MAY 5, 1999)
Written by Tony Blake & Paul Jackson
Directed by Craig Zisk</td></tr>
</table>

"Blind Sided"

(MAY 5, 1999)
Written by Tony Blake & Paul Jackson
Directed by Craig Zisk

When David, a friend's son, is kidnapped from his birthday party in the park, Prue suspends the boy and the demon abductor in midair. Surprised that her powers will channel through her hands, she freezes, which allows the demon to take the boy to his underground lair and steal his sight. As if that weren't bad enough, Eric Lohman, a tabloid reporter looking to make his mark, threatens to publish a damaging article about what he saw. Preoccupied with saving David, Prue denies everything and avoids his calls.

Phoebe is later told by one of the cops investigating the scene that David is the second boy to be kidnapped from the park recently. Strangely, the same thing happened twenty years ago—same park, two kids. Phoebe finds Brent Miller, one of those earlier victims, and gets him to talk about his ordeal. He tells her that the demons said something about seeing auras. This finally gives the Charmed Ones someplace to start looking for answers. Phoebe and Piper find a listing in the Book of Shadows for auras that includes a reference to demons named Grimlocks. They roam from city to city, killing powerful forces of good that are identified by the unique aura around them. The Grimlocks are able to see the auras with the sight they've stolen from Innocent children. The stolen sight, which works only as long as the child is alive, lasts twenty-four hours (hence the need to continue to kidnap children).

While Prue makes a potion to vanquish the Grimlocks, Piper and Phoebe locate their underground lair. Piper falls into a pit and gets knocked out, and Phoebe calls Prue for help. Finding her car disabled and Lohman still on the front steps, Prue doesn't have time to blow him off, so she admits she's a witch and lets the reporter come along. She warns him that it's too dangerous to follow her into the storm drains, but he ignores her and is killed by the Grimlocks. Before doing further Grimlock hunting, Prue raises the grate on which Piper was trapped and sends her out of the drains to safety. Andy joins the party after he learns about the storm drains while questioning Brent Miller. He witnesses Prue's power when she saves him from the Grimlocks. Prue's potion dissolves both demons, restoring all of the victims' eyesight.

Andy covers for the sisters with Morris. He and Prue try to discuss what he saw, but are interrupted by reporters wanting a story about the rescued boys. And Piper remains in emotional turmoil, because although she's dating Josh, she admits she thought about Leo while she was helpless in the pit.

"I feel like I should be cackling." **PRUE HALLIWELL**

"The Power of Two"

(MAY 12, 1999)
Written by Brad Kern
Directed by Elodie Keene

The tension between Piper's sisters mounts when she attends a convention. Phoebe is tired of handling the household chores and errands because she doesn't work, so she blows off everything her sisters left her and goes to Alcatraz with a friend. There, she sees Jackson Ward, the Ghost of Alcatraz, escape in the body of a security guard (killed by a ghostly entity called the Charon). Her concern seems frivolous until people who were responsible for Ward's execution are murdered. All the evidence points to the dead man. Andy enlists the Halliwells' help with the case, unaware that Internal Affairs is suspicious of him. Phoebe has been practicing calling her premonitions, so she deliberately evokes a vision from the murder weapon and identifies the next victim, a juror. When Andy, Prue, and Phoebe save the juror, the ghost recognizes Phoebe from Alcatraz. Prue is angry that Phoebe lied to her, but even angrier that she had to hear the truth from a ghost.

To save Ward's future victims, the witches cast a spell to call his ghost. But since an evil spirit can only be vanquished on the astral plane, someone would have to die to kill Ward. Prue concocts a "killer cocktail" that kills her instantly—though temporarily, as long as she's revived within four minutes. Ward responds to the summoning spell and shows up at the Manor. A battle ensues and Phoebe is knocked out just as Prue downs the potion. The dead Prue chants the spell. Andy arrives and sees Prue dead on the floor. He almost revives her before she can vanquish Ward, but somehow hears her spirit tell him to wait. Ward is disposed of and Andy returns Prue to the living. He now accepts that magic and demons are real, but knows he can't live in Prue's world. He will keep her secret, though, and gives her the police case files and evidence he's collected that implicate the Halliwells in several unsolved crimes.

"I'm not even married, and already I'm a housewife." **PHOEBE HALLIWELL**

"I've always believed there was another world behind or beyond this one. I even sort of believed in demons, but I never in my wildest dreams could have imagined that this existed." **ANDY TRUDEAU**

"Love Hurts"	(MAY 19, 1999) Written by Chris Levinson & Zack Estrin & Javier Grillo-Marxuach Directed by James Whitmore, Jr.

Leo returns to help Daisy, a future Whitelighter, evade the Darklighter Alec. Alec says he's looking for Daisy because he fell in love with her, but Leo argues that Darklighters aren't capable of love. Angered by Leo's attitude, Alec shoots him with a Darklighter's crossbow. The arrow is tipped with a poison fatal to Whitelighters. Leo orbs to the Halliwell attic, where Piper finds him writhing in pain. Prue telekinetically extracts the arrow from Leo's shoulder and the girls dress his wound. Piper is angry that Leo never told her what he was. Phoebe reminds Piper that she tried to tell them, but no one believed her. Leo explains that the sisters need to find and help Daisy and keep Alec away from her. He warns them that Alec's power is in his hands and he can kill with a touch.

Prue searches for Daisy, Phoebe looks after Leo, and Piper scours the Book of Shadows for a way to heal the Whitelighter. Since Leo can heal others but not himself, Piper casts a spell to switch their powers. With Leo's power to heal, she can save his life. The spell works, but also switches Prue's and Phoebe's powers. Each sister successfully masters the other's powers. Following Prue's premonition, they find Alec, and Phoebe telekinetically throws him to the ground. As he drops his crossbow, the girls pick it up and shoot him with it. Hit by his own arrow, Alec disappears in a puff of black smoke. Back at the Manor, Piper is increasingly frustrated by her inability to use Leo's power to heal him. He tells her that he understands how hard she's tried, and regardless of what happens, he loves her. When her sisters return with Daisy safely in tow, Piper tells them Leo died. She begins to cry and tells Leo that she loves him. Her tears soak her hand, which rests on Leo's body. A glow emanates from Piper's hand and Leo's eyes open. Love is the trigger to Leo's power, and until Piper expressed her love for him, it wouldn't manifest. She apologizes for not declaring her feelings sooner.

Meanwhile, Alec is gone but not vanquished. The sisters track him down again. Prue uses the power-changing spell to switch powers with him, and kills him with his own deadly touch. She quickly switches their powers back as the Darklighter disintegrates. The next day, Leo tells Piper about his past as a World War II medic and how he became a Whitelighter. He says he would gladly give up immortality to spend a mortal life with her, but Piper knows his work is too important to stand in his way.

While the witches were doing battle with Alec, Andy was fending off Internal Affairs. Fed up with the investigation of his actions, he turns in his badge. Still determined to get their man, Rodriguez and Anderson put a wire on Morris to trap Andy into incriminating himself, but Rodriguez is the one who reveals a secret: He's a warlock, and his ultimate goal is to kill the Charmed Ones.

"You know how Peter Pan has Tinkerbell? They're sort of like that only minus the tutu and wings."
PHOEBE HALLIWELL

"A couple of dates not picking up the check, that's a slump. This is more like a sucking void."
PRUE HALLIWELL

120

"Déjà Vu All Over Again"	(MAY 26, 1999) Written by Brad Kern & Constance M. Burge Directed by Les Sheldon

The day begins ominously when Phoebe has a premonition of Andy's death. Since they've been able to change the outcome of Phoebe's visions before, the sisters band together to prevent Andy from dying. What they don't know is the demon Tempus is after them, and he can keep replaying the day until he gets the outcome he desires. Tempus uses the warlock/fake Internal Affairs cop Rodriguez to carry out his plan.

The first time around, Rodriguez kills Phoebe before Prue can kill him. The second time the day begins, Phoebe gets an odd sense of déjà vu, but Rodriguez still manages to kill her and Piper before Prue kills him again. When they go around again, Phoebe's power helps her realize that this isn't déjà vu, but some sort of time demon after them. Prue warns Andy to stay away from the Manor because weird things are happening, and Rodriguez is in the middle of them. But Andy has suspicions about Rodriguez, and ignores her warning.

In the third version of the day, Rodriguez has learned from his mistakes. He fires his first fireball at Prue so she won't be around to save her sisters. The fireball misses its target, but when Prue dodges it, she hits her head and falls unconscious to the floor. Just then, Andy enters and sees an immobile and vulnerable Prue. He shoots Rodriguez, who retaliates with another fireball. This one is a direct hit and kills Andy instantly. His spirit visits the unconscious Prue and tells her she has let him die to end the time loop. If she doesn't, and keeps replaying the day, they will all die. Andy accepts his death as his destiny. It is not Prue's fault, and she needs to know that he will always be there for her.

Prue regains consciousness and is even more determined to defeat Tempus. According to the Book of Shadows, the only way to beat the demon is to speed up time, thus breaking the loop. They can only go forward, so there is no going back to save Andy. The sisters read the spell. Time speeds up, and as it passes midnight the next day, Tempus turns into a red mist and vanishes into a fire. Prue unties Rodriguez, who had been captured by Piper and Phoebe. He turns and throws one last fireball at the witches. Prue deflects it, killing Rodriguez with his own weapon.

The Charmed Ones mourn their friend Andy, and take some comfort in the fact that finally, his record and his name have been cleared.

"We do good things. Together."

PRUE HALLIWELL

The Charmed Episode Puns

When it comes to their episode titles, the writing staff at *Charmed* gets to have a lot of fun with puns, plays on words, old sayings, and pop culture references. Here are the episode titles from the **FIRST SEASON** along with their most likely origins.

SOMETHING WICCA THIS WAY COMES: "By the pricking of my thumbs, something wicked this way comes," is a line spoken by the Second Witch in Act IV, Scene 1, of Shakespeare's *Macbeth*. Wicca is a religious practice involving nature.

I'VE GOT YOU UNDER MY SKIN: A Cole Porter song most often associated with Frank Sinatra, who first recorded the hit in 1956.

THANK YOU FOR NOT MORPHING: "Thank You for Not Smoking" is a common phrase seen on signs in various public locations. "Morphing" is an ability to shift from one image into another.

DEAD MAN DATING: *Dead Man Walking* is the title of a 1995 movie starring Susan Sarandon and Sean Penn.

DREAM SORCERER: *"Dream Weaver"* is a song and album released by Gary Wright in 1975.

THE WEDDING FROM HELL: Common phrase used to describe an awful occasion; in this case, a wedding.

THE FOURTH SISTER: A random girl would like to join the Charmed Ones as a member of their family of witches, thus making her a new sister.

THE TRUTH IS OUT THERE . . . AND IT HURTS: Combination of the tagline of the TV series *The X-Files* and the cliché "the truth hurts."

THE WITCH IS BACK: A play on words of a phrase with a similar-sounding word announcing the return of a strong woman. Also, a play on an Elton John song.

WICCA ENVY: "Penis envy," from Freudian psychoanalytic theory, describes a perceived inferiority certain women have in regard to men.

FEATS OF CLAY: "Feet of Clay" is a phrase that refers to a person's weakness. Its origin is found in the Old Testament (Daniel 2:31–32): " . . . his legs of iron, his feet part of iron and part of clay."

THE WENDIGO: A malevolent spirit from Native American folklore.

FROM FEAR TO ETERNITY: *From Here to Eternity* is a 1953 film based on the novel about heroism and romance set during World War II.

SECRETS AND GUYS: *Secrets and Lies* is the title of a film from 1996, as well as a phrase commonly used to note untrustworthy situations.

IS THERE A WOOGY IN THE HOUSE?: "Is there a doctor in the house?" is a comic phrase that came into popularity in vaudeville routines.

WHICH PRUE IS IT ANYWAY?: *Whose Line Is It Anyway?* is an improvisational comedy TV series hosted by Drew Carey, based on a British series of the same name.

THAT '70S EPISODE: *That '70s Show* is a TV comedy series set, logically enough, during the 1970s.

WHEN BAD WARLOCKS GO GOOD: A play on the sensationalized phrase "When good [blanks] go bad."

BLIND SIDED: To be taken by surprise. To have something come at you from the direction you aren't looking.

THE POWER OF TWO: What's left when one of the Charmed Ones is removed from the Power of Three.

LOVE HURTS: A proverb stating the obvious. Also the title of numerous songs.

DÉJÀ VU ALL OVER AGAIN: "It's like déjà vu all over again," is a quote attributed to Yogi Berra.

Episode Guide

Season Two

(SEPTEMBER 30, 1999)
Written by Brad Kern
Directed by Craig Zisk

On the first anniversary of the Charmed Ones receiving their powers, the Book of Shadows mysteriously flips open to the Rite of Passage page, which instructs: "Fight it with the power of one, or else. . . ." The Book is promptly stolen by a demon, who seemingly comes out of a wall in the attic. The loss of their greatest magical tool causes the Halliwells to reevaluate matters of individual importance: Prue blames herself for Andy's death, Piper applies for a loan to buy a nightclub, and Phoebe develops an interest in traditional Wiccan ways. The sisters ask the Spirit Board for help. It gives them the name Abraxas, who Phoebe finds in one of her books about Wicca. Abraxas is a demon of the astral plane that destroys witches by demonizing their powers. Since the Book is their power, Piper deduces that Abraxas is reading it backward, giving power back to demons they vanquished. Phoebe reasons that since no one can remove the Book from the Manor except a Charmed One, it and the demon must still be in the house—just on a different plane of existence. The girls need to find the portal to this other plane before Abraxas gets to the front of the Book and reverses the incantation that gave the sisters their powers.

Acting on Grams's hints and Phoebe's new knowledge of Wiccan magic, they realize the Power of Three is strongest when they act together as one. Prue overcomes her doubts about the benefits of having magical powers, and they recite the Spell for Invoking the Power of Three around a stone altar. The Book of Shadows is retrieved, the spells are recovered, and Abraxas is vanquished. Phoebe and Prue secure a second mortgage on the house to finance Piper's club. While dealing with Abraxas, the Halliwells welcome Dan Gordon and his niece, Jenny, who move in next door.

"How can it be good to be witches if all it does is get the people we love killed?"
PRUE HALLIWELL

124

"Morality Bites"

(OCTOBER 7, 1999)
Written by Chris Levinson & Zack Estrin
Directed by John Behring

After using magic for revenge against an inconsiderate neighbor, Phoebe sees herself being burned at the stake in 2009. To prevent that, the Charmed Ones recite a one-use-only spell to move forward in time. Rather than being observers in a world where witches are persecuted, they inhabit the bodies of their future selves. Piper has a daughter, Melinda, and Leo is her ex-husband. Prue is a rich workaholic, and Phoebe used her power to kill a brutal murderer.

When Piper and Prue discover the return spell isn't in the Book of Shadows, they try to rescue their sister from prison. However Phoebe knows she has to pay for her crime. Their job is to protect the Innocent, not punish the guilty. When it's obvious she's willing to die, the Elders return the Charmed Ones to the moment before they used magic on Nathaniel Pratt, the inconsiderate neighbor and future witch prosecutor. This time they keep their powers holstered.

"The wrong thing done for the right reason is still the wrong thing."
PHOEBE HALLIWELL

"We can still make the good things happen. We just have to make the right choices."
PRUE HALLIWELL

"The Painted World"

(OCTOBER 14, 1999)
Written by Constance M. Burge
Directed by Kevin Inch

A 1920s painting of a castle intrigues Prue, especially after she sees a man in a lighted window write the word *help*. An X ray to authenticate the painting reveals words written in Latin under the paint. Prue reads the phrase and is drawn into the painting, where she meets Malcolm, the man trapped there. He helps her dodge fireballs, knowing their pattern after being stuck in the castle in the painting for seventy years.

While Prue tries to figure her way out of the painting, Phoebe is feeling inadequate after yet another attempt to get a job. The company has given her an aptitude test to take home, so she writes a twenty-four-hour Smart Spell to help her ace it.

The next morning, Piper realizes that Prue hasn't been home and Phoebe seems awfully well informed. Sensing that the painting is a link to the missing Prue, Piper brings it and the X-ray print of it home. Prue has come up with a plan to contact and warn her sisters, but she doesn't get the chance to implement it before a curious Piper reads the Latin phrase on the X ray. Phoebe is shocked to see her sister sucked into the painting. Working together, Prue, Piper, and Malcolm manage to send Phoebe the signal. Still supersmart, the youngest Halliwell understands it and finds the reference in the Book of Shadows. Thinking fast, she sends the cat into the painting with the escape phrase. That's when Malcolm exposes himself as a warlock who, with his warlock girl-friend, set up the whole scenario. They needed the power of the Charmed Ones to free Malcolm. He finds the exit spell in Kit's collar and chants it, leaving Piper and Prue trapped. Finally free, Malcolm now also wants the Power of Three. Time's run out on her Smart Spell, so Phoebe can't go into the painting to save her sisters because she can't remember the Latin escape phrase. When Malcolm's girlfriend sets the painting on fire, Phoebe reacts quickly once more. She reads the phrase on the X ray and drags the two warlocks into the castle with her. On the way, she picks Malcolm's pocket for the escape phrase. She then grabs her sisters and Kit and recites the spell. The Charmed Ones and the cat are thrown out to safety, and the painting—with the warlocks trapped inside—is destroyed.

During the whole warlock-in-the-painting ordeal, Piper also deals with a multitude of building code violations that block her club from opening. Since her new neighbor Dan is in construction, he agrees to help her bring everything up to code.

"She's a walking brain-trust, an Einstein with cleavage."

PIPER HALLIWELL ON PHOEBE

"I don't obsess. I think—intensely."

PRUE HALLIWELL

"The Devil's Music"

(OCTOBER 21, 1999)
Written by David Simkins
Directed by Richard Compton

B usiness is so slow at Piper's new club that Prue secretly arranges a loan with a private lender named Chris Barker. Before she seals the deal, Leo arranges for a popular band to appear at P3. The reason the band is so hot is that their manager feeds the souls of young female fans to a demon named Masselin in exchange for their success. Piper is upset that Leo didn't ask her before booking the band, but he did it so that the Charmed Ones can vanquish the demon and put an end to the soul harvesting.

Piper and Phoebe consult the Book of Shadows to find out how to vanquish Masselin. The plan is to feed him an extra-strength antacid to get him to "burp up" the souls. They can only get to the demon through the person feeding it the souls—the band's manager, Carlton. Phoebe plans to charm Carlton into getting her to Masselin so she can administer the medication. Throwing a curve into everything is the Halliwells' teenage neighbor, Jenny, who sneaks in to see the band. Realizing that Phoebe is a witch, Masselin has Carlton confiscate Phoebe's "antacid" and bring him Jenny instead. The potion spills all over Phoebe's dress in the ensuing altercation, but that doesn't stop the Charmed Ones. Prue hurls the potion off of the dress into the demon's mouth, dissolving him and freeing his victims.

Oblivious to all of this, the band plays on, and the crowd loves it. With the guaranteed success of P3, Barker decides to take over the club rather than just loan Prue the money. But after witnessing the events that vanquished Masselin, the businessman heeds Prue's warning to leave the club and her sisters alone.

Darryl, who has been investigating the disappearances of the fans, tells the sisters he needs and wants to know who and what they are. He insists that they stop protecting him.

Meanwhile, Piper is more than a little annoyed that Leo seems to be paying attention to her only because of business. She wonders if they can truly have a romantic relationship.

"You have time for baseball, but you don't have time to tell me about you-know-what before you-know-who shows up for you-know-where?" **PIPER HALLIWELL**

"She's a Man, Baby, a Man!"

(NOVEMBER 4, 1999)
Written by Javier Grillo-Marxuach
Directed by Martha Mitchell

While Piper wonders if Dan is interested in her and Prue wonders if a casual dating acquaintance, Alan, has lost interest in her, Phoebe is killing lovers in her erotic dreams. The victims are all pictured in a police file of murdered men Darryl gives Prue. Since her power is psychic, Phoebe is apparently mentally linked to a succubus—a sexual predator—that's targeting men from a dating service. There's no spell to vanquish the succubus, but there is one to attract it, after which it can be destroyed with fire. Prue casts the spell, but it doesn't attract anything—it turns her into a man! With no reverse spell in the Book, Piper figures that the way Prue is supposed to kill the demon is to remain a man and attract the succubus to her (him). The witches' strategy session is cut short when Dan shows up. Piper explains that ManPrue is Manny, the brother they never had.

Adapting quickly to her male persona, Prue learns a lot about how men think and feel. Manny's macho moves at a dating service mixer attract the predator's attention and he ends up in the succubus's bed despite their precautions. Still linked, Phoebe reverses the connection and speaks through the killer to remind Manny that he's really Prue, a woman. Prue hears Phoebe's pleas and uses her power to throw the succubus across the room, which starts a fire that consumes the demon. Mission accomplished, Manny turns back into Prue. Everyone's love life takes a turn for the better, including Piper and Dan's.

"It's starting to get weird? Where have you been?" **PHOEBE HALLIWELL**

"You know that I know you've got a secret." **DARRYL MORRIS**

"That Old Black Magic"

(NOVEMBER 11, 1999)
Written by Vivian Mayhew & Valerie Mayhew
Directed by James L. Conway

After the evil witch Tuatha is accidentally freed from her two-hundred-year-old entombment, the Charmed Ones are called upon to protect The Chosen One, the only person who can possess Tuatha's wand and destroy her. To their surprise, The Chosen One is a teenage boy named Kyle Gwydion. Leo brings the girls Kyle, and an auction at Buckland brings them the wand. It also brings Jack Sheridan, an artifact appraiser with an Internet auction house, to Prue. While Leo teaches Kyle to use his power, the Halliwells confront Tuatha, who strips their powers.

Realizing that the boy is their only hope, Phoebe arms her sisters with three vials: a sleep potion, a potion to repel an evil threat, and one of water, to put out a fire. When Kyle pits his will against Tuatha for the wand, Prue convinces him the water is a potion for courage. Although no such potion exists, Kyle believes Prue and believes in himself. He wins the wand and wishes Tuatha gone forever. Since Kyle succeeded on his own, Prue encourages him to remain confident, and if he does he can create whatever he wants for his life. Leo realizes he can't give Piper the normal relationship she wants. Prue, who has been resisting Jack's advances, relents and uses the broken wand as an excuse to see him.

"He's a jerk. How do I look?"   **PRUE HALLIWELL ON JACK**

"Maybe there's a lesson here for us, not taking our powers for granted."

PIPER HALLIWELL

"They're Everywhere"

(NOVEMBER 18, 1999)
Written by Sheryl J. Anderson
Directed by Mel Damski

Worried when Jack appears to blink and the cat hisses at Dan, Prue and Piper cast a spell to hear secret thoughts and see if the men are warlocks. They could have saved themselves the trouble if they had known what Phoebe later tells them—warlocks don't bleed.

While working at a medical care facility, Phoebe has a vision of two real warlocks using a needle to extract knowledge from a patient's son, Eric Bragg. The same process left Eric's father mindless weeks earlier. The warlocks are after Eric because he is the only one who knows how to translate the map to the Akashic Records, a detailed account of all of the significant events in history. Known as the Collectors, the warlocks want the Records because they also predict all future events. With that knowledge they will be able to upset the balance between good and evil. There is no vanquishing spell for the Collectors in the Book of Shadows, only the cryptic comment that "their hunger for knowledge is your ally."

Phoebe tries to keep Eric out of harm's way while figuring out how to get rid of the Collectors. Eric begins to see the Akashic Records as a threat, rather than a gift to humanity. If the outcome of all events is known in advance, there could be no need for—or exercising of—free will, and no world as we know it. Eric destroys the translation key tablet, leaving his knowledge the only link to the whereabouts of the Records. The Collectors offer Eric a deal: They promise to restore his father's mind in exchange for what he knows. The Charmed Ones arrive as the warlocks begin to drain Eric's brain. Phoebe is first on the scene and becomes another victim of the Collectors' extraction needle.

Piper quickly freezes the warlocks, and Prue telekinetically shifts them so that they drain each other out of existence. The effects of the partial brain drain leave Phoebe and Eric with no short-term memory, and although they don't remember the map key or each other, they experience a sense of familiarity when they meet again.

Piper and Prue successfully prove that neither Dan nor Jack are warlocks. Jack is a twin, however, which explains how he seemed to be in two places in a blink of an eye.

"With warlocks and demons coming out of the woodwork all the time, it's a wonder we trust anybody."

PIPER HALLIWELL

"P3 H20"

(DECEMBER 9, 1999)
Written by Chris Levinson & Zack Estrin
Directed by John Behring

Unknown to her sisters, Prue often visits the site of her mother's death, where she tries to cope with her fear of dying young. She sees her mother's killer, the Demon of the Lake, pull a man from a canoe, drowning him near the dock where Patty died. Prue tries to help the drowning man, but is told, cryptically, that he's already been taken. With Camp Skylark about to open again, the sisters are determined to vanquish the still-deadly water demon. They also want to investigate the strange man who warned off Prue. The camp owner says it must be Sam, a rather odd man who lives by the lake. The girls get Sam's address, and when they find him, they find much more. Sam was their mother's Whitelighter. When he couldn't save her from the demon in the lake, he was devastated. He clipped his wings and became human. A Whitelighter losing a charge is a difficult thing, but the Charmed Ones also know that it shouldn't have been so overwhelming as to cause Sam's extreme actions. Knowing they will be curious, Sam sprinkles some magic dust on the sisters and sends them home. The next morning, they don't remember Sam, the water demon, or anything about their trip to the lake.

Leo checks up on his charges, and when they are confused by his questions about the demon, he realizes what Sam did. A little refresher course is all they need to get back on the case. Prue and Phoebe go back to the lake. Since they hadn't warned anyone before talking to Sam, and didn't remember to afterward, the camp is reopening with a fresh crop of victims. Piper stays home with a case of poison ivy. She finds letters she had picked up at Sam's cabin and stashed in her pocket. She and Leo read them aloud and find they were love letters from Patty to Sam, which explains why he was so distraught about her death. Piper and Leo are extremely affected by the letters, and by the fact that they are not the first Halliwell witch and Whitelighter to fall in love. Leo breaks another Whitelighter rule to orb Piper to the lake so she can tell her sisters about Sam and Patty.

When the girls confront Sam about it, he tells them he blames himself for distracting Patty and causing her death. She froze him to protect him, so he didn't see how she was planning to kill the demon. Now Phoebe must return to the spot and try to get a vision of how it all happened. She sees her mother prepare to kill the demon with electricity—the only thing that separates water molecules—and when she turns to save Sam, the water demon engulfs her. It is up to Prue to try again, since she is the daughter most like her mother. History almost repeats itself as Prue calls for the water demon and the sisters distract her. But this time, Sam deliberately allows the demon to envelop him. As he struggles against it, he tells Prue to electrocute the demon within him. Finally accomplishing his goal of keeping the next generation of Halliwell witches safe from the water demon, Sam happily joins Patty in the spirit world. He has some parting words for Leo, who, like Sam, knows his love keeps him from doing his job. And like Sam, Leo knows he can't stop loving a witch.

"In case you didn't get the memo, I'm not one of the good guys anymore."

SAM WILDER

"Leo doesn't do personal anymore. He just does his job." **PIPER HALLIWELL**

"Ms. Hellfire"

(JANUARY 13, 2000)
Teleplay by Constance M. Burge &
Sheryl J. Anderson
Story by Constance M. Burge
Directed by Craig Zisk

It's another Friday the Thirteenth, and another opportunity for Barbas, the Demon of Fear, to kill thirteen unmarried witches and free himself from purgatory. The Halliwells' morning routine is shattered by a spray of bullets, which Prue repels, killing a human hit woman. After they admit to being witches, Darryl agrees to keep the body on ice. Although Prue's job is at risk under Buckland's new management, she and Piper stop by the hit woman's apartment to look for clues. What they find is a wardrobe Prue would kill for and roses with a card addressed to Ms. Hellfire. When three henchmen who work for someone named Bane Jessup mistake Prue for the hit woman, she pretends to be Ms. Hellfire and discovers that Barbas hired Jessup to arrange the deaths of thirteen witches, including the Charmed Ones. While Prue perpetrates her hoax, Phoebe and Darryl save another witch on Ms. Hellfire's list.

129

Under pressure at Buckland's and as a Charmed One, Prue feels the need to be in two places at once—and suddenly is. Her powers grow and she develops the power of astral projection, conveniently allowing Prue to be Ms. Hellfire and a Buckland's employee at the same time.

Barbas catches on to Prue's charade. Since Jessup can't get the job done for him, he'll have to do it himself. Barbas reads that Prue's greatest fear now is that someone will kill her sisters. Under Barbas's influence, Prue believes that the real Piper and Phoebe are imposters and she attacks with the intent to kill. After forcing Prue to astral project, Phoebe and Piper break the demon's hold. He is sent back to hell, and Jessup is sent to jail.

Dan fixes the windows shot out by Ms. Hellfire, and offers to let Piper move in with him—for safety reasons, and for any other reason she might think of. . . .

"Since when do demons use bullets?" **PHOEBE HALLIWELL**

"Heartbreak City"

(JANUARY 20, 2000)
Written by David Simkins
Directed by Michael Zinberg

Robbed of the ring that lets him influence love, Cupid seeks out Phoebe. He needs the Charmed Ones' help to stop the demon Drazi from spreading hate and killing him. He also helps Phoebe understand why she can't find love. Since everything is going great for her sisters and their respective beaus, Jack and Dan, Phoebe is constantly reminded that she's alone. Cupid explains that potential partners shy away from her closed heart, which has kept her safe from people leaving, as her mother did.

Unaware that Cupid's ring protected Drazi from their vanquishing potion so he wasn't destroyed, the sisters go to P3. Phoebe realizes the demon still exists when Cupid reacts to the lovers' quarrels between Piper and Dan and Prue and Jack. Phoebe helps fix the romantic damage with words, which weakens Drazi. When he tries to kill Cupid again, Phoebe switches the ring onto Cupid's finger. She throws the remaining potion on Drazi and the demon dies. The couples make up, but Dan admits he still has a problem with whatever secret Piper is keeping.

"Nothing like a night out on the town after a hard day of demon killing."

PIPER HALLIWELL

"The pain of love lost deepens if you don't deal with it." **PHOEBE HALLIWELL**

"Reckless Abandon"	(JANUARY 27, 2000) Written by Javier Grillo-Marxuach Directed by Craig Zisk

After asking Darryl to hire her as a police psychic, Phoebe takes temporary custody of an abandoned baby. The name Matthew is appliquéd on his baby blanket. A vision indicates that the baby's father, Gilbert Van Lewen, will be killed by a ghost. When Gilbert dies, a Web search reveals that the family chauffer, Elias Lundy, vanished just before the deaths of Van Lewen males began. The sisters believe Matthew was left at the police station to save his life. They visit the Van Lewen estate and their theory is confirmed. The ghost has vowed to kill every male Van Lewen as revenge for being spurned by Martha Van Lewen and shot by her husband. Armed with this information, the Charmed Ones consult the Book of Shadows and learn that a ghost can be vanquished by pouring a potion on its bones or destroying the object of its wrath. However, killing Martha Van Lewen, Matthew's grandmother, who rejected Elias's love years before, isn't an option. Lundy feels his bones being attacked, and sends them deep into the earth before the potion is applied. Upon learning that her death will destroy Lundy, Martha explains that she, not her husband, shot the chauffeur. To save her grandson, Martha throws herself over a second-floor banister. Her spirit ascends and curses Lundy to hell.

Piper is amazed at how good Dan is with baby Matthew, but worries that his perfection only points out her imperfection. And Prue knows that Jack isn't Mr. Right, but he'll do for now.

"There could be hundreds of dead people that are holding a grudge against them."
PHOEBE HALLIWELL ON THE VAN LEWEN FAMILY

"Awakened"	(FEBRUARY 3, 2000) Written by Vivian Mayhew & Valerie Mayhew Directed by Anson Williams

Piper is hospitalized with Oroya fever after being bitten by a sand flea in a smuggled fruit shipment to P3. When her doctor, Dr. Williamson, reveals that she may not survive, Prue and Phoebe call Leo. However, since Piper wasn't hurt fighting evil, the Elders won't let him cure her. Desperate, Prue and Phoebe cast an awakening spell that heals Piper, but also animates a ninja doll that spreads the disease through the hospital.

The Charmed Ones are alerted to the deadly consequences of using magic for personal gain when they're taken into custody by the Centers for Disease Control and Prevention after an outbreak of Oroya fever hits the hospital. They know that Piper can't survive at the cost of innocent lives, and she dies when the spell is reversed. In the ether between planes where the Elders can't stop him, Leo heals Piper. The doctor is mystified by her miraculous recovery. Dan is devastated when she calls for Leo and not him upon awakening. The Elders discover Leo's transgression and punish him by clipping his wings. As a mortal, Leo vows to fight Dan for Piper.

As Piper comes back to life her sisters make some major life changes. Phoebe enrolls in college, and Prue rejects the fraudulent business practices at Buckland's. She quits the auction house and leaves Jack.

"I had a little wake-up call, and I realized that life is way too short to be wasting my time doing something I really don't want to be doing." **PRUE HALLIWELL**

"The world is made up of almost-perfect. It's nothing but near-misses and necessary compromises." **JACK SHERIDAN**

"Animal Pragmatism"

(FEBRUARY 10, 2000)
Written by Chris Levinson & Zach Estrin
Directed by Don Kurt

In a study group, Phoebe advises women on how to create a love spell. Then the students, Andrea, Tessa, and Brook, use the spell to turn a pig, a rabbit, and a snake into human males for twenty-four hours. The guys look great, but they have the personalities and traits of their animal selves. Bored and unemployed, Prue helps Phoebe look for a man she saw nibbling a girl's neck in a vision. Piper preps for P3's Valentine party and copes with Dan's jealousy of Leo, who, with no human resources besides Piper, sleeps and works at the club.

After caging Tessa and killing Pig, poisonous Snake bites Andrea and Brook to force Phoebe to make him and Rabbit permanently human. Tracking them to P3, Phoebe writes an impromptu spell, which turns the ani-men and everyone else at the club into critters. Piper and Prue find the dying girls while Phoebe reverses the spell. Human again, Snake and Rabbit are taken to jail. Piper goes to dinner with Dan as planned, to celebrate Valentine's Day, but she imagines she's kissing Leo.

"Why do we seem to have a habit of gathering our men at the scene of a supernatural smackdown?" **PIPER HALLIWELL**

"Pardon My Past"

(FEBRUARY 17, 2000)
Written by Michael Gleason
Directed by Jon Paré

When Phoebe is attacked by an invisible assailant, Leo thinks it's a warning from the past. Under a past life spell, Phoebe's consciousness returns to 1924, where she observes a previous self and her warlock lover, Anton, plotting to kill her cousins, the past Prue and Piper. According to the Halliwell Family tree, evil P. Russell died February 17, 1924—the same day that Phoebe was attacked in the present. Further investigation reveals that the cousins cursed and killed P. Russell to prevent her from ever being with the immortal Anton. Without the protective amulet the warlock gave her previous self, Phoebe Halliwell will die.

To try to find the amulet, the sisters track down an elderly survivor of that day, but she doesn't know what became of it. Phoebe realizes that if she can physically return to 1924 she can hide the amulet for recovery in the present. She switches life forces with Past Phoebe, going to 1924 and sending the evil P. Russell to 2000; however, she arrives after the amulet is lost. What no one knows is that Anton had recovered the amulet. He gives it to P. Russell when he revives her in the present. Without the amulet, Present Phoebe is vulnerable in the past, so she says the spell to return, but it fails because P. Russell is wearing the magical necklace. Present Prue and Piper need to get the amulet to bring back their sister, and Present Phoebe needs to stay alive long enough to make it. Evil defeats itself once again when Prue kills Anton by deflecting a fireball thrown by P. Russell. She retrieves the amulet as Phoebe tries the spell one more time and succeeds. Prue places the amulet on Phoebe to make sure that she's not killed by anyone in either time frame. Phoebe survives the curse, but she makes an entry in the Book of Shadows warning her future selves about Anton and her apparent affinity for the dark side. Knowing he was part of Piper's past, Leo is certain they're destined to be together. Dan worries because Leo *has* no past.

"It's not like there's a fallen Whitelighter support group to join or anything."

PRUE HALLIWELL

"Would you like me to curse anyone for you?"

P. RUSSELL

	(FEBRUARY 24, 2000)
"Give Me a Sign"	Written by Sheryl J. Anderson
	Directed by James A. Contner

Bane Jessup is freed from prison by two demonic henchmen. Although he previously worked for Barbas, the Demon of Fear, Bane is not anxious to renew his relationship with the Underworld. That's fine with Litvack, an Upper-Level demon. However, Litvack still wants Bane dead, because the mortal knows that demons exist. After Bane eludes his liberators, he kidnaps Prue, needing her help to vanquish the demons that are hunting him. Despite the fact that Bane worked with Barbas to kill the Charmed Ones, Prue believes he honestly wants to break free of his evil connections.

Locating Prue is complicated by a spell Phoebe cast in the hope Piper would get a sign to help her decide between Dan and Leo. However, the signs Phoebe believes are related to Piper are actually about Prue. When the two younger Halliwells finally read the signs correctly, they track down Prue and Bane. Trusting their older sister's instincts about Bane's sincerity, they unite to vanquish Litvack, but he leaves them wondering about an evil entity he calls The Source. Piper no longer wonders where her love lies, though. She knows her heart belongs to Leo.

"To find a mortal, all you have to do is follow his dreams."

LITVACK

"We're rescuing you from the tall, dark, naked man."

PHOEBE HALLIWELL

	(MARCH 30, 2000)
"Murphy's Luck"	Written by David Simkins
	Directed by John Behring

415 magazine gives Prue an assignment to photograph a charity worker having a streak of bad luck. After saving Maggie Murphy from a suicidal fall, Prue casts a spell to restore her good luck. She is unaware that a Darklighter wants Maggie to kill herself so she can't become a

Whitelighter. Since the good luck will be voided if Prue dies, the Darklighter changes his focus. After cursing her with the bad luck that previously haunted Maggie, he plays on Prue's buried guilt about an old accident involving Phoebe and her self-doubt about becoming a professional photographer, trying to get her to kill herself.

Based on a vision, Piper and Phoebe intercept Prue at a bridge from her past, where the Darklighter has succeeded in driving her to the verge of suicide. Frustrated by his inability to help, Leo demands that the Elders give him back his powers. He wants to be with Piper now that he knows she loves him, but not if she has to lose a sister. Encouraged by her sisters, Prue breaks the Darklighter's hold on her mind. Leo orbs in, tackles the dark being, and orbs it out with him.

Back in action, Prue gets the shot of Maggie, and her first credit as a professional photographer. Piper faces having to tell Dan it's over.

"She was saved by some angel . . . that by her description bears no resemblance to Della Reese."
DARRYL MORRIS

"How to Make a Quilt out of Americans"

(APRIL 6, 2000)
Teleplay by Javier Grillo-Marxuach & Robert Masello
Story by Javier Grillo-Marxuach
Directed by Kevin Inch

The Halliwells are surprised when Gail Altman, an old family friend, reveals that she belonged to Grams's coven and knows their secret. She tells the girls she needs them to vanquish Cryto, a demon that's skinning corpses in her town. While the sisters confer, Gail steals the page from the Book of Shadows with the potion and spell to separate a witch from her powers. Having no clue that Gail has made a deal with Cryto to trade their stolen powers for youth and health, the Charmed Ones agree to help.

The sisters travel to Gail's house in Santa Costa, where they are served iced tea laced with the potion to make them susceptible to the power separation spell. Gail and her friend manage to restore Cryto to a body and give him the Charmed powers. Gail becomes young and healthy, but Cryto kills her friends so there aren't enough witches left to banish him again. While the demon trades youth for other souls in town, the sisters figure out that their powers are gone. Still wishing for a normal life, Piper doesn't want them back, but accepts her responsibility and relents. Cryto is tricked into astral projecting, which allows Piper and Prue to give him the potion. The sisters call back their powers and vanquish Cryto.

Learning a lesson about vanity, Phoebe accepts wearing glasses. And painful as it is, Piper finally breaks up with Dan.

"I'll just put my life on hold one more time and I'll be right there."
PIPER HALLIWELL

"Chick Flick"

(APRIL 20, 2000)
Written by Chris Levinson & Zack Estrin
Directed by Michael Schultz

The Demon of Illusion follows Phoebe home from her favorite film, a black-and-white classic called *Kill It Before It Dies*. Phoebe vanquishes him too easily, leaving the sisters to wonder what's really up. When riots break out at movie theaters playing the classic film, they realize the vanquish wasn't real. Leo tells them the Demon of Illusion uses magic to create violence in society. The Charmed Ones return to the revival house, the last place they saw the demon. It's not really work for Phoebe to watch the movie again because the hero, Billy, is her ideal man. In addition to the usual cast of characters, the sisters find the demon in the film this time. When he insults Phoebe, Billy defends her, and the ensuing tussle throws the two of them from the screen. Seeing illusion enter reality gives the demon a new plan. Luckily for everyone, Billy has experience being an illusion and some theories on how to deal with the impending problems, which only makes him brighter in Phoebe's eyes and heart.

Phoebe's encounter with her hero is in direct contrast to Prue's disappointment with hers, a pompous photographer. His histrionics are merely annoying, however, compared to the problems created by the demon. The Manor is attacked by Bloody Mary and an ax murderer, two characters from other horror films playing around town. The Charmed Ones find they can't kill movie characters because they don't really exist. However, Phoebe reasons, the characters will die if they meet the same fates in reality as they do in their films. The girls try it, and it works. With that problem solved, they refocus on vanquishing the Demon of Illusion. Piper and Phoebe drink a potion to enter the movie, but almost become trapped in the film as it ends. Prue rewinds the reel so they can escape and kills the demon by stopping the film. Stuck in the frame, he burns as the film catches fire.

Phoebe is sad to say good-bye to Billy offscreen, but is thrilled when Prue gives her a video of the movie. Piper and Leo go on their first real date as they try to start their "normal" relationship.

"It's the twenty-first century. It's the woman's job to save the day."

PRUE HALLIWELL

"Don't we usually start in some dark and dreary place and then end up here at the Manor for the big, old vanquish?" **PIPER HALLIWELL**

134

"Ex Libris"	(APRIL 27, 2000) Teleplay by Brad Kern Story by Peter Chomsky Directed by Joel J. Feigenbaum

Steering clear of Leo and Piper's romantic reunion, Prue ponders a saddened man who appears in several photos for a *415* article. Cleavant Wilson haunts the bus stop where his daughter was murdered, hoping to find a witness against the pawn shop owner who killed her. At the library Phoebe meets Charleen Hughes, who claims to have proven the existence of demons. Charleen is killed by a Libris Demon, a Reaper type that decapitates humans with unequivocal evidence that evil entities are real.

After much prodding and some concrete proof from Phoebe, Charleen accepts her death. She decides she wants justice so that her spirit can move on. The Charmed Ones vanquish the Libris Demon, but that doesn't release the ghost. It seems Charleen also needs to get justice for another. After she haunts the pawn shop and scares a confession from Gibbs, both Charleen and Mr. Wilson are able to move on.

While Phoebe is dealing with a ghost and Prue with a distraught father, Piper walks in on Dan and Leo in the middle of a fistfight. Dan warns Piper that Leo isn't who he says he is and gives her a folder with incriminating evidence. Although Piper already knows most of what's in the folder, she discovers that Leo was married to a woman named Lillian. Curious, Piper visits Lillian, who tells Piper that she loved Leo and probably always will in a certain way, because thanks to him, she had a happy life. After his death, Leo appeared to her in a dream, bathed in beautiful white light, and told her to move on because wonderful things were in store. Piper confronts Leo with what she's learned, and he agrees to be more honest with her.

"You keep trying because you never give up hope."   **LEO WYATT**

"How could someone not know that they're dead?"   **PHOEBE HALLIWELL**

"Astral Monkey"

(MAY 4, 2000)
Teleplay by Constance M. Burge &
   David Simkins
Story by Constance M. Burge
Directed by Craig Zisk

135

Dr. Williamson, who treated Piper's Oroya fever, has been doing some independent research. He runs tests on three lab chimpanzees using blood samples culled from the three Charmed Ones. As he is about to inject the chimps with a syringe containing the combined blood samples, the "Prue" chimp telekinetically injects the doctor instead. He begins to manifest all three Charmed powers.

When the real Prue sees a chimp astral project into her photo shoot, she knows something's amiss. The sisters snoop around Williamson's lab and find that he was doing research on all three of them to find a universal antibody for Oroya fever. But, as the monkeys clearly indicate by telekinetically sending bananas across the room and freezing them in midair, the doctor discovered something else. When they find Williamson, he's in the middle of several personal crises. His sister needs a kidney transplant and his brother-in-law just had a heart attack—one he saw moments before it happened, thanks to his newly found premonition abilities from Phoebe's blood sample. Desperate to save his sister, Williamson harvests a kidney from a drug dealer. This sets him on an organ-removal rampage, harvesting "spare parts" from any unwilling victim he can find. This brings Darryl into the mix, since the doctor is now on something of a crime spree. Leo explains that Dr. Williamson is going insane from his inability to cope with the Charmed powers.

Luckily, Phoebe is able to come up with a potion to strip their powers from the monkeys. When they try to administer it to Williamson as well, he uses the power he got from Prue and hurls them out of his way. Prue is drawn into a telekinetic battle of blades to vanquish the doctor. She wins, but it still takes a couple of bullets from Darryl's gun to kill him. The sisters take all of Williamson's files and destroy them so that his research on the Charmed Ones will never be found out.

Piper can't help but feel responsible for the destruction and death of Dr. Williamson. She feels that not only is Halliwell magic to blame, but if she had just gone in for the follow-ups he requested, she could have prevented things from going so far. Luckily, Leo is there to comfort her.

Meanwhile, Prue is having a hard time keeping her actions and her magic a secret after a tabloid photographer takes her picture with Evan Stone, a movie star and her latest assignment for *415*.

"He's kinda become the big brother I never wanted."   **PHOEBE HALLIWELL**

"He's using our powers in public?!"   **PRUE HALLIWELL**

| "Apocalypse, Not" | (MAY 11, 2000)
Teleplay by Sheryl J. Anderson
Story by Sanford Golden
Directed by Michael Zinberg |

Road rage and a run-in with a man who didn't freeze sends the Charmed Ones to the Book of Shadows. Grasping at straws, they think the Demon of Anarchy might be to blame. When they hunt for him, they find four demons waiting. Facing off with dueling spells, they open a vortex that swallows Prue and the demon that grabbed her. Using the Spirit Board, Prue lets her sisters know she's trapped on another plane with her captor. Cooperation might retrieve both from a netherworld between good and evil.

Leo infiltrates the demons' domain and learns that they are the Four Horsemen of the Apocalypse and are on a tight deadline for creating catastrophe. If they fail, The Source will kill them and select four more. Piper and Phoebe reject Leo's argument that saving Prue isn't worth losing the world. When Phoebe has a vision of nuclear holocaust, she knows Leo is right. She and Piper refuse to bring Prue back to save good, or to bring War back to perpetrate evil. Because of the sisters' selfless act, the vortex holding Prue should remain sealed, but The Source has no patience. He opens the vortex, and Piper and Phoebe recite the spell that retrieves Prue. The Horsemen, having failed their mission, are destroyed by The Source. The apocalypse is postponed because there's still too much good in the world to defeat.

"Well, who do we know who'd be keeping track of anarchy?" **PRUE HALLIWELL**

"Are you telling me evil called good and good answered?"
PHOEBE HALLIWELL ON COOPERATION
BETWEEN LEO'S BOSSES AND THEIR EVIL COUNTERPARTS

| "Be Careful What You Witch For" | (MAY 18, 2000)
Teleplay by Brad Kern & Zack Estrin &
Chris Levinson
Story by Brad Kern
Directed by Shannen Doherty |

Phoebe rubs the dust from a bottle left on the doorstep, releasing a genie who will not leave until he grants three wishes and wins his freedom. Although the sisters know every wish has a catch, he tricks them into making one. Prue wants to experience the thrill of first love again and becomes seventeen. Dan rapidly ages after Piper wishes he could move on with his life. Phoebe is suddenly able to fly, an active power the genie stole from a Dragon warlock who immediately storms the Manor demanding it back.

An evil council sent the genie to kill the Charmed Ones. When the Dragon warlock questions the genie's true intentions, he decides to take matters into his own hands. He lures Piper and Phoebe by threatening the teenaged Prue. When they come to rescue her, Dragon stabs her. They return to the Manor, but it's too late—Leo can't heal the dead. Devastated by the actions he set in motion, the genie willingly returns to his bottle, the only way to reverse the wishes and get back adult Prue and the Power of Three. Phoebe is once again earthbound, and Dan returns to his normal age, but even though Prue is no longer seventeen, she's still dead. The sisters need one more wish. Phoebe releases the genie again and he grants her wish to brings Prue back to life. The Power of Three vanquishes the Dragon warlock.

Piper had to reveal all to Dan about witches and Whitelighters to make him understand what had happened to him. After hearing that and seeing the demon vanquished firsthand, Dan has little trouble with finally letting Piper go. Feeling guilty about burdening him, Piper uses one of their remaining two wishes to grant Dan peace of mind and let him move on with his life without consequences. To reward his good deeds, the Charmed Ones use their last wish to give the genie his fondest desire—to be mortal.

Piper is frustrated that she's never seen where Leo goes when he orbs, or what her Whitelighter boyfriend's life is like when he's not on duty. So when They call, she goes Up There with him.

"Are we on some kind of list? And if so, how many points are we worth?"

PHOEBE HALLIWELL

"Prue, you are too hot to have to duty date."

PHOEBE HALLIWELL

The Charmed Episode Puns

THere are the episode titles from the **SECOND SEASON,** along with their most likely origins.

WITCH TRIAL: Traditionally a sham of a court case to determine the likelihood that a person (generally a woman) was a witch. The most notable witch trials were held in the seventeenth century in Salem, Massachusetts.

MORALITY BITES: *Reality Bites* is a film from 1994 starring Winona Ryder, Ethan Hawke, and Ben Stiller.

THE PAINTED WORLD: The Painted Desert is a brilliantly colored plateau region in Arizona.

THE DEVIL'S MUSIC: Rock and roll was once described as "the Devil's Music" by wary adults.

SHE'S A MAN, BABY, A MAN!: "She's not your mother, it's a man, baby!" is a phrase used by Austin Powers in his first film, *Austin Powers: International Man of Mystery.*

THAT OLD BLACK MAGIC: Song written by Johnny Mercer and Harold Arlen and performed by many artists.

THEY'RE EVERYWHERE: "They're here" is a phrase from the film *Poltergeist.*

P3 H2O: P3 is the Charmed Ones. H2O is the chemical composition of water (two parts hydrogen, one part oxygen). Title is likely a reference to the 1998 film *Halloween H2O.*

MS. HELLFIRE: *Mrs. Doubtfire* is a film starring Robin Williams.

HEARTBREAK CITY: A destination a person is said to be setting herself up for when expecting too much (particularly from another).

RECKLESS ABANDON: Taking actions without fear of repercussions.

AWAKENED: 1990 film *Awakenings,* directed by Penny Marshall.

ANIMAL PRAGMATISM: "Animal magnetism" is a phrase referring to a primal attraction between two people.

PARDON MY PAST: PARDON MY DUST is seen on signs during construction or remodeling.

GIVE ME A SIGN: Phrase often used when a person is hoping to have a decision made for her by an otherworldly power.

MURPHY'S LUCK: "Murphy's Law" is a belief that "if anything can go wrong, it will." The original postulate is credited to Edward A. Murphy Jr., one of the engineers in a 1949 Air Force experiment to test human acceleration tolerances.

HOW TO MAKE A QUILT OUT OF AMERICANS: *How to Make an American Quilt* is a 1995 film starring Winona Ryder.

CHICK FLICK: Slang for a film typically geared toward a female audience.

EX LIBRIS: Latin for "from the books," often seen on bookplates.

ASTRAL MONKEY: Astral Prue and monkeys.

APOCALYPSE NOT: *Apocalypse Now* is a 1979 Francis Ford Coppola film.

BE CAREFUL WHAT YOU WITCH FOR: "Be careful what you wish for" is a proverb warning that oftentimes people are not prepared for the reality of getting what they want.

Charmed®

Episode Guide

Season Three

"The Honeymoon's Over"

(OCTOBER 5, 2000)
Written by Brad Kern
Directed by James L. Conway

In the month since Piper and Leo orbed Up There, Prue and Phoebe have discovered that an Evil Triad is behind the numerous attempts on their lives, and that running a house and a nightclub with just the power of two is a daunting task. Their lives get even busier when they get a call from Darryl requesting their help with a murder suspect he thinks may be in league with a demon. Based on a rune carved into victims' foreheads, the sisters determine that a Guardian demon is protecting the mortal criminal, Emilio, in exchange for his victims' souls. With Darryl in hot pursuit of Emilio, Prue and Phoebe rush to the scene just as the police officer is attacked. Prue uses her powers to knock down the criminal and destroy his Guardian. Emilio is taken into custody, and the Halliwells are the only witnesses to the crime whose solution is not something easily explained to a judge. They formulate a plan, which is immediately ditched when Phoebe spots the handsome new assistant district attorney, Cole Turner. She volunteers to be a witness—and anything else Cole requires.

The combination of no murder weapon and the witches' shaky testimony causes the judge to dismiss the charges against Emilio. He gets a second Guardian and goes after Cole. When Phoebe gets a premonition about the attack, she and Prue rush to Cole's defense, where Phoebe finally gets her wish for an active power as she levitates fighting Emilio.

Meanwhile, Piper and Leo finally return with a problem. The Elders want them to break up or They'll reassign Leo so that the couple never sees each other again. Leo's solution is to ask Piper to marry him, reasoning that even They can't break up a holy union, especially if They don't know about it. The prospect of a quickie marriage doesn't thrill Piper, and leads to another argument between the witch and the Whitelighter. To keep peace, Leo is dispatched to see what he can find out about Emilio and his seemingly unlimited supply of Guardians.

It turns out that an Upper-Level demon is somehow assigning Guardians to criminals who are set free—all by the same judge. When all three Charmed Ones return to the courtroom for Emilio's arraignment for attacking Cole, Piper freezes only the Innocents, leaving anyone who moves as their enemy. Trouble is, only Leo, Darryl, and Cole freeze. The remainder of the courtroom turns on the sisters, led by the judge, the Upper-Level demon behind it all. With the Power of Three back in action, the mortals are defeated and freed from their Guardians. But as the girls fend off their attackers, they don't see Cole shimmer out and destroy the judge in a wall of flames.

Since she faced death yet again, Piper realizes that no matter the reason or method, she wants to be married to Leo.

"Is that why you asked me to marry you in a toilet?" **PIPER HALLIWELL**

"Oh, you know, witches and trials, it's that whole Salem thing." **PRUE HALLIWELL**

"Magic Hour"

(OCTOBER 12, 2000)
Written by Chris Levinson & Zack Estrin
Directed by John Behring

Piper is distressed that she has to have a secret wedding or lose Leo, but if the couple can consecrate their union before the deadline imposed by the Elders—midnight the following day—it can't be broken. They will be watching everything closely until then, so Leo cautions that no one can mention the word *wedding*. Piper comes up with the code word *rutabaga* for it instead. Phoebe is apprehensive about the whole thing, fearing the unspeakable wrath the Elders have threatened to manifest if Piper and Leo challenge them. The minimal preparations for a secret Handfasting are complicated by another pair of desperate lovers. Christopher exists as an owl by day, and Brooke as a wolf by night, because a sorcerer wants Brooke for himself.

The curse can be broken when there is "a night within a day," or if Brooke gives herself freely to the sorcerer. A total eclipse of the sun—night within the day—may be the answer to everyone's problems. When the couple, who are both human during the eclipse, kiss, the sorcerer is vanquished. And the celestial phenomenon keeps the Elders from tuning in to events down here, which shields the Halliwell wedding from Them. Phoebe's misgivings dissipate after talking to Grams, who presides over the ceremony. But despite the evasive action provided by the eclipse, Leo is forcefully orbed out before the ritual begins. It seems Cole alerted the Triad, who uncharacteristically joined forces with the other side and told the Elders.

"If I had a dollar for every time an owl turned into a hot guy on our porch . . ."
PHOEBE HALLIWELL

"The Charmed Ones are destined for greatness, but that fact doesn't keep a girl warm on a cold winter's night."
PENELOPE "GRAMS" HALLIWELL

"Once Upon a Time"

(OCTOBER 19, 2000)
Written by Krista Vernoff
Directed by Joel J. Fiegenbaum

Since the Elders took Leo, and ruined her life, Piper won't do anything for them. All her innocence and hope destroyed, she doesn't believe the Enchanted Kingdom of their childhood exists when Prue and Phoebe help a seven-year-old who's protecting a fairy princess named Thistle. Terrorized by trolls, Kate is vulnerable at midnight, a 'tween time she can't escape. Since only children can see fairies and trolls, and there's no listing for them in the Book of Shadows, which was written by adults, Thistle gives Kate fairy dust to sprinkle over Prue and Phoebe. They regress into childlike innocence and see the fairy and the real—and dangerous—trolls. Piper is dusted by her sisters, but it has no effect because she's hardened her heart.

The effects of the fairy dust are negated when a demon tries to steal the Book and trolls throw the sisters down the stairs. Prue writes a spell to allow the adult witches to see enchanted creatures, and Phoebe convinces Piper to help. They go after the trolls who have kidnapped Thistle and turned Kate into a fairy, but the spell doesn't work because Piper just can't believe in anything anymore. When she realizes that her bitterness is endangering the protection of Innocents, a fairy appears to the sisters and leads them to fellow fairies Thistle and Kate. The witches defeat the trolls and rescue the fairies. Piper convinces Kate to be a little girl again, even if life is unfair at times.

Impressed that Piper has found an understanding about the importance of the greater good and its place in a witch-Whitelighter relationship, the Elders send Leo back on probation. Everything will be reevaluated to see if the couple can be together without jeopardizing the Charmed destiny.

Cole continues his conquest of the Charmed Ones by attempting to conquer Phoebe.

"The tooth fairy is going to come and harass us all for not flossing?"
PIPER HALLIWELL

"All Halliwells' Eve"

(OCTOBER 26, 2000)
Written by Sheryl J. Anderson
Directed by Anson Williams

It's Halloween, the night when the veil between the dead and the living is the weakest and any number of magical things is likely to happen. At Halliwell Manor that means two Grimlocks suddenly unvanquishing, and a vortex that opens and transports the Charmed Ones to 1670 Virginia. They arrive as witches are being hunted and hanged, and one, Charlotte, is about to give birth. Prophecy states that the baby will usher in an era of good magic, so Cole follows them back to ensure that Charlotte's baby will be born into evil hands, thereby changing the future. But Prue deduces that the Elders want to ensure the prophecy, which is why she and her sisters are there. The only problem is there's no Power of Three, because technically, they haven't been born yet. Eva, one of the good witches of the coven that sent for the Charmed Ones, teaches them the magical tools of the time. Armed with this knowledge, they attempt to rescue Charlotte but are captured.

Hanged by the witch hunters, the Charmed Ones escape death when Micah, a colonial local, rigs the ropes so they don't strangle. They take Charlotte to a Wiccan altar, where they put their new knowledge to work. Piper acts as midwife for the birth of Melinda Warren, and Prue forms a protective circle with apples and herbs. Sweeping energy into a broom, Phoebe takes flight and scares off the hunters. Failing to sabotage the Warren line, Cole returns to the present. Successful, the Charmed Ones are sent home. The sisters remain unaware of Cole's evil nature, which he further disguises by showing up at P3 dressed as an angel.

"Personally, I'm offended by the representation of witches in popular culture."
PHOEBE HALLIWELL

142

"Sight Unseen"

(NOVEMBER 2, 2000)
Written by William Schmidt
Directed by Perry Lang

Prue is determined to catch the demon who tried to steal the Book of Shadows two weeks ago. Darryl, Piper, and Phoebe believe a break-in, broken mirrors, and missing items indicate a human stalker. Skeptical of that theory and unaware that Cole is the demon Belthazor, Prue sets a demon trap. Having made a deal with the Triad to kill the Charmed Ones, Cole is angry when they send Troxa to do the job. Trying to thwart Troxa, Cole is captured in the trap, which makes him furious with Prue, and Prue suspicious of him. He sets up Troxa to be captured in the trap. As the Triad vanquishes their hit man in a ball of fire, he warns the Charmed Ones of another demon named Belthazor.

Convinced the immediate threat is gone, Prue works on a photo assignment and is caught off guard when Abbey, a P3 bartender, blinds her with film developer. Holding Prue in the basement, Abbey explains that she wants to be Prue, proving sometimes humans can be as dangerous as demons. A phone call to Darren tips Piper and Phoebe to the potential threat Abbey poses. Phoebe has a vision in time to interrupt the almost fatal shooting. Despite Prue's reservations about Cole, Phoebe is thrilled that he wants to be more than friends.

Being under Their constant supervision all of the time makes it difficult for Piper to be alone with Leo.

"There are other evils in the world, and some of them are even human."

PIPER HALLIWELL

"Since we got back from Pilgrim times, she's been on a demon bender."

PHOEBE HALLIWELL

"Me, I'm on a mission."

PRUE HALLIWELL

"Primrose Empath"

(NOVEMBER 9, 2000)
Written by Daniel Cerone
Directed by Mel Damski

A series of signs leads Prue to a sensitive empath, Vince, whose pain is so great he won't leave a condemned building. Unaware that Cole is manipulating her and that Vince is a demon working for Belthazor, she recites a spell to free Vince from his gift. During the spell, he transfers the empathic ability to Prue. Although some people become immortal empaths after death, humans can't handle the input. Prue soon buckles under an onslaught of emotions she can't seem to escape, but Phoebe's emotional state is just fine after Prue "feels" Cole falling in love with her.

What Prue doesn't feel yet is that Vince is determined to find Father Thomas, the empath who cursed him. Cole warns his henchman off of his quest so they won't draw attention to the fact that Prue was set up, but Vince will not be deterred. Guided by Phoebe's vision, the sisters find Father Thomas in a mental institution. He brings them up to speed about Vince, or Vinceres, an immortal demonic hitman. The sisters can't just reverse the spell because Vinceres is immune to witches' magic—unless, like with the original spell Prue cast, it's to his advantage to let it work. Father Thomas uses his innate understanding of people to help Prue cope. He forces her to channel all of the emotions she's feeling into her power. When Vinceres finds Father Thomas at the Manor, Prue is ready for a fight. Since the gift augments her power, Prue matches Vinceres in a physical fight, and then astral projects into him. The intensity of so much human emotion destroys him. The empathic gift dies too, but Father Thomas now knows how to work without it.

Their growing emotions for each other finally draw Cole and Phoebe together. When she stays the night at his apartment, Phoebe notices Cole's suitcase is packed. Cole was ready to leave, thinking the empathic ability would kill Prue and destroy the Power of Three. When she finds him still there the next day, Phoebe has no idea that his plans changed because all of the Charmed Ones are still alive.

"Lunch is a cheap imitation of dinner."

PHOEBE HALLIWELL

"Sometimes being magical kind of takes the magic right out of things."

PIPER HALLIWELL

"I was looking for a power boost to fight Belthazor. Maybe this is it."

PRUE HALLIWELL

143

"Power Outage"

(NOVEMBER 16, 2000)
Written by Monica Breen & Alison Schapker
Directed by Craig Zisk

Expecting another attack, the Charmed Ones practice their response, which includes procuring a slice of Belthazor's flesh for a vanquishing potion. With the Triad vowing to kill him if he doesn't destroy the witches, Cole calls upon Andras, the Spirit of Rage, for help. The tension created by the sisters' busy schedules primes them for angry exchanges that escalate. When they use their powers against each other, the Power of Three is severed.

Phoebe goes to Cole for consolation. Although he tries, Cole can't kill her, so Andras possesses Belthazor to finish the job. Knowing the mortal rift must be repaired to fix the magical bond, the sisters stand together when Belthazor attacks, and the Power of Three is restored. Prue repels an energy ball, which throws Andras out of Belthazor, who kills him. Piper gets a piece of demonic flesh before Belthazor is hurled through a window. Injured, Cole shimmers away unseen, summoned by the Triad. However, rather than accept death for showing sympathy to the witches, Cole kills the Triad.

"Leo, you obviously don't have sisters. One minute you're arguing about something, and then suddenly you're arguing about who took whose Malibu Barbie in 1979."
PIPER HALLIWELL

"Sleuthing with the Enemy"

(DECEMBER 14, 2000)
Written by Peter Hume
Directed by Noel Nosseck

The Charmed Ones finish the vanquishing potion and summon Belthazor. A demonic bounty hunter named Krell arrives instead and tells the sisters that they're all after the same thing. He explains that since Belthazor killed the Triad, The Source wants him dead for his betrayal. Krell proposes they work together because Belthazor will still be after the sisters to save himself from being killed by The Source.

Phoebe finds the missing and injured Cole in his apartment and his demonic nature is revealed when Leo can't completely heal his wound. Phoebe stays to confront Cole. Meanwhile, Prue makes the Cole/Belthazor connection, and with Piper and Leo, breaks into Cole's apartment to find Belthazor holding Phoebe at knifepoint.

Belthazor shimmers Phoebe to the cemetery and explains that his father was human. Loving Phoebe has awakened his humanity. Krell tracks them and his taunts confirm Cole's confession to Phoebe. Cole destroys Krell with an energy ball and saves Phoebe. Because she believes in their love, Phoebe uses Cole's shirt, his blood, and the potion to fake his destruction. Her family sympathizes with her loss and assumes she did her duty, which makes the lie more troubling.

"We're going to vanquish Phoebe's boyfriend? That's going to cause some problems."
PIPER HALLIWELL

"Coyote Piper"

(JANUARY 11, 2001)
Written by Krista Vernoff
Directed by Chris Long

Piper's high school insecurities surface when she holds a ten-year reunion party at P3. But that's the least of the Charmed One's worries after an evil life essence steals her body. An Alchemist demon created the life essence Terra, but she desperately wants to escape from him. Terra decides that the body and power of a Charmed One is her chosen destination. She kills the body given to her by the Alchemist, which allows her life essence to escape. When Piper needs to escape an intimidating ex-schoolmate during the reunion planning, Terra finds her mark. Knowing the Alchemist will come looking for her, she joins with an unsuspecting Prue and Phoebe to destroy him. As the Power of Three vanquishes the Alchemist, he tells the sisters that "she" will destroy them. Piper/Terra returns to P3 to finish the party preparations as Prue and Phoebe ponder the meaning of the dying demon's words.

Putting together Piper's odd behavior and the Alchemist's warning, Prue realizes that Piper is possessed. If they don't do something very soon, Piper's soul will die. Prue and Phoebe attempt a spell to dispossess their sister, but it requires the Power of Three. Using information from the Book of Shadows, Prue devises a bold and dangerous plan—the only one possible—to save her sister. A knife to Piper's heart causes Terra's essence to transfer to Leo, who uses the Alchemist's power to raise Piper from the dead. Then the Power of Three drives Terra from Leo into nonexistence.

While vanquishing demons and saving Piper, Phoebe also worries about Cole. She visits the mausoleum where she last saw him, hoping for some answers. There, a vision reveals Cole's demon mother killing his human father. This spurs Phoebe to do research on Cole's family, and she discovers that her love was born in 1885. Although she can't tell her sisters that she didn't vanquish Cole, Phoebe is forced to admit that she still has feelings for him. Tormented by her secret, Phoebe almost tells Leo the truth.

"With my sister dead, I have nothing left to lose."   **PRUE HALLIWELL**

145

"We All Scream for Ice Cream"

(JANUARY 18, 2001)
Written by Chris Levinson & Zack Estrin
Directed by Allen Kroeker

A tune playing in Prue's head leads her and Phoebe to an ice-cream truck Prue saw once in a nightmare. Trying to save a little girl they believe to be an Innocent, they are pulled into a winter playground inside the truck. A young boy runs onto the playground and begs for their help to save him from The Nothing. It attacks everywhere and when it gets you, there's Nothing left. Prue is powerless in this mysterious place, but as they pass the playground's swing set, Phoebe gets a vision of a six-year-old Prue being saved by their father from The Nothing. It points her in a direction for their escape. The sisters get the children safely out of the truck only to see their little friend burn the hands of the ice-cream man who had originally entrapped him. They realize the children they thought were Innocents are really demons, and they've now released them back into the world.

When they get home, the girls check the Book of Shadows. The song Prue heard is called the devil's chord. It attracts child demons who can only be vanquished by The Nothing. According to the Book, only mortals can open the truck's door. But the ice-cream man is hurt and trapped inside the truck. Prue recalls Phoebe's vision in which Victor, the girls' father, saved little Prue from The

Nothing. Too bad the only person with experience and ability to get into the truck is never around when you need him, Prue complains. Phoebe tells her sisters that Victor actually *is* around. He's in town for a job interview. The girls enlist his help.

It's a race between the demon children, who want to destroy the ice-cream truck, and the Charmed Ones, who need to put it back in business. Victor and Prue make it to the playground. They try to save the ice-cream man, but he knows his time is up. Just before he dies, he gives Victor the part needed to restart the truck. In a hasty escape, Victor saves Prue from The Nothing again. She reciprocates as the demon kids try to kill him before he can repair the truck. With the part in place, the devil's chord is struck again. The little demons are yanked back into the playground, unable to resist the song, just as Leo shows up with Caleb, the new ice-cream man. Victor explains that he left shortly after the first bout with The Nothing because he couldn't protect his girls if he had no powers. Now that they can protect themselves, he wants to be around more, so he takes the job in San Francisco.

"Why couldn't you get a boy-band song stuck in your head like everybody else?"
PHOEBE HALLIWELL

"Blinded by the Whitelighter"
(JANUARY 25, 2001)
Written by Nell Scovell
Directed by David Straiton

The Halliwell household is disrupted when Leo's coworker Natalie arrives to brief them on a witch killing. Eames, a shape-shifting warlock with other stolen powers, seems less threatening than the no-nonsense Natalie. Piper's annoyed by Leo and Natalie's close working relationship, and Natalie disapproves of the Charmed Ones' undisciplined methods. When their impulsive approach allows Eames to get a Darklighter's bow, Leo steps aside, and the sisters try things Natalie's way.

The witches stick to Natalie's plan against their better instincts, and Eames infects Natalie with Darklighter poison. With Natalie's power to orb Up There, Eames can eliminate all Whitelighters, leaving witches defenseless. To avert that, Leo orbs the Charmed Ones "up" to vanquish Eames. As a result the Elders give permission for Piper and Leo to marry. Phoebe deals with Inspector Davidson regarding Cole's disappearance and admits to Leo that he's alive.

PIPER: *"She doesn't like our clothes."*
NATALIE: *"You need outfits that are loose and move. That means no more braless, strapless, fearless attire."*
PRUE: *"Okay, but then I have nothing to wear."*

"Wrestling with Demons"
(FEBRUARY 1, 2001)
Written by Sheryl J. Anderson
Directed by Joel J. Feigenbaum

Morris calls the sisters to protect an Innocent, but when the demon attacks, Prue lets him escape. She recognizes him as Tom Peters, a guy she dated in college. Investigation reveals that a demon called Kellman runs a training academy. He poses as a business manager, primarily to former athletes, and makes Faustian deals with mortals, which destroys their humanity. The deal is sealed when the demons-in-training kill an Innocent. Since Tom has yet to kill anyone, he can still be saved.

But first, the sisters need to find him. Conveniently, Phoebe has a Lost and Found Spell she

146

wrote to bring back Cole, although she has never used it. When they recite the spell to find Tom, it spirals out of control, bringing back more stuff to the Manor than anyone wanted: hundreds of socks lost in the dryer, Grams's lost dog, and Phoebe's brown hair. It also brings Tom, but Prue has no luck reviving his humanity. She allows him to escape and follows him to Kellman's Underworld hideout, where the sisters find him battling Wrestler Demons. Piper freezes Tom to buy them some negotiating time, and Kellman agrees to let Prue and Phoebe wrestle his demons to release Tom from his contract. Phoebe chooses the moment before the battle to tell Prue that she didn't vanquish Cole, which piques the eldest Halliwell's anger and helps her defeat the demon wrestlers. As the fight ensues, Kellman seriously injures Piper. This breaks the freeze on Tom, allowing Kellman to take the demon trainee to kill his Innocent and seal his fate.

With their match over, Prue and Phoebe are able to get Piper back to Leo in time for him to heal her. They discover that the Innocent Tom is to kill is his own mother. The Charmed Ones set up a meeting at the Manor, where Mrs. Peters' love and Prue's words restore Tom's humanity. He saves his mother and himself when he turns against Kellman and kills the demon.

Although Phoebe apologizes to Prue for lying about Cole, Prue can't help feeling betrayed. And luckily for Leo, the Lost and Found Spell retrieved Piper's mother's ring that he misplaced during an orb.

"Innocents and alleys. Don't they ever learn?"
PRUE HALLIWELL

"If I could freeze you two, I would. Often."
PIPER HALLIWELL

"Bride and Gloom"	(FEBRUARY 8, 2001) Written by William Schmidt Directed by Chris Long

147

To gain the Charmed Ones' powers, a Dark Priestess, Dantalian, uses the warlock Zile in a plot to turn Prue and her sisters evil with a Black Wedding. After the ceremony, Dantalian doesn't need Zile anymore, so she paralyzes him to take possession of the Book of Shadows herself. Piper and Leo's disagreements about their wedding are set aside when Prue goes missing. Playing a hunch, Phoebe finds Cole in the mausoleum and asks for help to find Prue. He agrees, even though he might be caught and killed by The Source.

Since the Charmed Ones' powers are connected, as Prue turns toward evil, so do Piper and Phoebe. The two younger Halliwells enjoy the freedom evil brings. Annoyed when Leo lets the Dark Priestess escape with the Book of Shadows, they kill him and blink to Prue's location. Dantalian awakes Zile and evil Prue to fight them. Zile shape-shifts into Prue, causing some confusion, but Piper and Phoebe devise a way to determine their true sister. They kill Zile, and the Charmed Ones and the Book of Shadows are restored. Their evil deeds are undone, and Dantalian is vanquished with the Power of Three.

Phoebe loves Cole, but she knows he can never escape the evil within him, which will always be a problem between them.

"You may not need wedding planners, but I do. I don't want to have to worry about anything. That way if I have to fight a demon in the morning, I know that the flowers will still be there on time."
PIPER HALLIWELL

"I gotta tell you I really like this whole think-and-it-happens deal. Think of the time we'd save not chanting."
EVIL PHOEBE HALLIWELL

"The Good, the Bad, and the Cursed"

(FEBRUARY 15, 2001)
Written by Monica Breen &
Alison Schapker
Directed by Shannen Doherty

Victor takes Phoebe to a ghost town he's thinking of buying, hoping she can prove or disprove the ghost stories connected to the property. Phoebe becomes psychically linked to Bo Lightfeather, a Native American from 1873 who has visions. Phoebe not only sees the past events that cast the town into a time loop, she sustains Bo's fatal injuries. To save her life, Cole shimmers Prue to the town that exists in a parallel plane. Sutter, a vicious mortal, was given town property in exchange for bringing the railroad. As the sisters search for him, he rules the town with fear, and he resents Bo, who will not be cowed.

Phoebe's condition worsens, but Prue realizes that healing Bo won't help. The curse is the result of the townspeople's inaction, not Bo's death. When Sutter torments him, a scenario that endlessly repeats itself, Prue's and Cole's encouraging words convince the bartender to interfere. Bo is saved, Sutter is jailed, and the time loop is broken. Phoebe recovers when Bo is no longer injured.

Victor spends some time getting to know his future son-in-law, Leo, who he thinks is a mortal. He tells Leo he blames Patty's Whitelighter for his failed marriage. After finding out the truth about his daughters' beaus, he's not sure what's worse: Leo being a Whitelighter, or Cole being a demon.

148

"You can't trust the Whitelighters, Leo. They're sneaky little bastards."
VICTOR "DAD" BENNETT

"Just Harried"

(FEBRUARY 22, 2001)
Written by Daniel Cerone
Directed by Mel Damski

Prue's unexplained exhaustion and Victor's disapproval of Leo don't hamper preparations for Piper's wedding. No one, including Prue, knows that her astral self is skipping out while Prue sleeps, or that a man she fought outside a bar is dead. Since Piper threatens to call off the wedding if one more thing goes wrong, everyone tries to keep life as normal as possible. Victor steps in as Leo's best man, and Piper is thrilled when the Elders allow Patty to attend. With Grams's spirit presiding, Piper glows as she joins Leo at the altar. Everyone is stunned when astral Prue's boyfriend, T. J., drives in on his bike to save Prue from the cops and tears everything apart.

Convinced she and Leo are not supposed to marry, Piper leaves. While Patty and Victor go after her, Leo and Cole look for the real killer. Cole's knowledge, demonic senses, and Belthazor's image convince the murderer to confess. Using her psychology studies, Phoebe realizes that Prue has denied her own desires in order to keep the family going for years; Astral Prue rebelled. Prue becomes whole with that understanding, Piper returns, and the wedding takes place just before midnight.

"All I am is yours." — **LEO WYATT**

"I was born to love you, and I always will." — **PIPER HALLIWELL**

"The women keep their names in this family." — **PENELOPE "GRAMS" HALLIWELL**

"As Halliwells, we are blessed as witches, and we are cursed as women." — **PIPER HALLIWELL**

"Death Takes a Halliwell"

(MARCH 15, 2001)
Written by Krista Vernoff
Directed by Jon Paré

While Prue pursues a shadowy essence stalking a woman working with Inspector Davidson, Phoebe deals with Davidson's ongoing investigation into Cole's disappearance. Cole's landlady is found dead, the work of vampire-like Seekers who retrieve information from brain stem cells. The situations intersect when Phoebe and Cole visit his old apartment. A vision reveals that Davidson dies while Prue turns away.

Death confronts Prue, who has been angry since her mother died. He takes only those whose time has come, a fact of life Prue must accept. Phoebe and Piper are locked out of a cemetery building when the Seekers kill Davidson, an event Death forces Prue to witness. She's torn apart by the loss, but knows she couldn't interfere. Having fed off Davidson, the Seekers know that Cole can be found at the Manor. The Charmed Ones arrive in time to save him and vanquish the demons.

149

"I can orb you because you're my wife, but I'm not a cosmic taxi for the whole family." — **LEO WYATT**

"I am not good or evil. I just am. I'm inevitable." — **DEATH**

"Pre Witched"

(MARCH 22, 2001)
Written by Chris Levinson & Zack Estrin
Directed by David Straiton

Acat familiar is transformed into a warlock after killing its witch. To become immortal, he must shed the nine lives inherent to his previous existence within two days, a service only the Charmed Ones are strong enough to perform. Attacking and killing, the cat, Shadow, forces them to eliminate his lives while Piper and Leo prepare to move out.

Flashbacks reveal that Piper and Prue moved back into the Manor when Grams was sick. Separated by conflicting personalities, misunderstandings, and grudges, the sisters were not close. Knowing the divide would endanger them when their powers were restored, Grams made a potion to stop their powers from manifesting, but died before she used it. Weakening the Charmed unity now doesn't feel right, and Piper and Leo move back in. Shadow is vanquished by a potion and spell that combine the pain of his nine deaths.

"What are we? Like in the <u>Warlock's Guide to San Francisco</u>?" **PIPER HALLIWELL**

"Sin Francisco"

(APRIL 19, 2001)
Written by Nell Scovell
Directed by Joel J. Feigenbaum

Piper tries to be SuperWife out of fear that the Elders will split her and Leo again, while Phoebe copes with Cole popping in and out, and Prue looks for demons to vanquish. Prue comes across an Innocent who is killed by a bus while chasing down a mysterious box. Prue retrieves the box, which contains sin balls of each of the Seven Deadly Sins. The sin balls corrupt paragons of good, causing the victims to self-destruct, whereupon the box's owner, an Infector Demon named Lukas, can collect the seven souls he needs to free himself from The Source. Lukas comes after his box and infects the Charmed Ones and Leo with the sins to which they are most predisposed. Unless the effects are neutralized, they will all self-destruct within hours.

Stricken with gluttony, Piper goes on an eating binge and shopping spree, while Leo gives in to sloth on the sofa in front of the TV. Phoebe, given lust, flirts with every man she meets, and pride causes Prue to feel infallible and invincible and to act recklessly. The sins weaken the witches' powers, and they fall in a fight with an Innocent who is infected with anger. When Piper, Phoebe, and Leo care more about helping each other rather than protecting themselves, their selfless acts purge the effects of the sins. But Prue is captured by Lukas during the battle. Too proud to help Lukas, she willingly jumps into the Bottomless Pit of Everlasting Torment rather than tell him where another victim is hidden. Since she jumped for the greater glory of Prue, she is not freed of the sin ball's effect. Leo orbs Piper and Phoebe to Lukas' lair. Piper freezes the demon while Leo rescues Prue from the Pit. Lukas is vanquished when the Charmed Ones hit him with several sin balls and he jumps into the Pit. The act expunges the sins from the remaining victims, including Prue.

"You do know that charming the pants off someone is just a figure of speech?"
PRUE HALLIWELL TO PHOEBE

"Why? You never listen to me, anyway." **LEO WYATT TO PRUE**

"The Demon Who Came in from the Cold"

(APRIL 26, 2001)
Written by Sheryl J. Anderson
Directed by Anson Williams

Alerted by a street prophet, Cole risks exposure in the Underworld when he rejoins the Brotherhood of the Thorn to uncover its plans. The elite organization, currently directed by the demon Vornac, is loyal to The Source and spreads evil by infiltrating businesses. At Cole's request Phoebe works on a potion to strip his powers; at the same time, she has to deal with her sisters' mistrust of his motives. After they identify the Brotherhood's corporate target, the Charmed Ones intervene so Cole's energy ball isn't fatal. However, Vornac assumes the CEO's identity and replaces him to vote yes on a merger.

To protect himself, Cole plays on everyone's suspicions. Vornac, still suspicious, believes that

Cole is working with the witch he loves. Vornac poses as Cole when the Charmed Ones show up to vanquish the CEO imposter. Phoebe asks a question knowing what Cole's answer should be. She gets the wrong answer and figures out that Vornac is impersonating Cole, so she vanquishes him. Unaware that another "brother" is watching, Cole reveals his true feelings for Phoebe. His admission costs him when he returns to the Underworld to cover his tracks but is rendered unconscious by an angry Raynor.

"Wouldn't it be nice to save the world at a decent hour?" **PHOEBE HALLIWELL**

"You taught me not to walk away and let evil win, to fight the good fight."
COLE TURNER

"Exit Strategy"

(MAY 3, 2001)
Teleplay by Peter Hume and Daniel Cerone
Story by Peter Hume
Directed by Joel J. Feigenbaum

Phoebe stakes out the mausoleum in case Cole returns, and Leo balks at getting a passport since they have to falsify his birth certificate. Raynor, leader of the demonic Brotherhood of the Thorn, plots to destroy the love that turned Belthazor soft and turn him back to the dark side, where they can use his knowledge of the Charmed Ones to destroy the witches. To convince him to work for evil, Raynor threatens to give Cole's father's soul to The Source. Still playing along to protect those he loves, Cole takes half a protective amulet from a witch as instructed, but leaves her alive. Raynor kills her just before Phoebe and Prue arrive, which sets up Belthazor/Cole to take the blame later and plant doubt in the sisters' minds about Cole's true loyalties.

Meanwhile, Piper and Leo spend a frustrating few hours waiting to get Leo's passport. Just as they get to the front of the line, Leo is called away. Piper's rage causes her to blow up a wall clock with her hand.

Cole is sent to get the other half of the amulet because when both halves are brought together, its protective power is increased. Jenna, the witch in possession of the other half of the amulet, is taken to the Manor for protection, where she helps finish the potion to strip Cole's powers. Brotherhood member Tarkin shows up at the Manor and engages the sisters in a fight downstairs. At the same time, Raynor shimmers into the attic, where Janna, Leo, and Cole are planning their next move. He knocks out Leo and goads Belthazor to emerge. Phoebe sees Belthazor kill Janna and knows her love is lost. Since Cole would be able to use the amulet if he were human, the sisters believe it to be the real reason behind him wanting his powers stripped, so Phoebe destroys the potion. Piper kills Tarkin with the new power she can't quite control.

"Every time I try to freeze, I flame." **PIPER HALLIWELL**

"We need to detox a demon." **PRUE HALLIWELL**

151

"Look Who's Barking"	(MAY 10, 2001) Teleplay by Curtis Kheel & Monica Breen & Alison Schapker Story by Curtis Kheel Directed by John Behring

 fter an Innocent is killed, the sisters determine it was the work of a Banshee, a demon who feeds on souls in great emotional pain. The demon emits a piercing scream undetectable by the human ear that shatters glass and blood vessels, and can be heard by animals, including dogs. There is no spell to vanquish a Banshee, but there is one to track it. Phoebe and Piper recite the spell, which turns Prue into a dog.

In denial about her feelings toward Cole, Phoebe is susceptible to the Banshee's scream. The Elders tell Leo that since the Banshee is a former witch, her scream doesn't kill witches—it turns them into Banshees. Piper manages to blow up the original Banshee, but not before Phoebe is transformed and begins hunting for anguished souls.

Determined to purge his feelings for Phoebe, Cole enlists an Alchemist to transmute his blood, making him immune to the vanishing potion but not necessarily cured of his love.

A first kill will condemn Phoebe to being a Banshee forever. Hoping Cole's love will neutralize the Banshee effect, Piper summons Belthazor, trusting her instincts. When Cole refuses to help, she has no use for another demon and uses the vanquishing potion, but it doesn't work. Drawn to Cole's pain, Phoebe the Banshee attacks, and he shimmers her to the mausoleum. His declaration of love breaks the Banshee's hold and returns Prue to human form. Cole explains that Raynor cast a spell to turn him toward evil and destroy Phoebe's faith in him. Phoebe decides there's still good in Cole, and vows to renew their relationship.

"Am I okay? Prue is a dog and Phoebe is a Banshee. I am not even in the vicinity of okay."
PIPER HALLIWELL

"All Hell Breaks Loose"	(MAY 17, 2001) Written by Brad Kern Directed by Shannen Doherty

 he Charmed Ones bring a doctor to the Manor to protect him from Shax, The Source's assassin. Shax attacks Prue and Piper, and is then wounded by Phoebe's vanquishing spell. Prue and Piper track and try to destroy the demon again on a neighborhood street. Believing that the problem is solved, Phoebe goes to the Underworld to neutralize the black magic spell that turned Cole against her. Things quickly deteriorate when Shax's vanquishing appears on TV and a media mob gathers outside the Manor. Once exposed, the Charmed Ones can no longer carry out their destiny to do good. The only way to fix things is having the demon Tempus turn back time. Since neither good nor evil forces want to be exposed, they need to cooperate on this. Leo goes to the Underworld to arrange things. He isn't able to be contacted Down There, and while he is gone, a wannabe witch from the mob outside the Manor shoots and kills Piper.

Since demonic evil has been exposed, The Source agrees to let Tempus reset time, but only if Phoebe turns evil and remains in the Underworld. If she doesn't, one of her sisters will die. Phoebe accepts the terms because she has no choice, but she has one condition: Piper and Prue must be warned before Shax attacks. The Source agrees. Leo returns and is in agony over Piper's death.

Then, just as a SWAT team is about to kill Prue, too, time reverses back to the moment before Shax attacked. As promised, Prue has a flash of warning. But this time, when the assassin hurls Piper and Prue through a wall, Phoebe is not there to stop him with a spell. Shax swirls out in a gust of wind with Prue, Piper, and the doctor left for dead.

"You're not an easy girl to dump."

COLE TURNER

The Charmed Episode Puns

Here are the episode titles from the **THIRD SEASON**, along with their most likely origins.

THE HONEYMOON'S OVER: Phrase noting that the newlywed portion of a marriage is over as the couple settles into their life together facing the day-to-day realities. Also signifies the ending of any period of ease.

MAGIC HOUR: The periods of twilight before dawn and after sunset.

ONCE UPON A TIME: Traditional opening line for fairy tales.

ALL HALLIWELLS' EVE: The name Halloween is derived from "All Hallows' Eve," the evening before "All Saints' Day."

SIGHT UNSEEN: Phrase referring to an item purchased without previous inspection.

PRIMROSE EMPATH: "Primrose path" refers to a pleasurable lifestyle. The phrase comes from Ophelia's line in *Hamlet,* Act I, Scene 3, "Himself the primrose path of dalliance treads." An "empath" is one who can sense the emotions of others.

POWER OUTAGE: Formal phrase to describe a blackout.

SLEUTHING WITH THE ENEMY: *Sleeping with the Enemy* is a 1991 film starring Julia Roberts.

COYOTE PIPER: *Coyote Ugly* is a movie that was released in 2000.

WE ALL SCREAM FOR ICE CREAM: Phrase from a childhood rhyme.

BLINDED BY THE WHITELIGHTER: "Blinded by the Light" is a song released in 1973 written by Bruce Springsteen.

WRESTLING WITH DEMONS: A person suffering personal turmoil is said to be "wrestling with her inner demons."

BRIDE AND GLOOM: Pun off the more familiar "bride and groom."

THE GOOD, THE BAD, AND THE CURSED: *The Good, the Bad, and the Ugly* is a film starring Clint Eastwood, released in 1966.

153

JUST HARRIED: A play on the traditional phrase written on signs and attached to the back of the cars of newlyweds.

DEATH TAKES A HALLIWELL: *Death Takes a Holiday* is a film from 1934.

PRE WITCHED: *Bewitched* is a TV series that ran from 1964 to 1972, starring Elizabeth Montgomery. The title also refers to the flashbacks to the Charmed Ones' pre-witch years.

SIN FRANCISCO: A pun off the name of the city in which the Charmed Ones live, San Francisco.

THE DEMON WHO CAME IN FROM THE COLD: *The Spy Who Came in from the Cold* is a film from 1965.

EXIT STRATEGY: Military term referring to the plan for evacuating a location once the mission has been accomplished.

LOOK WHO'S BARKING: *Look Who's Talking* was a film that allowed the audience to hear the thoughts of babies.

ALL HELL BREAKS LOOSE: A colloquial expression meaning an event of confusion or violence. The phrase is originally from John Milton's epic poem *Paradise Lost*: "Wherefore with thee came not all hell broke loose? . . ."

Episode Guide

Season Four

156

Inconsolable after Prue's death, Piper tries several spells to bring back her sister, including one To Call a Lost Witch. At the funeral, Phoebe has a feeling of familiarity when she meets social services worker Paige Matthews and gets a vision of Paige being attacked by Shax. Phoebe wants to help Paige, but now that there is only the Power of Two, Piper is convinced that their Charmed destiny is over. She becomes more depressed when a demon hunter and a homicide detective crash the funeral and reception. Phoebe is not willing to let Innocents die, though. She and Cole follow up on her premonition, hoping the combined powers of a witch and a demon will be enough. Staking out the rooftop Phoebe foresaw, they watch as Shax attacks. Paige surprisingly orbs out of harm's way.

Looking for an explanation when even the Elders have no knowledge of an apparent Whitelighter, Piper summons family spirits. The girls learn that Paige is their half sister. Patty Halliwell had a child with her Whitelighter, Sam Wilder. The baby had to be given up for adoption so that the Elders wouldn't know of their forbidden union. Paige will reconstitute the Power of Three. The nosy police inspector, Cortez, interrupts the family meeting. When he sees the ghosts of Patty and Grams, Phoebe sends him to Timbuktu to prevent him exposing the witches.

Sensing her family connection, Paige comes to the Manor. When Piper takes Paige's hand, the three sisters are bathed in light from above, signifying the rebirth of the Power of Three. Shax strikes again a moment later, and Paige helps vanquish the assassin with a spell, then runs away, shocked by what she's become.

"Your destiny still awaits."　　　　　　　　　　**PENELOPE "GRAMS" HALLIWELL**

"And I thought my family was screwed up."　　　　　　　**COLE TURNER**

"Charmed Again, Part Two"

(OCTOBER 4, 2001)
Written by Brad Kern
Directed by Mel Damski

The Power of Three can't be fully revived until Paige chooses to use her powers for good. The Source possesses her boyfriend, Shane, and a suspected abusive father to influence Paige before the window of opportunity closes. Confused, she seeks out Sister Agnes, a nun who believes Paige was brought to the church as a baby by angels. Piper and Phoebe track down Paige at the church and Piper freezes the nun. They try to explain to Paige that they had trouble believing and accepting that they were witches at first too. They ask Paige to trust them, but she fears that maybe they're the forces of evil (after all, they froze a nun). Phoebe begins to break through to her half sister when she mentions that the third Charmed One has the power to move objects with her mind. That intrigues Paige, who discovers she can orb things. But she's still suspicious of her sisters, and when the possessed Shane finds her at the church, she leaves with him, not realizing he is really the evil entity.

157

Because they know that The Source is luring Paige toward the dark side, Piper and Phoebe need a way to easily see the good and bad guys. A spell in the Book of Shadows enchants an old pair of sunglasses that allow Phoebe to see a black aura around forces of evil. The sisters seek out Paige at her office to see what The Source is up to. The Source, who previously possessed the body of an abused boy's father and taunted Paige, now convinces her if she orbs the heart out of the man's body, the problem will be resolved. Leo orbs Paige to the Manor before she makes the irreversible mistake of killing the man, which would turn her evil. Paige is convinced she's evil nonetheless and orbs household objects at Leo and her sisters. The Source appears as various people to finish claiming his prize. But when he attacks Phoebe, Paige turns against him to save her sister and the Power of Three, proving she is ultimately good and a Charmed One. The Source leaves to fight another day, but not before attacking Inspector Cortez, who came back from Timbuktu more wary than ever. He drops his murder investigation, however, after Leo heals him and he realizes the Halliwells are a force for good, just as Darryl said.

To further strengthen their new sisterly bond and assuage Paige's anxiety, Piper and Phoebe summon their mother to meet her youngest daughter.

"I guess blood's a little thicker than evil."   **PIPER HALLIWELL**

"When I wanted to find out who I was, I didn't want to find out I was a freak."
                                                                        PAIGE MATTHEWS

"Hell Hath No Fury"	(OCTOBER 11, 2001) Written by Krista Vernoff Directed by Chris Long

Driven by her anger over losing Prue, Piper pursues any evil she can find, with no concern for safety, no desire to help Paige adjust, and no control over a power that will either freeze or blow up her targets. Paige, wanting to learn more about witchcraft and being a witch—and getting little help from her preoccupied sisters—defies Phoebe's order that the Book of Shadows not leave the Manor. She throws it out of the attic window, but when she gets to work, she finds it can't be photocopied. So she just uses the original. Enjoying her newfound abilities, Paige casts spells for personal gain and learns the hard way why it's prohibited.

Meanwhile, Piper's frame of mind makes her susceptible to her latest demon. The Furies, who punish evildoers, sense a kinship with the pained Piper and make her one of their own.

After Phoebe helps Paige reverse the spells she cast and returns everything to normal, they work to recover Piper. Paige's innate compassion and understanding of human nature prove vital to the process. Since the Furies are attracted to evil, Paige proposes using the still half-demon Cole as bait to lure Piper and her Fury companions to the Manor. They add a drop of Cole's blood to the spell to call a lost sister, and Piper responds with her fellow Furies in tow. Phoebe and Paige try to keep them from destroying Cole, while finding a way to reach the real Piper. Paige knows that Piper is furious with Prue for leaving and explains that it's okay to hate her older sister for it. When Piper's anger is expressed, the Fury within her is vanquished, and she begins to accept Paige.

"I think Prue being killed counts as a pretty big glitch in the system."
                                                                        PIPER HALLIWELL

"Enter the Demon"	(OCTOBER 18, 2001) Written by Daniel Cerone Directed by Joel J. Feigenbaum

Cole helps Phoebe hone her martial arts skills to fight The Source, and Piper tutors an unenthusiastic Paige in basic potions and magic to protect her from the dangers of being Charmed. While shopping for ingredients, Piper sees a young Asian woman, Anling, use supernatural ability to steal the Dragonblade, a magical knife. Outside the shop, an Asian man, Yenlo, stabs Anling's father, the Zen Master, and escapes into a puddle with the old man. Yenlo is angry because he used his power for evil and wasn't chosen to be the new Zen Master. The puddle is a portal to Limbo, where a wounded Yenlo and Anling's father won't die or move on.

At the Manor, an accidental spell and Paige's experimental potion cause her to switch bodies with Phoebe. As Phoebe, Paige tells Cole he'll lose her if he doesn't lighten up on the training. Something in "Phoebe's" tone and the sisterly concern of the lecture makes him realize that somehow Paige and Phoebe are switched. Piper discovers the switch when Yenlo comes to the Manor. The inevitable fight ensues, but "Phoebe" can't figure out how to levitate. In her anger, Piper realizes the switch may be the answer to their problem with Yenlo. She switches Phoebe and Paige back into their own bodies, and uses Paige's potion to change places with Anling's father. With his knowledge, Anling, Paige, and Phoebe enter Limbo, defeat Yenlo, and free the Zen Master to enter the portal to reincarnation.

"Now wipe that look off my face."

PHOEBE (IN PAIGE'S BODY)

"Size Matters"

(OCTOBER 25, 2001)
Written by Nell Scovell
Directed by Noel Nosseck

iper hires a new club manager, who begins tearing P3 apart. Phoebe endures another humiliating job interview because she can't explain why she needs flexible hours. They both dismiss Paige's feeling that something's amiss in a creepy house. When Leo urges Phoebe to support Paige, they agree to meet at the rundown house later. Phoebe arrives early, just in time to confirm Paige's suspicions. A demon called the Collector uses a wand to shrink her to five inches tall.

Leo and Piper search the house for Phoebe but find nothing. She's locked up with Claudia, another shrunken young woman, and is too small to make her presence known. The couple returns to the Manor to look up Gammill in the Book of Shadows. Armed with the knowledge, they orb back to the creepy house and find Paige, who had sought out Finn, the handsome Golem created by Gammill to lure young women into his trap. Finn reveals that Gammill shrinks his victims. So it's back

159

to the Manor to find an unshrinking spell. When the sisters return to Gammill's house, he's waiting for them. He destroys Finn and shrinks Piper and Paige. With everyone immobilized in clay for his kiln, Paige alone has a useable power. She orbs free of the drying clay and calls Gammill's wand, which the still-tiny witches use on the demon. A spell finishes off the shrunken fiend, and Claudia is saved. So is P3 when Piper decides being too hip is bad news for the club.

"I am not having the best day of my life. It began with an interview woman who made me feel this big, and now I __am__ this big." **PHOEBE HALLIWELL**

"Oh, he's way too big for my tiny magic." **PIPER HALLIWELL**

| "A knight to Remember" | (NOVEMBER 1, 2001)
Written by Alison Schapker & Monica Breen
Directed by David Straiton |

The presence of a Shocker Demon at the Manor prompts Piper and Phoebe to ask Paige to move in as a Power of Three spell is needed for a vanquish. Annoyed after they busted in on her and Glen that morning, Paige just wants to quickly check the Book of Shadows and leave. She is thrilled to find a reference to her favorite fairy-tale villain, the Evil Enchantress, until she recites the spell that brings an adoring prince through a portal.

Paige soon learns she can't elude the prince and the Evil Enchantress, who is actually Paige in a past life. The Charmed Ones must prevent the Evil Enchantress from being impregnated by the prince or Dark Magic will reign forever. Since Paige's previous life cannot be vanquished without affecting her present, everyone goes back in time to bind the evil witch's powers. Paige taps into her old power to render the Evil Enchantress harmless. Paige moves into Prue's old room, and the Shocker Demon is vanquished by the Power of Three.

"Because it's your damn fairy tale, and it's alive and frozen in our kitchen." **PIPER HALLIWELL**

| "Brain Drain" | (NOVEMBER 8, 2001)
Written by Curtis Kheel
Directed by John Behring |

The Source can defeat the Power of Three if a Charmed One relinquishes her powers, so he kidnaps Piper. Playing on her fears and desires with information collected by a chameleon demon, he creates an illusion in Piper's mind in which she's a patient at Halliwell Hospital, a mental institution. Dr. Alaster, the human form adopted by The Source, tries to convince her that she's just been living in a delusional magical world since her grandmother's death. Paige and Phoebe are just fellow patients, and the Book of Shadows is only a notebook of childish scribblings.

Since the Relinquishing Spell was burned after they used it to give Rex Buckland their powers three years ago, it only exists in Piper's mind. Paige realizes that's where The Source will look for it. While Cole and Leo look for Piper in the Underworld, Paige and Phoebe use a mindlink to enter Piper's mind. Cole allows himself to be captured because finding The Source means finding Piper. Leo follows, and fights with The Source to break his connection to Piper's mind. Maintaining his illusion weakens The Source, so Cole is able to injure him with an energy ball. The real Leo, Paige, and

Phoebe convince Piper not to finish reciting the spell that will strip their powers. Although Piper will never have a normal life, she realizes that wanting one keeps her sane.

"What do you say we click our heels and get out of this crazy joint?"

PAIGE MATTHEWS

"Black As Cole"

(NOVEMBER 15, 2001)
Teleplay by Brad Kern & Nell Scovell
Story by Abbey Campbell
Directed by Les Landau

Cole's marriage proposal weighs heavily on Phoebe's mind, especially when a series of witch killings focuses attention on his demonic past. The MO of the murdering demon matches Belthazor's methods. Paige can't help but suspect Cole because she has trouble dismissing his murderous past, regardless of the good he's done recently. The sisters lay a trap, but the black-and-red demon escapes when a mortal, Emma, tries to knife him. Emma explains that a demon killed her fiancé and she's been hunting him ever since. She will not stop until he is dead.

Leo accompanies a witch he's guarding to a meeting requested by Assistant District Attorney Sykes. He sees Sykes's demonic aura and realizes he's the demon who is emulating Belthazor. Leo saves his charge and orbs back to the Manor to warn the Charmed Ones. Sykes follows, and during the ensuing fight, Paige gets a piece of Sykes's demon flesh, but it takes Belthazor to stop his imitator. Witnessing the battle between the demons, Emma identifies Belthazor as her fiancé's killer.

At Cole's request, Phoebe prepares the potion to vanquish Belthazor. He knows he will have to become his demon half to beat Sykes, and he's afraid he might not able to morph back. Anticipating Sykes's next move, Cole realizes his enemy will strike Phoebe to get to him. Cole allows Belthazor to emerge. He stabs Sykes and kills him, and then turns on the Charmed Ones. Piper is about to throw the vanquishing potion when Emma, seeking vengeance, runs in and throws a potion she found in Phoebe's purse. Belthazor goes up in flames, but the human Cole emerges. Phoebe explains she made a power-stripping potion rather than the vanquishing potion Cole requested. She couldn't kill him, just as he could never bring himself to harm her. Cole is no longer a demon. He is completely human, which leaves him feeling vulnerable and a bit befuddled.

"You were a demon and a lawyer? Insert joke here."   **PAIGE MATTHEWS**

161

	(DECEMBER 13, 2001)
"Muse to My Ears"	Written by Krista Vernoff
	Directed by Joel J. Feigenbaum

Now human, Cole worries because he can't protect Phoebe from evil. Underworld factions will form to challenge the injured Source, and the best way to gain support is to kill the Charmed Ones. When Muses begin disappearing, the Charmed Ones' Muse, Melody, explains that a warlock named Devlin is capturing them with a Ring of Inspiration. Uninspired, the world of good will be weakened. Melody's presence makes passions run high at the Manor as they take steps to deal with Devlin's warlock faction.

When a plan to lure Devlin results in losing the Ring and Melody, Leo gives the Charmed Ones a pep talk to reinspire them. Phoebe writes a spell to take them to Melody in the Ring—which is still on Devlin's finger. Expecting to wind up in the Underworld, the witches are surprised to orb into P3. This means Devlin and his faction are at the club. Leo and Cole orb to the club as backup. Piper turns on the strobe lights to keep the warlocks from blinking and freezes the Innocents so her sisters can vanquish Devlin's followers. Devlin is deserted by his minions after they see the Charmed Ones in action. The warlock, who had morphed into Melody, morphs back and attacks the sisters. Cole throws him down with a human tackle and takes the Ring. Devlin is vanquished by Phoebe's spell and the Muses are released.

PAIGE: *"Who's trying to kill us?"*
PIPER: *"No one."*
PAIGE: *"That's new."*

162

"Corporate party, big money, total nightmare."
PIPER HALLIWELL ON A CLIENT PARTY AT P3

	(JANUARY 17, 2002)
"A Paige from the Past"	Written by Daniel Cerone
	Directed by James L. Conway

To help Paige reconcile her guilt about her parents' deaths, Leo takes her back in time to relive the events. During their passage, the ghosts of Frankie and Lulu, two 1950s jewel thieves, escape into the present and possess Phoebe and Cole. Piper and Darryl follow them from one robbery to another, removing any evidence that will incriminate their loved ones.

Paige was a troubled teen who skipped class, picked fights, and partied hard. She tries to change her parents' impression of her on this second time around, but learns instead that they never thought she was bad, just lost. Despite Leo's warnings, she tries to avert the accident that took their lives, but she fails. Paige orbed out of the car without realizing it at the time and survived. As they arrive back in the present, the surly spirit that controls temporal journeys captures the ghosts of Frankie and Lulu. Leo heals Cole, who was shot by Darryl while he was still possessed by Frankie. To heal Paige's lingering pain, Leo brings her parents back to see how well she turned out.

"Next to the Charmed Ones, I'm a potted plant."　　　　　　　　　**COLE TURNER**

"Trial by Magic"
(JANUARY 24, 2002)
Written by Michael Gleason
Directed by Chip Scott Laughlin

Phoebe's jury duty is complicated when the murder weapon evokes a vision proving the defendant, Stan, is innocent. Stan also has visions, but seems guilty because he led the police to his wife's body. While Paige, Piper, and Leo hunt the real killer, Phoebe must prove to her co-jurors that magic is real so they don't replace her with an alternate. When Glen returns from Australia, Paige invites him to stay at the Manor over her sisters' objections. Snatches of conversation and spell ingredients in the fridge lead Glen to the attic and the Book of Shadows. After confessing she's a witch, Paige accidentally casts a spell that gives Glen the ability to stretch as though he's made of rubber instead of stretching his imagination to accept her powers, as she'd planned.

Piper and Paige get a taped confession from the killer before he disappears from the magic club in a puff of stage magic smoke. He reappears in the club basement where a rat demon in human form turns him into a rat and other rat demons kill him. Piper and Paige help Phoebe summon Angela, the dead woman, who clears Stan. The jury votes for acquittal, but the rat demons Angela planned to expose for their money laundering are holding Glen. Demons need money to infiltrate the mortal world, so Paige offers the rat pack a deal. They'll turn over the taped confession and keep quiet so the demons can continue their operation in exchange for Glen. Leo erases the jurors' memories of the spirit's testimony, but since Paige trusts Glen, he's allowed to remember everything.

"When nothing happens, you can drag me off to the funny farm and tell them I've been brainwashed. Believe me, I can use the vacation." **PAIGE MATTHEWS**

"Demons you can handle, but not rats?"　　　　　　　　　**LEO WYATT**

"We all need to believe that magic exists."　　　　　　　　　**PHOEBE HALLIWELL**

"Lost and Bound"
(JANUARY 31, 2002)
Written by Nell Scovell
Directed by Noel Nosseck

Cole gives Phoebe Grams's ring, making their engagement official. Although Phoebe loves the ring and the gesture, she can't help but feel like she's giving up her identity to become Mrs. Cole Turner. At the same time, the other happy couple in the Manor argue whether to bind their eventual child's magical powers. Leo feels strongly that they should, but Piper argues that her

163

own experience indicates otherwise. Not only did she miss out on twenty years of magic, she had a hard time coping with everything when her powers were finally restored.

While her sisters work on their issues, Paige just goes to work, which brings another crisis. A young boy named Tyler appears to start fires with his mind. He's freaked out by the power and can't control it, and doesn't want to go back to his foster home. Paige takes him to the Manor, since dealing with an uncontrollable Firestarter is pretty much business as usual there. Before the Charmed Ones can find out much, Tyler's foster parents show up at the Manor and hurl an energy ball at Piper, which causes Tyler to set them ablaze. Piper and Paige discover that the boy's foster parents were demonic bounty hunters who were going to give him to Ludlow, a demon that runs an academy that trains Firestarters for The Source. After Piper vanquishes another bounty hunter, she realizes that they'll just keep coming until they get what they want. She and Leo decide to pose as bounty hunters to confront and vanquish Ludlow. Tyler wants to help, but Piper warns that it's too dangerous. The boy won't be denied, and he hitches a ride on Leo's orb. Once at the academy, Ludlow takes Tyler and tells Piper and Leo that The Source will kill the boy for his powers. He then transports the witch and Whitelighter outside the gates, and they can't reenter. They orb home because rescuing Tyler will take the Power of Three.

However, the Power of Three isn't readily available. Phoebe, who has been acting strangely domestic since she slipped Grams's ring on her finger, has completely transformed into Samantha Stephens, the witch/housewife from the 1960s TV show *Bewitched*. She believes she is only Mrs. Cole Turner, the perfect wife. Cole realizes that the problem started when he gave Phoebe the ring, and that Grams must have cursed it. Paige orbs the ring off of Phoebe's finger, restoring her sister's sense of self and her powers.

The Charmed Ones return to Ludlow's academy and recite Paige's first Power of Three spell, a haiku, which vanquishes the demon. Tyler is saved and Paige finds him a good foster family. Before he leaves, the boy requests Piper bind his powers. She does, and tells Leo she now understands his point of view regarding the subject

"That's not how powers work. They're not good or bad by themselves. It's how we use them."
PIPER HALLIWELL

"Any excuse to spend a little extra time in the kitchen."
SAMANTHA STEPHENS/PHOEBE HALLIWELL

"Charmed and Dangerous"

(FEBRUARY 7, 2002)
Written by Monica Breen & Alison Schapker
Directed by Jon Paré

Phoebe has a vision of Cole intercepting an energy ball to save her from The Source. When a stream of black particles escapes a defeated demon, and Piper's powers are suddenly gone, they realize the Hollow, a force that consumes magic, has been released. Paige leaves a client facing a last chance to get custody of her son, and the three sisters prepare to face The Source. Ignoring the Seer's warnings that the Hollow will destroy everything good and evil eventually, The Source sends a Darklighter to kill Leo so he can't heal his charges. The Darklighter shoots Leo and absorbs Paige's power when she fights back.

Cole is pulled into the Underworld by the Seer. She preys on his sense of helplessness and his love for Phoebe. To save her, Cole must work with the Seer to defeat The Source. She says that Cole

must take in the Hollow and its ability to consume powers, so when The Source attacks, Cole can absorb his powers as well. Left defenseless, The Source will then be able to be vanquished. The Seer will then join forces with the Charmed Ones to banish the Hollow back into its crypt before it consumes everything, and Cole will return to normal. Cole agrees, believing it's his only chance to save Phoebe.

At the Manor, The Source corners the witches in the attic. They activate a crystal demon trap, but he breaks it, having absorbed Paige's power to call objects. He hurls an energy ball at Phoebe, but Cole shimmers in to take the hit. The powers Cole absorbed from the Hollow make him impervious to the weapons ball, and also give him back the demonic ability to create them. He fires at The Source and weakens him, allowing the Charmed Ones to cast a spell that calls on the power of all Halliwell witches. It works, and The Source is vanquished. Paige channels Leo's healing power to save him. Phoebe and the Seer send the Hollow back where it belongs, and when Paige questions what happened to The Source's powers, the Seer says they went into "the void." But as Cole hugs Phoebe, his eyes flash black, indicating a more specific location for the powers.

"We are talking about the Source of All Evil. Maybe measured optimism is best."
PIPER HALLIWELL

"The Three Faces of Phoebe"

(FEBRUARY 14, 2002)
Written by Curtis Kheel
Directed by Joel J. Feigenbaum

Cole can't fight the power of The Source emerging within him. However, since his love for Phoebe strengthens the human half, The Source lets it exist to be exploited. Worried about Cole's reticence, Phoebe casts a spell to see if she should marry him. Two other Phoebes appear, one age ten and the other from forty years in the future. Old Phoebe won't say anything to alter her past. Young Phoebe reminds Phoebe of her childhood dreams, which included Cinderella and finding Prince Charming.

Casting her lot with Cole, the Seer convinces an ambitious demon named Kurzon to attack the Charmed Ones. She tells Cole it's to protect him, but she wants the bond with Phoebe severed. The allegedly human Cole saves Young Phoebe from Kurzon, who escapes without a fight, a deed that arouses Paige's suspicions. When the sisters leave to vanquish Kurzon, Old Phoebe asks Cole if he can be saved. That may be why she was sent back, to save him instead of destroying him and living a life of regret. When she dies to save Cole from Kurzon, Phoebe has the answer she's looking for. Paige's orbing power advances, and she's able to control her flight.

"I'm ten. I'm not stupid."

YOUNG PHOEBE HALLIWELL

"Nobody's going to take you seriously until you stop dressing like a tramp."

OLD PHOEBE HALLIWELL

"Marry-Go-Round"

(MARCH 14, 2002)
Written by Daniel Cerone
Directed by Chris Long

Since holy matrimony will keep Cole from reigning as The Source, the emerging evil within him plots with the Seer to stop the wedding by sabotaging Phoebe's trust in Paige. The wedding dress Paige picked up is too big, it has the wrong name tag, and her tarot reading for Phoebe predicts despair and death. Phoebe wakes up with severe acne from Paige's face cream, and Paige's spell to vanish the blemishes makes Phoebe invisible. Paige transfers the invisibility to herself, but a Lazarus demon crashes the wedding, ending it.

Phoebe is not consoled by the fact that Piper tried three times before she married Leo. Unaware that a matrimonial trap has been set by Cole, the sisters and Leo bury the Lazarus demon in the cemetery so he won't be resurrected. When the demon claims that Cole commanded him to disrupt the wedding, Cole morphs into the Seer to cast blame on her. The wedding party is convinced the Seer is guilty when they find Cole in the mausoleum, where he flamed a moment before. When they find a chapel and a waiting priest in the cemetery, Phoebe marries Cole without realizing it's a dark ceremony that seals their fate with evil.

"My wedding dress could double as a circus tent."

PHOEBE HALLIWELL

"In the end, all that matters is that you marry the guy you love. If you managed to do that, your wedding was perfect."

PIPER HALLIWELL

"The Fifth Halliwheel"

(MARCH 21, 2002)
Written by Krista Vernoff
Directed by David Straiton

Cole lands a lucrative job with a law firm, which is really just a front for his new position as The Source. But more importantly, he's busy arranging for a demonic conception. His plans are disrupted when Phoebe brings home a hysterical woman named Karen Young who has no memory of what happened to her. Phoebe gets a vision of Karen being attacked by demons, and Cole says he'll do whatever he can to help. Thinking he's alone, the allegedly human Cole tries to magically pull the information from Karen's mind, but Paige arrives just in time to see his hand glow, reaffirming her suspicions that he's still demonic. Piper and Phoebe return with what they found in the Book of Shadows. They connect the light ball Phoebe saw in her vision with demonic Power Brokers. The light ball contained a demonic power that is now being stored in Karen until a buyer for it is found. The human in whom the demonic power is stored will become confused and frightened and ultimately die. Luckily there is a potion that will pull the power out of the Innocent. Piper starts making the potion, but Karen is worried about her job, so Phoebe takes over her newspaper advice column while she is incapacitated. Phoebe, Piper, and Leo save Karen's life with the potion and her job with the copy Phoebe writes. Then Leo and Piper orb to Hawaii for the honeymoon that their "loving" brother-in-law Cole arranged for them.

Knowing that Paige is on to him, Cole needs to get her out of the picture. He has a Power Broker infect Paige with a demonic power. Cole's honeymoon arrangements for his in-laws and himself assure that the youngest Charmed One will be home alone and die before she can alert anyone about her infection. He sticks around the Manor long enough to taunt Paige so that the demonic powers manifest themselves and hasten the process. He then shimmers to Phoebe, who's waiting in a hotel suite. Determined to let Phoebe know what she knows—the truth about Cole—Paige interrupts the newlyweds and tries to kill her demonic brother-in-law. Cole breaks the only remaining bottle of potion, and not even Leo and Piper, who were called back from Hawaii, are able to save Paige. Phoebe's despair when faced with losing another sister drives Cole to command the Power Brokers to remove the power from Paige. Luckily for the new Source, when Paige recovers she doesn't remember anything that happened.

167

Karen quits her job, recommending that Phoebe replace her. Phoebe's joy is marred when she realizes Paige's attack was prompted by real hatred or mistrust of Cole.

"I'm going for that kind of we're-married-but-we're-not-dead look."

PHOEBE HALLIWELL

"I think being so Charming, as we are, is a full-time job." **PIPER HALLIWELL**

"Saving Private Leo"

(March 28, 2002)
Teleplay by Daniel Cerone
Story by Doug E. Jones
Directed by John Behring

Phoebe yearns for peace and quiet to write her new advice column. Cole is creating annoyances so she'll want to move out of the Manor, which will separate her from her sisters and weaken the Power of Three. Piper wonders why Leo refuses to attend the sixtieth anniversary of Guadalcanal. He doesn't talk about the place where he died or about his posthumous Medal of Honor. Piper learns that Leo feels guilty for leaving his lifelong friends Rick and Nathan Lang in a tent that was blown up. Leo avoided dying with them because there were others who needed his help more, so he returned to the field, only to die there after saving many more lives. The ghosts of Rick and Nathan have been honing their corporeal skills, waiting for a chance to get revenge on Leo.

When Rick and Nathan find Leo, they kill a teacher he's guiding. Guilt causes Leo to break down and lose his powers. Driven to take everything from him, the ghosts attack and mortally wound Piper. Phoebe and Paige call Leo to no avail. Piper's spirit casts the spell to vanquish ghosts, which can only be chanted by the dead. Leo runs in and his powers are restored in time to save Piper. Posing as his own grandson at the reunion, Leo meets some of the men he saved because he wasn't killed in the tent. Their children and grandchildren all exist because of him.

"Leo poses as a heavenly handyman."　　　　　　　　**PIPER HALLIWELL**

"Bite Me"　　　(APRIL 18, 2002)
Written by Curtis Kheel
Directed by John Ketchmer

Life changes for the Charmed Ones as Phoebe moves with Cole into the luxurious penthouse offered by Cole's "law firm." Piper misses not having her to talk to, and although Paige tries to help, she knows she still doesn't share the same bond with her sister that Phoebe does. Forgetting Cole's new "no orbing into the penthouse" policy, Paige pops in looking for Phoebe. What she finds is Cole winding up a meeting with a vampire named Rowan. The witches still don't know that Cole is a demon again, although Paige continues to have her suspicions. In order to make his reign as The Source as powerful as possible, Cole holds meetings with various Underworld factions to get them to work together toward their common goal—the triumph of evil over good. Rowan had been meeting with Cole to discuss bringing the vampires back into the fold. They had been exiled by the old Source, and the vampire Queen, sensing a return of her power, is willing to talk to the new one.

Paige has no idea what she orbed in on, but Rowan recognizes the value of his Queen having the Charmed Ones on her side. He makes a date to see Paige at P3 that night. When she's apparently stood up, Paige heads home and is bitten by a swarm of bats in the parking lot. After a short stay in the emergency room, Leo heals Paige at home. Knowing that Rowan probably has something to do with this, Cole suggests that she was attacked by vampires. His theory is proven correct when the others see Paige turn into a bat and fly out the window. Consulting the Book of Shadows, Piper learns that if the vampire Queen is killed, her entire flock will die as well. Transformation into a vampire isn't sealed until a first kill is made, so if they can get to the Queen before Paige bites anyone, they can save their sister. Cole didn't know that killing the Queen kills all her vampires, and is more than a little annoyed that none of his demonic factions had shared that information. He senses a coup, and figures that the vampires are plotting with a demon named Keats who had shown him resistance during his meetings. He tracks down Keats and tortures him until he reveals the location of the vampire Queen.

Meanwhile, the Queen sends Vampire Paige off to convert her sisters. She goes in for the kill just as Cole finds the Queen and kills her. Her minions go up in flames, and Paige, still a virgin vampire, is returned to her normal state. She says she knows the new Source is the one who killed the Queen, because he visited her cave, but Paige never got a look at him. With Phoebe on her way to the penthouse, Paige tells Piper that she met Rowan at Cole's. Piper has to agree that something demonic is up again with their brother-in-law.

Through all of this, Phoebe hasn't been feeling very well. It turns out that the plan the Seer had for her to conceive the heir to The Source worked—Phoebe's pregnant.

"I'm living proof that magic happens when witches and Whitelighters hook up."
PAIGE MATTHEWS

PHOEBE: *"Should we be worried?"*
PIPER: *"No, not til after dinner."*

"The demonic electoral college is meeting. They're gonna vote in a new Source."
PIPER HALLIWELL

| "We're off to See the Wizard" | (APRIL 25, 2002)
Written by Alison Schapker & Monica Breen
Directed by Tom Lonsdale |

The last known wizard contacts the Charmed Ones to steal the *Grimoire*, the black magic version of the Book of Shadows, without which the new Source's coronation can't happen. Ignoring her sisters' lack of enthusiasm about her pregnancy and Paige's accusation that Cole is evil again, Phoebe honors her Charmed responsibility and goes to the Underworld with her sisters to retrieve the *Grimoire*, where she kills a guard by throwing fire—something only demons can do. Unnerved by this new power, Phoebe looks for comfort in Cole's arms, but when he hugs her, she has a series of visions that he is The Source. She pulls away and runs off to the Manor.

When the distraught Phoebe comes home, she tells her sisters that not only is Cole working with demons, he is a demon again. Focused on Phoebe's problem, the witches don't realize that the wizard uses an illusion to steal the *Grimoire*. The loss of the book becomes even more important when Leo returns with information from the Elders that wizards are evil, and the wizard plans to use the *Grimoire* to become the new Source.

The girls search for Cole to get some answers, but find Julie, Cole's demonic assistant, at the penthouse. A fight ensues, and Phoebe kills her. Then Phoebe is summoned below, where the Seer persuades her to embrace her evil destiny to save Cole and their unborn baby. Phoebe doesn't realize Cole is giving up The Source's power to keep her, and misunderstands when she walks in on him transferring his powers to the wizard, thinking his powers are being stolen. She kills the wizard, sealing Cole's evil fate. Phoebe informs her sisters that she has a new destiny—to be Queen of the Underworld—and flames Down There for the coronation. Since they can't vanquish The Source or the Seer without the Power of Three, Piper and Paige are helpless to save their sister.

"I can't believe we let that slimy Lord of the Ring wannabe use us!"

PIPER HALLIWELL

"[The Source] didn't die. He was reborn—into a new sorry ass."   **WIZARD**

"Long Live the Queen"	(MAY 2, 2002) Written by Krista Vernoff Directed by Jon Paré

Phoebe starts killing Cole's best demons in snits of irritation and dumps the Seer's foul health tonic when her back is turned. Upset by her sisters' rejection, Phoebe uses a vision as an excuse to visit. Piper has shut down her emotions and armed herself with potions to use against Phoebe if necessary. Paige and Leo agree to give Phoebe a chance when she offers to help save an Innocent. When Phoebe lets the attacking demon go, Piper and Leo say that she has to choose—she can't be aligned with evil and do good. Cole agrees. Phoebe's good deed has weakened his hold on the Underworld.

While Paige guards the Innocent, Leo tries to reassure Piper that she's not a failure because Phoebe chose evil, but Piper freezes him to get some peace. The baby, aided by the evil tonic, gets stronger while Phoebe weakens. Then Cole confesses to killing the Innocent she tried to save. When her sisters arrive, trusting her to restore the Power of Three, Phoebe makes the crucial choice she's faced off and on since becoming a witch. She kisses Cole good-bye, rejects the dark side, and helps her sisters vanquish The Source—again.

"I'll always love you."   **COLE TURNER**

"She's like Piper Lite. All the personality with none of the messy feelings."

PAIGE MATTHEWS

"Womb Raider"	(MAY 9, 2002) Written by Daniel Cerone Directed by Mel Damski

The Seer stops the coronation of the High Council's choice for the new Source, Cole's former right-hand man, Dane, because he is not linked by lineage or magic, so they will give the Seer until that night to produce The Source's heir—or the throne will belong to Dane. The unborn child begins using its power independent of Phoebe. It throws Paige out a window, almost electrocutes a doctor, and tries to incinerate a cop when Phoebe files a missing person report on Cole. Because she needs that baby, the Seer sucks Phoebe through a portal in Cole's

170

closet, but the Charmed One is able to get away. With the clock ticking, the Seer goes to the Tall Man, a seven-foot demon banished to live in a cage for all eternity. She offers him freedom in exchange for Phoebe.

When the Tall Man gets to Halliwell Manor, the sisters find their magic doesn't work on him. He grabs for Phoebe, but the baby kicks Paige into him. Paige falls through the Tall Man and they both vanish. The Book of Shadows explains the mysterious disappearance occurred because the Tall Man serves as a portal to other dimensions. When he reappears, Phoebe taps into the baby's evil powers to vanquish him. The Seer lets them know what she's done with Paige when she sends Phoebe a premonition of her sister being killed in a cage.

Phoebe flames into the Underworld to save Paige, her eyes black with The Source's evil magic. She allows the Seer to perform a ceremony to transfer the baby into her womb, after which she reveals that the baby was never Cole's—it is The Source's, and it is pure evil. Phoebe is put in the cage with Paige, helpless because no magic can escape the confinement. They are forced to witness the coronation of the Seer as the new Source. As she begins taking the oath, Paige and Phoebe use the To Call a Lost Witch spell to bring Piper to them. Even though no magic can escape the cage, it can get in, so they make the Seer tap into the baby's full power. As she shoots premium-grade evil at the cage, the Charmed Ones chant a Power of Three spell to repel it with equal amounts of good. The power of Baby Source is too much for the Seer to withstand. It overcomes her and she explodes, taking all of the demons in the coronation chamber with her. The dueling magic created a rip in the cage that allows the sisters to escape, having vanquished another potential Source.

When they return to the Manor, Piper and Paige give Phoebe a letter they found for her at the penthouse. As she reads Cole's words, she mysteriously hears him calling to her from beyond the grave.

"Unborn babies don't perform magic tricks."   **PIPER HALLIWELL**

"That kid needs a serious time out."   **PAIGE MATTHEWS**

"Witch Way Now"

(MAY 16, 2002)
Written by Brad Kern
Directed by Brad Kern

As a reward for vanquishing The Source, the Angel of Destiny offers the Charmed Ones the chance to give up their powers to lead normal lives. Paige is against it, but Piper and Phoebe have been through too much to reject the idea out of hand. While they consider it, FBI Agent Jackman begins a surveillance of the Manor. When Phoebe astral projects to Cole in demon purgatory, she is snared by the Beast that roams there absorbing the demonic powers of the vanquished. Piper and Paige perform a reversal spell to pull Phoebe back, after they hear her scream and Jackman gets the incantation on tape. He has a dossier on the Halliwells, which he shows them. If they help him catch a serial witch killer named Selena, he'll destroy it.

The Charmed Ones battle Selena's bodyguards, capture her, and turn her over to Jackman after he acquires a warrant. Since they've decided two to one to forsake magic, Phoebe tells Cole she will no longer have the power to save him. He doesn't tell her that the Beast is dead or that he has new and improved demonic powers. All is resolved until Leo discovers that Jackman is the real witch hunter. Since Jackman uses amulets to keep magic from working, the sisters use human skills to save Selena. Cole materializes to save Phoebe from Jackman's bullet, and the sisters decide they can't renounce their Charmed destiny.

"It's no longer really a choice for us. This is who we are." **PIPER HALLIWELL**

"How can I move on with my life when I keep being haunted by his afterlife?"
PHOEBE HALLIWELL

The Charmed Episode Puns

Here are the episode titles from the **FOURTH SEASON,** along with their most likely origins.

CHARMED AGAIN: To reclaim the Power of Three.

HELL HATH NO FURY: " . . . like a woman scorned." The line referring to the anger of a woman who feels she has been taken advantage of comes from William Congreve's play, *The Mourning Bride.* It originally read: "Heaven has no rage, like love to hatred turned, nor hell a fury, like a woman scorned."

ENTER THE DEMON: *Enter the Dragon* is a film released in 1973 starring Bruce Lee.

SIZE MATTERS: A common misconception.

A KNIGHT TO REMEMBER: *A Night to Remember* is the name of a 1958 film about the sinking of the *Titanic.*

BRAIN DRAIN: Loss of talented and educated people of a country to another country where conditions are better.

BLACK AS COLE: "As black as coal" is a simile used to describe something very dark in either color or mood.

MUSE TO MY EARS: In Greek mythology a muse is any of the nine sisters presiding over and inspiring song, poetry, and the arts and sciences. "Music to my ears" is a common phrase noting when particularly pleasant news is heard.

A PAIGE FROM THE PAST: "Taking a page from the past" refers to using a past example for something in the present.

TRIAL BY MAGIC: "Trial by fire" is a phrase that means attempting to do something without practice, usually in an emergency situation.

LOST AND BOUND: Play on "lost and found."

CHARMED AND DANGEROUS: "Armed and dangerous" is a way police refer to a particular suspect on the loose.

THE THREE FACES OF PHOEBE: *The Three Faces of Eve* is a film from 1957 starring Joanne Woodward.

MARRY-GO-ROUND: A merry-go-round is a spinning circular platform for children (and the occasional adult) to ride.

THE FIFTH HALLIWHEEL: "The fifth wheel" is a phrase used to describe the odd person out when two couples are joined by a fifth, unattached, person.

SAVING PRIVATE LEO: *Saving Private Ryan* is a Steven Spielberg movie released in 1998 starring Tom Hanks.

BITE ME: Phrase used when telling someone off.

WE'RE OFF TO SEE THE WIZARD: "We're off to See the Wizard" is a song from *The Wizard of Oz*.

LONG LIVE THE QUEEN: Traditional cheer for royalty.

WOMB RAIDER: *Tomb Raider* is a popular video game (and movie) centering on the character Lara Croft.

WITCH WAY NOW?: "Which way now?" is a simple phrase used when trying to figure out direction.

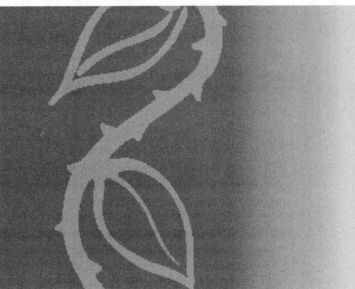

Episode Guide

Season Five

"A Witch's Tail, Part One"

(SEPTEMBER 22, 2002)
Written by Daniel Cerone
Directed by James L. Conway

Preparing for their baby's arrival, Leo builds a nursery and Piper goes through a box of baby clothes, where she finds her baby book. She is saddened to see that it ends when she was five and her mother died. Piper develops an overwhelming fear that she too will die and leave her baby, the way her mother left her.

Phoebe files divorce papers only to have Cole show up at the last minute and contest her allegation that he deserted her. Phoebe is furious and doesn't believe Cole's assertion that he is good again. She also doesn't have time to argue with him. The success of her advice column has made her something of a celebrity, with her face on billboards and interviewers wanting time with her.

And Paige finally gets the promotion to full-fledged social worker that she's been lobbying for so hard.

Things seem to be going along as usual for the Charmed Ones, until a mermaid named Mylie changes everything. Mylie made a pact with a Sea Hag so that if Craig Wilson, the mortal Mylie loves, expresses his love for her, Mylie will become human. If not, she owes her immortality to the Sea Hag, who in turn promised the eternal life to the demon Necron. Recognizing a billboard photo of Phoebe as a Charmed One, Mylie turns to the sisters for help. Unfortunately, even the Power of Three can't keep Craig from running out the door when Mylie reveals her mermaid nature. Sensing Mylie's defeat and desperate for the immortal life force, the Sea Hag kidnaps her.

Paige writes a spell to find the Sea Hag, but it turns Phoebe into a mermaid. The Charmed Ones use this to their advantage. Phoebe quickly takes to the sea and locates the Sea Hag's underwater cavern. But a panic-stricken Piper stays behind when Leo and Paige orb to Phoebe. Without the Power of Three the girls are defenseless against the Sea Hag. Thinking quickly, Paige orbs a leech-like auger shell off of Mylie before it drains her life. Phoebe swims in and throws the discarded auger shell at the Sea Hag. It sticks to her chest and reduces her to salt. Leo orbs in with Craig, who finally declares his love, which turns Mylie human.

It's time to return to the Manor to see what's wrong with Piper, but Phoebe decides to heed the call of the sea and swims off.

"Nothing perks up a girl's career like sending her husband straight to hell."
PHOEBE HALLIWELL

"What's life like under the sea? Does your skin get all wrinkly? Does algae pose a personal hygiene problem?"
PAIGE MATTHEWS

"A Witch's Tail, Part Two"

(SEPTEMBER 22, 2002)
Written by Monica Breen & Alison Schapker
Directed by Mel Damski

Leo has no luck capturing MerPhoebe. When he and Paige return to the Manor, they find Piper full of self-recrimination about her panic attack. Leo tells her she needs to focus on getting over her fear. Piper secretly casts a Fearless Spell on herself that eradicates not only her worry but also her good sense.

Necron chases MerPhoebe and injures her, and she is caught by fishermen, which finally allows Leo to sense her and orb her home. Piper, afraid of nothing, acts recklessly and is captured by Necron when he comes looking for MerPhoebe.

In an attempt to save Phoebe, Darryl and Paige separately talk to Cole. Darryl tells him if he truly loves Phoebe, he should give her what she wants— her freedom. Paige tells him that initially, she thought Phoebe was the one who was turned into a mermaid because her heart was cold—purposely frozen so that Cole couldn't hurt her again. But Paige realizes now that it's not Phoebe's hate but her love for Cole that has made her harden her heart. Without his help they may never break the sea's hold over Phoebe, and she will remain a mermaid forever.

The troops regroup to vanquish Necron. Buoyed by the fearless spell, Piper doesn't panic when Necron subjects her to an electric eel shock. But when he telekinetically throws her across the grotto and injures her, she instinctively fears for her baby and the spell is broken. MerPhoebe and Leo rush to Piper's aid, and try to keep Necron at bay until Paige gets there with the vanquishing spell. Late because of her talk with Cole, Paige finally orbs into the Sea Hag's cavern. The Charmed Ones destroy Necron with the vanquishing spell, but the recoil from his demise knocks everyone unconscious. Piper is dragged underwater. Her mother appears to her and tells her to have faith that she will survive for her baby. Patty's spirit leads Piper back to the surface, and before Leo can get to her, the baby heals Piper from within. She now truly believes that she will not leave her baby as she was once left. Seeing all is well with her sisters, MerPhoebe takes off again for the call of the open sea.

Paige finally gets back to the social services office, but realizes there isn't enough time in a day to be both a good social worker and a good witch. Because she knows her sisters and their battles need her more, she quits her job to become a full-time Charmed One.

On the beach, Cole magically calls Phoebe to him and convinces her to admit that she loves him. When she does, she becomes human again. She tells Cole that although she will always love him, it doesn't change anything. She still cannot be with him.

"Happily Ever After"

(SEPTEMBER 29, 2002)
Written by Curtis Kheel
Directed by John T. Kretchmer

Piper reads fairy tales to her unborn baby, just as Grams used to do for her. When budding superwitch Paige questions her, Piper says that she believes that there is some truth in all fairy tales. Little does she know how right she is.

At a mountain fortress, the Keeper of the Fairy Tales accidentally bumps the mirror that houses the evil witch. It falls to the floor and releases her. She immediately kills the Keeper and imprisons his apprentice, Osgood, in the mirror. The evil witch needs a little affirmation and asks the mirror who the most powerful witch of all is. Since whoever is in the mirror cannot lie, Osgood lets it slip that there are three more powerful witches than she. The evil witch now has a mission: to kill the Charmed Ones. She calls forth characters from fairy tales to bring the sisters to their demise.

Meanwhile, Piper frets about her abilities to raise a magical baby. She demands that Leo orb in Grams to help her. He can't, but apparently the baby can, as the little one makes Grams corporeal. Grams listens to Piper's pleas for help and meets Paige for the first time. Although Paige is reluctant to embrace Grams as her relative, the two bond over potion making and their shared stubbornness. While they are making the potion to kill the evil witch, the woodsman from Snow White bursts into the house and goes for Paige. Piper vanquishes him. When they find his picture in the fairy tale book rather than the Book of Shadows, Grams tells the girls that fairy tales are real, or at least they once were. They can be rewritten if they fall in to evil hands, and will be changed forever.

Having failed with the woodsman, the evil witch takes matters into her own hands. She leaves a poisoned apple in the kitchen for Paige, who succumbs. Cinderella Phoebe can't control a pair of glass slippers that the witch left for her. They send her straight to a ball with the charming Adam Prinz, who is now under a spell cast by the evil witch. Finally, the witch sends the big bad wolf to eat Grams, then morph into her form. When he eats Piper, too, she saves Grams and herself by blowing up the wolf from the inside. Calling the seven dwarvfs to look after Paige, Leo orbs to the ball to warn Phoebe, who suspects Cole is behind whatever in the world is going on. Adam manages to keep her from her Whitelighter and at the stroke of midnight, he morphs Phoebe's carriage into a pumpkin, with Phoebe still inside. Cole shows up just in time to stop Adam from smashing the pumpkin to bits.

Piper, in complete control of the situation, dons Little Red Riding Hood's cloak to stop the evil witch. Using the fairy-tale book as a portal to the Keeper's castle, she vanquishes the witch with the potion concocted by Grams. Killing the witch releases Phoebe, Paige, and Adam from her magic and frees Osgood from the mirror. Piper gains confidence, Paige accepts the truth of the fairy tales, and Phoebe learns that she can't necessarily trust her judgment.

(OCTOBER 6, 2002)

"Siren's Song"

Written by Krista Vernoff
Directed by Joel J. Feigenbaum

Leo is too busy to indulge Piper when she complains she's nauseated and burping white light, producing flower petals instead of explosions. Paige is so focused on honing her magical skills and practicing potions that she's also inattentive to her sisters. But when news of an attack with demonic overtones intrudes on family issues, Leo orbs home long enough to turn on the TV news coverage of Cole rescuing a woman from a burning building. He explains that the woman, Melissa, is a future Whitelighter, and the Elders want him to watch her until the danger passes. The

demon that was after Melissa also sees the news, and heads to the hospital to finish her off. She finds Leo in her way, and tries to take him out as well. Fortunately for Leo, Paige finally notices something's wrong with Piper and orbs them to the hospital. Unfortunately for the Whitelighter, he is in a lip-lock with the alleged demon when his wife arrives.

After fighting the demon, Paige, Piper, Leo, and Melissa orb back to the safety of the Manor. Still not able to see the other's point of view, Piper and Leo argue while Paige consults the Book of Shadows. She finds that the demon is a Siren. As a mortal, the Siren fell in love with a married man. The town punished her affair by burning her to death. Her rage turned her into a Siren: a being who seduces married men with her song, and then destroys both husband and wife with the very flames that consumed her. Paige figures they can handle her with a potion, but Leo argues that her power is very strong. Piper makes a crack about him kissing the Siren, which sets off another argument. A swirl of orbs suddenly explode after appearing around the fighting couple, switching their powers. Piper's a Whitelighter, and Leo's got her powers—and their baby. They figure the baby switched the powers because its parents were constantly bickering.

Piper realizes that Leo hears his charges all the time, and he can't ignore their calls. Leo experiences how difficult it is to control Piper's power. He also realizes the "crying thing" is caused by hormones.

While Piper and Leo sort out their issues, and Paige works on vanquishing the Siren, Phoebe has problems of her own. After Cole's heroics, Elise wants Phoebe to interview her ex for the paper. Phoebe reluctantly agrees and keeps it purely business, despite Cole's efforts to steer the conversation to the two of them. Sensing Phoebe's rejection of Cole's efforts, the Siren sees a way to defeat the Charmed Ones, because they are just like any women in love. The Siren seduces Cole and calls Phoebe, but Cole isn't killed by her lung-searing kiss. Piper, Paige, and Leo arrive to find him strangling

Phoebe. As soon as Leo blows up the Siren, the spell is broken. Even though Cole swears he wants to be good, he realizes he can't always control the evil inside him.

With everyone safe and with a better understanding of each other's needs, the baby switches Piper's and Leo's powers back to their proper places. Paige learns the importance of combining her Whitelighter compassion with her superwitch strength. And Phoebe knows that her love for Cole may be true, but it also may be fatal.

"Woman to woman? If you're still describing this guy as the love of your life, then the can's open, the worms are out, and you may as well use them to go fishing."
ELISE ROTHMAN

"We also need to teach your half-witch baby the joy of maiming and killing demons."
PAIGE MATTHEWS

"Witches in Tights"

(OCTOBER 13, 2002)
Written by Mike Wilding
Directed by David Straiton

The Charmed Ones cross paths with Kevin, a teenage artist, when his drawing of a superhero named The Aggressor comes to life and shows up at the Manor. A warlock named Arnon has no powers of his own, and is looking to pick up a few. He senses great power in Kevin, who can not only draw characters, but bring them to life as well. Arnon also knows that a retiring Elder named Ramus will be passing on his powers before the end of the night, and that

Ramus is at Halliwell Manor. Arnon wants Ramus's powers before they are transferred, and instructs Kevin to bring The Aggressor to life to steal the powers. The evil superhero shows up and the sisters make quick work of him, so Arnon forces Kevin to draw a stronger, invincible Aggressor who can handle the witches. He does, but unbeknownst to Arnon, Kevin also draws the sisters with superpowers to rival The Aggressor.

Phoebe is also in a fight with slumlord Edward Miller, who is evicting his tenants. When she confronts him, her clothes suddenly morph into a superhero costume. Phoebe uses her newfound superpowers to intimidate Miller. At the same time, Piper and Paige are looking for clues about the identity of The Aggressor. When their clothes also magically morph, they too attain superpowers. Pleased with their new and improved abilities, the girls reconvene at the Manor to compare notes. They notice that when they remove their masks, they remove the high brought by the new powers. Piper reasons that their better judgment was masked as well as their faces. They decide to leave off the masks, but find the outfits alone still give them superpowers when The Aggressor shows up again and is defeated. As he's dying he morphs into Kevin, who thanks them for stopping him. Leo heals Kevin, who explains his powers and Arnon's plan.

Kevin leads the Charmed Ones to Arnon. When the warlock sees them, he tears up the picture of the superhero witches. This voids the magic of the drawing and the witches have only their regular powers left to use. Normally, that would be enough, but Arnon forces Kevin to draw him with powers. He morphs into Arnon the Aggressor and attacks, knocking out the sisters. Arnon then heads for the Manor and Ramus, where he steals Ramus's powers and kills the Elder. Paige orbs in with her sisters and Kevin, who tells the girls the drawing is in Arnon's boot. Paige orbs the boot to her and rips up the picture. Once Arnon no longer has superpowers, Piper blasts him into smithereens. The powers he stole from Ramus flow into Kevin, who was always supposed to receive them because he is the new Elder.

But everything is not quite over. Cole tells Phoebe that Edward Miller has a videotape of Super Phoebe that he's threatening to use to expose her. As Phoebe is on her way to meet Miller, the slumlord makes Cole so angry that he incinerates him before she can get there.

"I'm pregnant, not terminal." **PIPER HALLIWELL**

"The Eyes Have It"

(OCTOBER 20, 2002)
Written by Laurie Parres
Directed by James Marshall

ince months have passed without a premonition, Phoebe seeks help from a psychic gypsy, Madam Tereza, who is later killed, her eyes gouged out. A partial vision at the funeral leads the sisters to Lydia, another gypsy. The premonition saves Lydia from Cree, a demon gypsy hunter who is set on avenging his father, Orin. Orin was blinded by the gypsies and will only see again when he gets the eyes of the last Shuvani, or gypsy princess. Lydia works with the Charmed

Ones to make a potion that will vanquish Cree, but she worries about her niece, Dr. Ava Nicolae, who doesn't believe in magic. Piper is happy to go see Ava because she's desperate to talk about her pregnancy. Lydia teaches Paige and Phoebe to read tea leaves, and when Paige sees danger coming to Ava, Lydia vanishes in a puff of smoke.

Rushing to save Ava, Lydia again runs into Cree, but isn't so lucky this time. As she dies, Lydia appears to Ava as Amulo—the living dead—and warns her not to give up her powers. The Charmed Ones investigate and discover the family talisman, which indicates that Lydia's eyes are the magical Evil Eye that Orin, Cree's father, wants.

Touching the talisman, Phoebe feels as though she's in two places at once: the present, and the future she envisions where Orin kills them all. Her present self suffers the injuries incurred by her future self. Knowing they can't stop Orin alone, the Charmed Ones combine their power with Ava's gypsy magic and The Source's vanquishing spell. The invoked spirits repel the power of the stolen Evil Eye, destroying Orin. Ava tutors the sisters in how to deliver the baby at home.

LEO: *"Since when are prenatal yoga and home-birthing videos your idea of a good time?"*
PAIGE: *"Since I became a friendless loser with no life."*

"Sympathy for the Demon"	(NOVEMBER 3, 2002) Written by Henry Alonso Myers Directed by Stuart Gillard

When Cole imagines using his powers on demons who aren't there, he asks for help before he hurts someone. What Cole doesn't know is that Barbas, the Demon of Fear, has returned, this time in spirit, not flesh, since he is still in the purgatory to which the Charmed Ones previously banished him. Barbas plans to divide and conquer the sisters, manipulating them into providing him with enough power to enable him to break free of his prison.

Phoebe, reluctant to help Cole, is further deterred when Barbas tells her that Cole will only drag her into his world of evil again. Piper and Paige agree to help, only to have Barbas talk Piper out of it before she begins. That leaves Paige as Cole's unlikely champion. She comes up with a partial solution: to strip Cole of his powers so that he can't hurt anyone while he's delusional. Cole worries that without his powers he won't be able to defend himself, but Barbas manipulates him into relinquishing them. Conveniently, Barbas is there to absorb Cole's powers as they leave his body. They make him corporeal, and he throws the defenseless Cole through a window before dematerializing. When Paige tells her sisters what she did, they are furious with her. With Cole's powers, Barbas is now even more of a threat. Cole comes to Paige's defense, though, and they all realize that he is only human again, and therefore their Innocent.

Leo orbs Cole to safety, leaving the sisters alone in the house, where Barbas traps them with their fears. He casts an illusion over Paige so that when Phoebe looks at her, she sees Barbas instead. Phoebe attacks "Barbas"/Paige with an athame, only to find that she really knifed her sister. Piper realizes she and Phoebe must conquer their fear to beat Barbas and save Paige. When she overcomes the natural fears of all expectant mothers, and Phoebe rejects the idea that she's evil, the trap crumbles. Leo heals Paige, but Barbas still has Cole's immense powers. The Charmed Ones catch Barbas by surprise and use the power stripping potion again, transferring the powers back to Cole. Evil energy doesn't just dissipate, it needs somewhere to go, so rather than taking the chance of the powers transferring to some unknown opportunistic demon, Cole willingly takes the powers back to save them and vanquishes Barbas permanently.

"Going against your sisters is pure suicide."　　　　　**LEO WYATT**

"Desperate demons call for desperate measures."　　　　**PIPER HALLIWELL**

"A Witch in Time"	(NOVEMBER 10, 2002) Written by Daniel Cerone Directed by John Behring

Piper worries that Phoebe's new love, Miles, is just a rebound dalliance. Phoebe has a premonition that Miles will be killed in gun battle. She and Piper save him, not realizing that with Phoebe's expanded power, and triggered by her emotional involvement, she has foreseen an ordinary, destined event rather than a supernatural threat that she is intended to prevent. She saves Miles from a warlock's athame at dinner, and from falling off his apartment balcony later. Cole gets a visit from a warlock named Bacarra who claims to be from the future. He says that future Cole sent him back to stop Phoebe from saving Miles. The Angel of Death has marked Miles to die, and if Phoebe continues to prevent that, she will die herself. Cole tries to warn Piper, but she sends him away.

Unknown to Cole, Bacarra conspires with his present self to take over the Underworld. Armed with a spell from the future and a potion of Charmed blood, they cloak themselves in good and are able to steal the Book of Shadows. Utilizing the spell To Disempower a Witch, the Bacarras steal the girls' powers and turn Paige and Phoebe to dust with energy balls. Leo orbs Piper out to the alley where Miles was supposed to die. The portal created by Bacarra's ripple in time will stay open until the warlock enters again. Piper enters and arrives back in time, just before the shooting. Knowing how to prevent it, she chooses to allow it to happen this time. Phoebe doesn't save Miles, and everything that happened from that point on is erased.

"One's a premonition. Two's a pattern."   **LEO WYATT**

"Warlocks we can handle. Demonic ex-husbands we can't."   **PIPER HALLIWELL**

"Sam I Am"

(NOVEMBER 17, 2002)
Written by Alison Schapker & Monica Breen
Directed by Joel J. Feigenbaum

Piper interviews magical nannies while Paige tackles her first Whitelighter assignment. When she learns that her drunken charge is her bitter father, she seems indifferent. Giving her up was the hardest thing Sam ever did, but since the Elders forbade his union with Patty, he had no choice. After that, and after Patty died, Sam didn't care about anything, especially about being a Whitelighter. Saving Prue brought back a little pride—and his wings—but he's fallen into his old bad habits again.

A renegade Darklighter named Ronan comes after Sam. With a little help from Cole, Ronan becomes invincible. He shoots a Darklighter arrow that magically separates into three: one each for Leo, Paige, and Piper's baby. The first two find their marks, but the baby throws a force field around Piper, who leaves to find Sam. Love for Paige pushes Sam to heal himself, and then he heals Paige and Leo. Paige and Sam come to terms with their relationship. She tells him that because of his sacrifice, she had a great life, with great parents, and now she has a great life as a witch and a Whitelighter.

Meanwhile, Cole is slowly going crazy. He can't have Phoebe, so he doesn't want to live. As if he isn't confused enough, two beings calling themselves the Avatars approach him. They say they are beings of pure power who are beyond good and evil. Cole tries to incinerate them with energy balls, but they are unharmed. It is futile to fight them, they say, because they are invincible. And, they add, it's only a matter of time until he joins them. Cole gets an idea: He'll have the Charmed Ones vanquish him and put him out of his misery. He materializes at the Manor and overhears the Sam/Darklighter saga. Putting his unique spin on the situation gets the sisters mad enough at him to take him out. They prepare the strongest vanquishing potion ever made, and hunt Cole down at the penthouse. Piper and Paige throw their vials, but before Phoebe throws hers she realizes that Cole wants to die. She tells him she will not help him kill himself. Cole telekinetically pulls the potion free from her hands and onto himself. There is an explosion, but Cole remains standing. Sadly, he realizes he's unvanquishable.

"Didn't you even read the Whitelighter manual?"   **SAM WILDER TO PAIGE**

"I can't go good. I won't go evil. What the hell do you want from me?"

COLE TURNER

"Y Tu Mummy También"	(JANUARY 5, 2003) Written by Curtis Kheel Directed by Chris Long

Darryl's promotion is jeopardized when a killer escapes a locked room, leaving a mummified victim. Realizing this is not a normal crime scene, he calls the Charmed Ones for help, but before they can do anything the mummy disappears from the morgue. Piper and Paige check the Book of Shadows and find information on Jeric, an ancient Egyptian demon that keeps looking for a body to house his lover, Isis. Since two spirits can't occupy the same body, the invading spirit overloads it. Jeric hopes to find a witch with enough magic for Isis to use so that she can dispossess the host spirit and remain in the human shell. As the previous bodies that have housed Isis die under the strain, Jeric mummifies them so that they will hold Isis's spirit until he can find a replacement. Now that they know Jeric's intentions, Paige scries for his next victim, and the crystal points to Phoebe.

When Jeric takes Phoebe to Egypt and transfers Isis's spirit to her body, Piper and Paige turn to Cole for help. He decides to make a deal with Jeric. If the Egyptian demon will mummify Phoebe's body for Cole, he will provide Paige's body and the Power of Three to fix the Isis burnout problem. Cole gets to keep Phoebe, and Jeric will get to spend eternity with Isis in Paige's body. Jeric accepts and lowers the protections on his lair so that the witches can find their sister. When they arrive, he raises the barriers again, preventing Paige from orbing everyone to safety. In fact, her attempt knocks her unconscious. Cole then creates a vortex that sweeps Piper back to the Manor. As agreed upon, Jeric transfers Isis's spirit into Paige and mummifies Phoebe.

Piper is now raging mad and summons Cole to the Manor. He tells her that she has to choose between her sisters—only one can be saved. To make matters worse, only Isis knows the spell to demummify Phoebe, and she will only recite it if Piper casts a spell to eject Paige from her own body so that Isis can remain. Leo orbs Piper to the Egyptian tomb and she says she has decided to save Phoebe. When offered a spell written by Isis, Piper elects to use one of her own. It appears that Paige has been vanquished, but in fact, it was Isis. Not only that, Paige retains all of Isis's knowledge, including the spell to reverse the mummification process. Once everyone is safe and in their own bodies, Piper blows up Jeric. The Charmed Ones agree that Cole is not only dangerous, but completely crazy, and it's time they figure out what to do about him.

184

During all of the body swapping, Piper deals with body issues of her own. She finally accepts that she looks pregnant, and it's okay. And thanks to a little extra help, Darryl gets his promotion.

"It's taken me a long time to lose the freaky-deaky rap."   **DARRYL MORRIS**

"Just because it's creepy doesn't mean it's demonic."   **PIPER HALLIWELL**

"Couldn't you just let me not-die in peace?"   **COLE TURNER**

"The Importance of Being Phoebe"

(JANUARY 12, 2003)
Written by Krista Vernoff
Directed by Derek Johansen

The *Bay Mirror* is being sued by a letter writer who wants Phoebe fired. When Paige's fender bender inexplicably puts the other driver in the hospital, she gets arrested—just as P3 fails a third health inspection because of a rat infestation. The girls quickly deduce that the seemingly ordinary problems are the result of Cole's sabotage. What they don't know is that he's reorganizing the Underworld and wants the power of the Spiritual Nexus that lies beneath the Manor.

Phoebe confronts Cole about what he's doing, but he uses that as another chance to try to rekindle the love between them. She storms out, just missing a shape-shifting demon, Kaia, on her way in. Kaia's specialty is morphing into Phoebe, which causes problems on both the good and evil sides of the equation. Deciding to have it out with Cole as well, Piper and Paige (who's temporarily orbed out of her jail cell) arrive in time to see their former brother-in-law in a clinch with "Phoebe."

Shocked, they don't stick around long enough to see Kaia morph back into her own form. Likewise, a demon working for Cole spots the real Phoebe leaving Cole's office and thinks it's Kaia playing tricks again. When he realizes his mistake, he also realizes he's said too much, so he kidnaps the Charmed One and locks her in the penthouse. Cole kills his henchman for the mistake, but decides to use it to his advantage. He keeps Phoebe locked up and sends Kaia to the Manor to pose as his ex-wife. Truly befuddled trying to be Phoebe, Kaia convinces her "sisters" that she's a threat to the Power of Three. After seeing the kiss, Piper thinks that Cole has cast a spell on Phoebe, so she agrees when Kaia suggests removing her powers to prevent them from being misused. This, of course, leaves the real Phoebe defenseless.

To cement his plan, Cole kills the woman who was in the accident with Paige, and she is charged with vehicular manslaughter. Her bail is set at fifty thousand dollars. Kaia, as Phoebe, suggests they go to a bail bondsman to get the money. Piper realizes that the only way they can do it is to use the house as collateral, and hands the deed to the Manor over to Cole. When she returns home, Cole has already taken over the house and refuses to let her in. Kaia morphs back into her regular form, and Piper and Leo realize they've been completely duped. Piper agonizes to remember the spell she used to remove Phoebe's powers so that she can reverse it. She does, just as Phoebe is about to be finished off by Kaia. With her powers restored, Phoebe turns the tables and vanquishes the shape-shifting demon. She then pulls another switch, pretending to be Kaia pretending to be Phoebe so she can get access to Cole inside the Manor. She finds him in the basement, where he has taken the Shadow of the Nexus into himself. Phoebe recites a spell that causes a vortex to pull Cole, his demons, and the Shadow back into the earth. Everyone and everything is vanquished, except the invincible Cole, who rematerializes after the smoke clears.

Once Cole's plot is undone, all of the dilemmas the girls faced are solved, including the one in Phoebe's heart. She realizes that she felt nothing when she thought Cole was dead—she is truly over him.

"Forgive me for not anticipating the demonic foreclosure." **PIPER HALLIWELL**

"Are you going to be okay? Because I have to go get fired." **PHOEBE HALLIWELL**

"Centennial Charmed"

(JANUARY 19, 2003)
Written by Brad Kern
Directed by James L. Conway

Determined to find a way to vanquish Cole, Paige practices on Leo until she hits on a solution. Orbing inside her target, she will explode him from the inside out. It works, but as usual, the indestructible Cole's particles reassemble. He flings Paige out the window, across town and into the bay, giving her a magical cold. Every time she sneezes, she orbs.

Frustrated by his situation, Cole decides to join the Avatars so that he will have the power to change reality. He feels if he could just go back in time to when he and Phoebe were the happiest—before Paige arrived on the scene—everything would play out the way he wants it. As Cole recites the spell, the sisters are at P3 celebrating Darryl's promotion. Paige sneezes and orbs out as Cole finishes his incantation, and orbs back in to a completely different world. Neither her sisters nor Leo know who she is. Piper and Leo are divorced, but Phoebe lives at the Manor with Cole. Since Prue's death, Piper has dedicated herself to hunting down and killing Shax, and she'll take out any demon that gets in her way. Paige tells them that Shax was vanquished, but they don't believe her. Hoping she'll have better luck with Phoebe, Paige heads towards the Manor.

Cole is surprised by what he finds as well. He is still Belthazor, and married to Phoebe, who is his Dark Queen. However, there is no love between them, and each is cheating on the other—not exactly the happy state of affairs he had hoped for.

Paige shows up at the Manor, but Phoebe doesn't believe her either. And since this sister is evil, she has no qualms about hurting Paige. Instinctively, Paige calls for Leo, and he orbs her out. He explains that the reason no one knows her in this reality is that The Source killed her before she could meet her sisters and reconstitute the Power of Three. They meet up with Piper, who followed Paige's advice to get rid of a Lazarus Demon, and now accepts that there may be something to Paige's story. They head back to the Manor to try to set things right.

Since Cole is merely Belthazor in this reality, he can be vanquished. Piper's and Paige's presence at the Manor sets off a battle in which they are able to slice off a sample of Cole's flesh. They orb to P3 to make the vanquishing potion and return to the Manor to finish the job. Paige urges Phoebe to grab Piper's hand, which reconstitutes the Power of Three. Phoebe throws the vial, and Cole is vanquished. The spell is broken, reality reverts, and Cole is finally gone.

"I guess it just wasn't meant to be."

PHOEBE HALLIWELL, ON HER RELATIONSHIP WITH COLE

"I may be dead, but it still hurts."

LEO WYATT AFTER PAIGE BLOWS HIM UP FROM THE INSIDE, PRACTICING TO DO THE SAME TO COLE.

187

"House Call"	(FEBRUARY 2, 2003) Written by Henry Alonso Myers Directed by Jon Paré

Residual energy from all the demons the Halliwells have vanquished in the Manor coalesces into an evil, poltergeist-like manifestation. Since it's not as harmless as Leo thought, they summon a witch doctor to cleanse the house. He looks more like an accountant than a witch doctor, but he wields a skull artifact that vacuums the demonic spirits and accomplishes his task.

Concerned that the Charmed Ones will eventually become evil because they are magnets for evil and easily distracted by petty, personal concerns, the witch doctor has the Council of Witch Doctors devise a plan to eliminate them. The witch doctor whom the Charmed Ones summoned puts a hex on the Halliwells using items he stole from the Manor, which turns their character flaws into obsessions.

Another paper's advice columnist taunts Phoebe. Once the spell kicks in, she will do whatever it takes to kill the competition—including turning him into a turkey and fattening him up for slaughter. Paige is thrilled that her old friend Glen is back in town. She thinks that this time their relationship may become romantic, but her hopes are dashed when Glen introduces her to his fiancée. Obsessed with having Glen for herself, Paige morphs into the bride-to-be and orbs the real one to purgatory. Piper is fixated on cleaning. The spell drives her to throw out dishes because they'll never be clean enough, wash the roof of the house, and eventually just make the whole Manor disappear—with Phoebe inside.

Paige is the first to realize the emotional impact of what she's done. It breaks the witch doctors' voodoo, and she goes to Leo to help break the spell on her sisters. When Piper realizes that she's made Phoebe disappear along with the house, she too is released from the magic. She recites a spell to rebuild the house. Phoebe is back, but she's still chasing the turkey with a cleaver in her hand. Leo keeps her away from her prey while Paige and Piper pay a visit to the witch doctor. They convince the Council that the powers of the Charmed Ones are good and will always stay that way, and that despite outward appearances, they are always focused on their magical destiny. The head councilman reverses the hex on Phoebe.

The sisters correct all ill effects of their magic, and learn that even though life isn't always perfect, it is always Charmed.

"Slipcovers to keep the furniture clean. Although I'm thinking we should just stand from now on."
PIPER HALLIWELL

"Piper, listen to me, you can't just vanquish an entire house, especially our house! People are gonna notice."
PAIGE MATTHEWS

"Sand Francisco Dreamin'"

(FEBRUARY 9, 2003)
Written by Monica Breen & Alison Schapker
Directed by John Kretchmer

A Sandman enhances Phoebe's dreams so she'll visit a campgrounds to save him. When a Tracer demon attacks, she is overdosed with dream dust that makes the masked chainsaw killer in her nightmare come alive. To please an Upper-Level demon, the Tracer kills the Sandman and overdoses everyone with dust. Deprived of dreams, people will act on their anger and frustrations during their waking lives, thus spreading evil. The Charmed Ones are affected when their dreams manifest themselves. The leading man in Piper's favorite soap romances her. Paige's clown doll comes to life, insisting there will be no guests at the baby shower she's throwing for Piper.

Phoebe runs from the murdering chainsaw guy, and suddenly, Leo's the one who's pregnant!

The manifestations will dissipate if they confront the meaning of the images. While everyone tries to figure out their inner demons, the all-too-real dream demons are contained in crystal traps. The Charmed Ones go under a sleep spell, and Leo uses the Sandman's remains to induce dreams. People walk away from the newborn in Paige's dream because it's not Piper's baby, it's Paige—and she is hurt. She was a secret no one could celebrate. Piper's leading man turns into Leo, the symbol of romance she doesn't want to lose. And Phoebe learns she's been running from herself, afraid to move on after Cole. Leo just wanted to be closer to the baby. After he feels it kick, it finds its rightful place in its mother's womb. Once everyone's issues are resolved, their nightmares disappear, and the Tracer demon hoping to take the Charmed powers arrives. No longer distracted by dreams, Piper gets to work and blows him up.

"The guy in my dream should be a piece of cake, even with power tools."

PHOEBE HALLIWELL

"The Day the Magic Died"

(FEBRUARY 16, 2003)
Written by Daniel Cerone
Directed by Stuart Gillard

Stricken with toxemia, Piper is sent to bed for rest with no stress. Consequently nobody mentions that there's a dead demon in the closet, a unicorn in the basement, and magic isn't working. When Victor shows up with a new bride, Doris, Piper's sisters leave her in the care of their stepmother. They have to cope with the demon Cronyn, who says that good and evil must work together to save magic. Armed with chem-lab weapons, Paige and Phoebe go to the "peace summit" at a pizzeria, where evil waits in ambush. The witches fight their way free and learn that the mystical signs Paige noticed were prophesied centuries ago regarding a twice-blessed birth. They also find out that Cronyn is after Piper's baby.

When Piper realizes the baby is coming, Leo leaves to find her sisters. Doris stabs Victor, and greets Cronyn just as Piper goes into serious labor. In league with the demon, Doris plans to raise the child as a force for evil. Piper tries to run, but she's stopped on the stairs. When Cronyn threatens her with a knife, Victor overcomes his pain to fling the demon clear. A spell, combined with the pure magic of shavings from a unicorn horn, vanquishes Cronyn, Doris, and the deceased messenger in the closet. Victor is healed, the baby is born, and surprise! It's a boy!

189

"This is like the entire universe is practically screaming at us to get our attention."

PAIGE MATTHEWS

"I may be stuck in bed, but I'm not stuck on stupid."

PIPER HALLIWELL

"Baby's First Demon"

(MARCH 30, 2003)
Written by Krista Vernoff
Directed by John T. Kretchmer

Jason Dean, a young dot.com millionaire, takes over *The Bay Mirror* and complicates Phoebe's life. He wants to expand her profile at the paper, but she doesn't want to leave the baby. Besides, the family needs her Charmed presence at home. A Hawker demon tried to kidnap the baby to sell. The demon is dead, but who wanted the baby—and why? And what exactly is that force field the baby can raise to protect himself? Confident that the baby is safe, Paige defies Leo and Piper's warnings and poses as a customer to infiltrate the Demonic Market. Before she can learn anything, she's disabled by Parasite demons that absorb her powers. Rather than kill her, they'll use Paige as bait to draw Piper and Phoebe to the market, leaving the baby unprotected.

Injured in the original kidnapping attempt, Piper hesitated to go demon hunting. However, after she kills a Parasite making another attempt to take the baby, she overcomes her anxiety to help

Phoebe save Paige and end the threat. They blast their way through the Market and arrive just as a Crone kills the second Parasite. The Crone explains that since the Underworld can't fight the baby's power, a law will be passed that forbids evil beings from harming the child.

After agonizing over what to name their son, Piper comes up with the perfect solution: Wyatt Matthew Halliwell—Wyatt for his daddy, Matthew in honor of Aunt Paige, and of course Halliwell, because "demons fear it and good magic respects it."

"You have a crush—on the boss?"   **LEO WYATT**

"The few neighbors who didn't already think we were crazy have changed their minds, but the house is now surrounded with apples and sage."   **PAIGE MATTHEWS**

"You have proven that the costs of this war will far outweigh the benefits."
                                                                                          THE CRONE

"Lucky Charmed"	(APRIL 6, 2003) Written by Curtis Kheel Directed by Roxann Dawson

Paige thinks magic should reimburse expenses incurred on Charmed duty and casts a spell to find luck. She finds Leprechauns, whose luck is being stolen by Saleel, a reptile demon. Since Saleel is elusive but easy to vanquish, Shamus, one of the Leprechauns, gives the Charmed Ones luck to find him. The sisters find Saleel, but he kills Shamus and steals their good luck. Their bad luck gets worse when a demon sent by Saleel takes Piper. Phoebe and Paige travel the rainbow and convince the Leprechauns they need their combined good luck to fight back. Hit with multiple doses of bad luck, Saleel is vanquished by a meteor and Piper is saved.

Phoebe may get lucky in other ways. Even though every word he speaks gets under her skin, Jason is still her boss, so Phoebe honors his request and researches online dating for an article. She claims she doesn't buy into the whole thing, but she seems to have fun corresponding with someone named Cyrano73. When Shamus suggests that taking a risk could turn her luck around, Phoebe accepts a date with Cyrano73 only to find that it's Jason. Annoyed, but surprisingly somewhat taken with his charm, she agrees to a drink. Maybe the Leprechaun was right after all.

"You can get books on the Internet, news, purses even, but not dates."
                                                                             PHOEBE HALLIWELL

"It ain't the cereal, but it's the best I can do."
                                     PAIGE MATTHEWS ON HER LUCKY CHARMS

"Cat House"	(APRIL 13, 2003) Written by Brad Kern Directed by James L. Conway

An Innocent named Katrina fights off a warlock, while Piper and Leo just fight. Phoebe recounts family history to Paige but is interrupted when Leo walks away from the latest fight, and Piper blows up the wall. The sisters decide it's time for a little marriage counseling.

Piper and Leo meet with Dr. Berenson, but it's hard to talk about their problems without revealing their magic. Losing patience, Piper freezes Dr. Berenson and casts a spell allowing her to relive the memories she shares with Leo. As she does this, Katrina finds her way to the Manor. She interrupts Paige's visit with Phoebe at work when she calls the Charmed Ones for help. Although Phoebe doesn't know her, Katrina appears to know an awful lot about the Halliwell homestead, and clearly seems like an Innocent. Paige orbs them home just in time to save Katrina from the warlock again. Before they can find out who he is and why he was sent, a blast of light engulfs them, and when it's gone, Paige, Phoebe, and the warlock are gone with it. They reappear on the front porch, and the warlock takes advantage of the witches' disorientation to blink out. Phoebe surveys her surroundings and quickly deduces that they are somehow in the past, witnessing prior events that have occurred in the Charmed Ones' lives. Figuring this to be the work of the warlock, they try to get to the Book of Shadows without disturbing history. Their efforts keep getting thwarted as the past scenes keep changing. The different venues are nerve-racking and inhibit their ability to vanquish the warlock, but Paige says she's happy she finally gets to share some of her sisters' memories.

This sparks Phoebe to realize that the memories aren't the warlock's, they're Piper and Leo's. Her revelation is interrupted when their long-lost cat, Kit, flies into the attic, followed by the warlock. He kills the cat, who morphs into Katrina. Destroying the Halliwell familiar in the past changes ensuing events, so the sisters need to find a way to change them back. Phoebe calls to Piper from within the memory to replay the past few minutes. Piper hears her and does. This time, Phoebe and Paige are ready for the warlock. They vanquish him and save Kit's and their futures. Piper undoes her memory spell and releases her sisters from their journey through her mind. Once safe, Katrina explains that she moved on from being the Charmed Ones' familiar once Paige was united with her sisters and she wasn't needed any longer. She was made human to guide other familiars. Leo explains that this transformation is a rare and special gift—much like love, family, and friendship. Apparently that marriage counseling is working!

"You know, come to think of it, she does look awfully familiar to me."
PAIGE MATTHEWS IN REFERENCE TO KIT, AKA KATRINA

"Nymphs Just Wanna Have Fun"

(APRIL 20, 2003)
Written by Andrea Stevens & Doug E. Jones
Directed by Mel Damski

Piper objects to the infringement on her territory when new superwitch Paige reorganizes their herbs and color-codes the Book of Shadows. They are diverted from their issues by a report about the Godiva Girls, three scantily clad women who have been seen frolicking all over the city. What mortals don't know, but the Charmed Ones discover, is that the women are really nymphs, who have come to the city looking for a new satyr. The demon brothers Tull and Xavier killed the nymphs' old satyr, hoping the sprites would show them the location of their Eternal Spring. The Spring, which is only able to be found by nymphs, will make the demons immortal and invincible. When the nymphs won't cooperate, Xavier kills one of them. The remaining two, Miranda and Daisy, need to replace their sister because there must be three nymphs to dance to hear the satyr's call. Sensing Paige's irritability with Piper and her repressed free spirit, they turn the youngest witch into a wood sprite, thereby completing their number, but leaving the other Power of Three one short.

Piper and Phoebe use one of Paige's spells (previously rejected by Piper) to track down their sister. Packing a vanquishing potion, they kill Xavier, but Tull, who has mastered the satyr's song, is urging the nymphs toward the Spring. Paige's conflicted witch/nymph nature knows that something isn't right, but by the time Tull reveals his true, demon self he's already drunk from the Spring. Paige tries to stop him from doing any further damage, but he sends her flying with his new and improved powers. Daisy and Miranda help the witches find their mutual sister. Using her trademark creative thinking, Paige determines that demons aren't the only immortal things. There are plenty of them in nature as well, so she chants a spell turning Tull into a tree, where he can live forever but remain harmless. The nymphs realize that they don't need a satyr after all, and finally appreciating Paige's abilities, Piper agrees to share head witch duties with her youngest sister.

Phoebe finds herself getting closer to nature—and to Jason as well. After he throws a party to celebrate Phoebe's Columnist of the Year award, she spends the night with him. Although they're both a little uncomfortable about it at first, they decide they want to make the relationship work. This is especially helpful when Jason gets pictures of Nymph Paige and agrees to not publish them out of respect to Phoebe.

PHOEBE: *"Morning. Never mind. Don't ask."*
PIPER: *"Hey! Somebody's doing the walk of shame!"*

"He's going to try to fry us, and we're gonna have to dive out of the way, get all dirty, and we're just going to end up vanquishing him anyway."
PIPER HALLIWELL EXPLAINING WHY THEY SHOULD CUT TO THE CHASE AND JUST VANQUISH XAVIER

"Maybe you should fire you." **PHOEBE HALLIWELL TO JASON DEAN**

"Sense and Sense Ability"

(APRIL 27, 2003)
Teleplay by Daniel Cerone & Krista Vernoff
Story by Brian Krause & Ed Bokinskie
Directed by Joel J. Feigenbaum &
Stewart Schill

A monkey touches the Charmed Ones at a street fair, and each one loses a physical sense at a crucial moment. Phoebe goes deaf during a meeting about syndicating her column. Paige tries to sing for a new romantic interest, Nate Parks, and loses her voice. Piper goes blind while driving and crashes into a pole. They find the Monkey Totem reference to see, hear, and speak no evil in the Book of Shadows, but they do not know the Crone sent the creature to incapacitate them. Driven by the desire to know Wyatt's future and the powers he will wield, the Crone needs to touch the baby. Once she sees what is to come, she can better prepare the leaders of the evil factions to fight.

Using Paige's stolen voice, the Crone sings to Wyatt, which makes him trust her and lower his protective shield. Leo runs in and yells to his son. The shield goes up again, and the angry Crone shimmers out with Leo in tow. Phoebe and Paige rush to the kitchen to make the Crone a vanquishing potion they found in the Book of Shadows. Blind Piper stays with baby Wyatt, and is tricked when the Crone comes back. Using Paige's voice again, she tells Piper that it's safe to leave the baby. When Piper gets to the kitchen she realizes that something is wrong. By the time the sisters get back to Wyatt's room, the Crone is holding the baby, having convinced him that she is Aunt Paige. She keeps up the charade, telling him that they are being attacked, which causes Wyatt to raise his protective shield around himself and the Crone. She places her hands on his head and gets the vision she was hoping for, but in the meantime, the Charmed Ones have blended their powers and remaining senses to invoke the Power of Three. They cry out to Wyatt, who responds to his true family, drops the force field, and orbs to Paige. Phoebe throws the potion and vanquishes the Crone, and the girls' senses return. Little Wyatt is able to sense his father, and he orbs Piper to the Crone's lair, where she frees her husband and reunites his family.

"So all that monkey business about, you know, speak no evil, hear no evil, see no evil, is real?"　　**PIPER HALLIWELL**

"Maybe someday I can have a date that doesn't end with, 'Sorry, Nate, you can't stay, 'cause I have to clean some demon guts off the ceiling.'"　　**PAIGE MATTHEWS**

"Necromancing the Stone"

(MAY 4, 2003)
Written by Henry Alonso Myers &
　Alison Schapker & Monica Breen
Directed by Jon Paré

No one is prepared for the difficulties Grams presents when she's summoned to preside over Wyatt's Wiccaning. He's the first boy born into the family in three centuries, and she feels his birth must be a mistake that will have dreadful consequences. She refuses to bestow the Matriarchs' Blessing on the baby. In the middle of an ensuing family argument, Grams is taken by the Necromancer Armond, a demon ghost who plans to resurrect himself by consuming the Charmed matriarchs' spirits. Grams was the Necromancer's lover when she banished him back to the spirit realm sixty years before.

Grams is not the only Halliwell woman with man problems. Paige casts the Truth Spell to see how Nate would react to dating a witch and learns he's married with two kids. Jason asks Phoebe to join him in Hong Kong for six months, which she considers but rejects. Grams realizes her bitterness toward men has harmed the family. Being a ghost, she is able to vanquish the spirit, Armond, and finally welcome Wyatt as a blessed member of the Warren line.

"They'd be better off with a dog. More loyal and they die sooner."　　**PENELOPE "GRAMS" HALLIWELL ON WHY PETS ARE BETTER THAN MEN**

"I don't want to hear about a dead demon doing the dirty!"　　**PIPER HALLIWELL**

"Don't make the same mistake I did. Don't ever give up on love."　　**PENELOPE "GRAMS" HALLIWELL**

"Oh, My Goddess, Part One"

(MAY 11, 2003)
Written by Krista Vernoff & Curtis Kheel
Directed by Jonathan West

Phoebe isn't adjusting well to Jason's absence, and a heat wave makes the prolonged separation harder to take. Paige thinks the weather may be connected to her fire-and-brimstone dreams, which have left her tired and cranky. Piper's happiness is marred when a Whitelighter goes missing and Leo leaves to investigate the disappearance. Paige figures out that everything is a result of the Titans, ancient Greek gods, having escaped their entombment. Their main goal is to steal Whitelighter orbing power to be able to go Up There and change the ruling structure. Since the Elders were somewhat responsible for banishing the Titans, they will have to pay. Paige orbs to attract the Titans and Phoebe is ready to attack, but her potions have no effect. Chris, a young Whitelighter, orbs in to help, but the Titan called Meta turns Paige to stone. Many magical beings gather at the Manor for protection. The elf nanny appoints herself to watch Wyatt, while a dwarf, leprechaun, and fairy hack away at the stone and finally free Paige.

Chris tells the witches that he came from the future to stop the Titans from ruling the world. The Elders have the power to stop this, but they won't make the mistake they made three millennia ago when they empowered mortals to defeat the Titans. The mighty mortals succeeded, then made humanity worship them, making them no better than those they were sent to stop. When Piper realizes the Titans want revenge on the Elders, Leo gets Up There too late to warn them. The magical beings disperse to guard the surviving Elders, but Leo doesn't know if Chris is really helping them or is manipulating events for his own purposes. Chris says the Elders had to die so that they wouldn't stand in the way of Leo doing what they couldn't do—empowering mortals to vanquish the Titans forever and save the future. Having no choice, Leo makes a painful decision: He unleashes the power and turns the Charmed Ones into goddesses.

"Y'gonna scry for Mother Nature and have a Wiccan word with her?"

PIPER HALLIWELL

"An earthquake! Did I call that or what?!"

PAIGE MATTHEWS

"At the end of the day, even we can't change what's meant to be."

CECIL, AN ELDER

"Look who's not stoned."

PHOEBE HALLIWELL

"Oh, My Goddess, Part Two"

(MAY 11, 2003)
Written by Daniel Cerone
Directed by Joel J. Feigenbaum

Piper, Goddess of the Elements, stops Phoebe, Goddess of Love, and Paige, Goddess of War, from indulging their new powers and desires to flirt and build armies. The remaining Elders hide in a sanctuary, but the Charmed Ones don't survive any of Paige's battle simulations against the Titans. They need Leo to bolster their confidence. Finally convinced, Chris orbs Up There as cover so Leo can return undetected.

Leo believes, unlike the ancient Greeks, that the Charmed Ones can handle the powers. They are the greatest force of good he knows. Phoebe survived the darkest love, and Paige has never let power consume her. Piper is everything good and beautiful in the world. When Piper realizes she's losing Leo to the Elders, her power manifests in wrath. She opens a rift in the earth and sends the Titans, Cronus and Demetrius, to their fiery doom. Then she unleashes a storm that reflects her pain and fury. Guided by love for her sisters and Wyatt, Piper accepts the inevitable. Leo can't deny his new destiny, and he erases her pain. Piper's uncharacteristic nonchalance about the loss alarms Phoebe. Leo appoints Chris Perry as the Charmed Ones' new Whitelighter, a moment before Chris appears to secretly flick him out of existence.

> *"If I had a choice in any of this, I'd choose you, Piper. I always have."*
> **LEO WYATT**

PAIGE: *"'Reason and judgment are the qualities of a leader.' Tacitus, one hundred A.D."*
PHOEBE: *"'Love will keep us together.' Captain and Tennille, nineteen seventies."*

> *"You expect us to beat the Titans dressed like this?"*
> **PIPER HALLIWELL ON THE IMPROMPTU TOGA PARTY**

The Charmed Episode Puns

Here are the episode titles from the **FIFTH SEASON,** along with their most likely origins.

A WITCH'S TAIL: An intentional misspelling to combine a story about a witch with the fact that the witch in question has grown a mermaid's tail.

HAPPILY EVER AFTER: Traditional ending to fairy tales to describe the way the characters lived after the story was over.

SIREN SONG: An enticing plea. The phrase comes from the Greek epic *The Odyssey,* in which the sweet singing of the Sirens lured sailors to their deaths.

WITCHES IN TIGHTS: *Robin Hood: Men in Tights* is a Mel Brooks film released in 1993.

THE EYES HAVE IT: "The ayes have it" is a phrase noting that the votes in favor of a given proposition are in the majority.

SYMPATHY FOR THE DEMON: "Sympathy for the Devil" is a song released by the Rolling Stones in 1968.

A WITCH IN TIME: "A stitch in time saves nine" is a proverb espousing the power of preventative action.

SAM I AM: A character from Dr. Seuss's classic story *Green Eggs and Ham.*

Y TU MUMMY TAMBIÉN: *Y Tu Mama También* is a film released in 2001.

THE IMPORTANCE OF BEING PHOEBE: *The Importance of Being Earnest* is a comic farce written by Oscar Wilde, first performed in 1895 and made into a feature film in 2002.

CENTENNIAL CHARMED: The one hundredth episode of *Charmed.*

HOUSE CALL: When a doctor visits a patient at home.

SAND FRANCISCO DREAMIN': "California Dreamin'" is a song released by The Mamas and the Papas in 1966.

THE DAY THE MAGIC DIED: "The day the music died" is a line from Don McLean's song "American Pie," and refers to February 3, 1959, the day Buddy Holly, Ritchie Valens, and J. P. Richardson (the Big Bopper) died in a plane crash.

BABY'S FIRST DEMON: Oftentimes parents take special note of a baby's "firsts" (as in first smile, first step, or in this case, "first encounter with a force from the Underworld").

LUCKY CHARMED: "Lucky charms" are trinkets thought to possess the power of luck. (It's also a cereal with marshmallows in various colors and shapes.)

CAT HOUSE: Another name for a brothel.

NYMPHS JUST WANNA HAVE FUN: "Girls Just Wanna Have Fun" is Cyndi Lauper's signature song.

SENSE AND SENSE ABILITY: *Sense and Sensibility* is a 1995 film based on the Jane Austen novel of the same name.

NECROMANCING THE STONE: *Romancing the Stone* is a film from 1984 starring Michael Douglas and Kathleen Turner.

OH, MY GODDESS: The female empowered version of the exclamation "Oh, my God!"

GLOSSARY OF CHARMED TERMS

ALTAR: raised structure for ceremonies; holds flora offerings, candles, and incense used in rituals

AMULET: a small object, usually metal or stone, inscribed with magical symbols and endowed with the power to protect or create a beneficial effect, such as good luck

APPLE: when it has a pentacle at its heart, with the addition of a laurel leaf, blocks path of evil

ATHAME: ceremonial knife; often used by evil entities to kill magical beings

AURA: a psychic energy field that surrounds all living things; only visible to some

BANISH: to remove evil effects of magic from a being, thing; to send into exile

BINDING: spell or ritual to prevent something from occurring

BLESSED BE: a phrase of greeting or parting; used to seal a ritual

BLINK: warlock's ability to move in "the blink of an eye"

BROOM: used to sweep evil from the path; use east to west as the sun travels with knowledge and reverence to connect with the power. (Witches riding on broomsticks is a myth that was created by Phoebe when she empowered a broom, embracing the cliché, and rode through the sky in 1670 to scare witch hunters.)

CIRCLE: group of Wiccans; those not in a coven

CONICAL HAT: a spiritual point that facilitates channeling magic, keeps the wearer focused and centered

CONSECRATION: act of cleansing

COVEN: a group of witches or warlocks, usually thirteen, who band together to use magic and perform rituals

CRAFT: witchcraft; magic or magick

CROSS: predates Christian times, when it was worn as an amulet to protect from evil, a jinx, and bad luck

CUPID'S START: aromatic herb

DEMON: an evil being with a specific or general agenda; powers, appearances, and substances of endless varieties

EMPATH: a highly sensitive being that's returned after death as an immortal empath to help and heal

ENERGY: the power within all beings and things natural

EQUINOX: when the sun is positioned to produce equal hours of darkness and light in a day; occurs twice a year

FAMILIAR: witch's attendant spirit in animal form

GHOST: spirit of a dead person; resisting transition because of unfinished business that may be good or evil

GLAMOUR: 1. type of spell; 2. the ability to change one's appearance

GOLEM: an artificially created man

GRIMOIRE: the evil equivalent of the Book of Shadows; a book that contains spells and rituals, learning

INCANTATION: words or rhymed phrases spoken to create a magical result; also called chants, spoken charms, and runes

LAUREL LEAF: if placed over heart of apple cut in half, will block evil's path.

LAVENDER: a protection herb

LIMBO: mystical place between life and death that souls pass through on the way to reincarnation, the nature of Limbo reflects the soul of the being occupying it; temporary state of souls after death

MAGIC: manipulation of natural energies for change or effect

MASK: worn on Samhain or Halloween so one may walk among demons and spirits without being recognized

PENTAGRAM: a symbol of good energy until evil stole it; traditionally is a five-point star symbol that represents the four primal elements and spirit; used in spells and rituals

POIGNARD: a dagger or knife

POPPET: doll; representative of a specific person in rituals

PRIMAL ELEMENTS: five elements of Earth, Fire, Water, Wood, and Metal; traditionally there are four elements—Air, Earth, Fire, and Water, with Spirit as the fifth

PUMPKIN: carved and lighted, will chase away evil spirits; traditionally used to light the way back to the other world so spirits can return on All Hallows' Eve.

RAGGED ROBIN: magical herb

ROSEMARY: protection herb

RUNE: 1. mystical symbolic writing, usually derived from the Greek; 2. something inscribed with such symbols

SABBAT: seasonal Wiccan festivals

SAINT-JOHN'S-WORT: medicinal herb

SAMHAIN: (Pronounced SOW-en); also called Halloween or All Hallows' Eve, the night when the veil between worlds is thinnest, and passage between is possible; demons who are capable may return for revenge; on this night magical power is strongest for all who tap into it

SCRYING: locating a witch or a witch's power with a crystal and a map; cannot scry for warlocks, but in "Hell Hath No Fury" random evil or demons can be located; traditionally is the interpreting of the future, past, or present in a crystal ball, candle flame, pool of water, or gazing mirror

SHIMMER: a demon's mode of moving between locations, including between the mortal realm and Underworld

SOUL: see spirit

SPELL: incantation or ritual performed to create a desired result for good or evil

SPIRIT: 1. the knowledge, will, and character of an individual's immortal essence, existing within or separate from the physical body; 2. soul

TALISMAN: any object thought to have magical power; usually but not always used to repel evil.

TARO ROOT: magical herb

TAROT: an ancient form of fortune telling using a deck of twenty-two pictorial cards of allegorical figures; the true depth of tarot cannot be defined in a few words

TOTEM: a doll made of husks or other natural fibers; signifies the power and wisdom of women

TRIDENT: weapon of the Greek gods, a three-pronged spear.

TRIQUETRA: the symbol for the Power of Three as it appears on the Book of Shadows, Wyatt's baby blanket, and the cat's collar; from *triquetrous* meaning "three-pointed"

WARLOCK: evil being with one purpose: to kill good witches and steal their powers; traditional—old English, meaning untrustworthy, oath-breaker

WHEEL OF BEING, CELTIC: a design of four intertwining circles signifying the four elements in balance and connected

WICCA: wise ones with a reverence for nature with some ability to manipulate the elements for effect; Wiccans—those who adhere to the precepts of Wicca

WITCH: practitioner of magic with a respect for Wicca

BEHIND THE SCENES

INTRODUCTION

The cast and crew of *Charmed* produce twenty-two episodes a season. That's twenty-two episodes consisting of eight-day weeks and twelve-hour days or more. By the time the production reaches the final episodes of a season, everyone is exhausted and looking forward to their hiatus—summer vacation. It's not the best time to come around trying to pump them for information for a book on their show. But in the midst of filming the two-part season five finale "Oh, My Goddess," the cast and crew still managed to welcome the Book of Three into their family—in between creating the heavens and destroying parts of Halliwell Manor one more time.

The staff is split between the writers' offices at Spelling Entertainment, in Los Angeles, and the production stages in the San Fernando Valley. We were able to spend two days visiting the soundstages and speaking with the cast and crew, and from the start, it was clear that this was a production team with history.

The combined talent involved in *Charmed* boasts an extensive résumé. Many have been "in the business" for decades, and are second- or even third-generation creative artists. We not only talked about Spelling's previous hits, *Beverly Hills, 90210*, *The Love Boat*, and *Charlie's Angels*, but we also heard about work on movies like *Camelot* and *Jaws*, TV series such as *I-Spy* and *Murder, She Wrote*, and family connections to personalities like George Burns and Buster Keaton. Needless to say, everyone is rather proud to know that all that history is now going into creating *Charmed*.

A CONVERSATION WITH
Aaron Spelling
and E. Duke Vincent,
Executive Producers

Long before he was "Tori's father," Aaron Spelling had an extensive Hollywood career. As a writer, producer, and actor, his name has been attached to some of the most notable hits in television history. From *The Mod Squad* to *Dynasty* and from *Melrose Place* to *7th Heaven*, Aaron Spelling has had a hand in a diverse list of television shows that have proven to stand the test of time. But he has not done this alone.

203

E. Duke Vincent has been collaborating with Mr. Spelling for over twenty years. Their names are constantly linked in the credits of their series as the executive producers and the men behind the shows. Along with Spelling Entertainment President, Jonathan Levin, they head a team of production personnel unrivaled in Hollywood.

Mr. Spelling and Mr. Vincent, however, are very different from other Hollywood executives. They aren't the buttoned-up, stiff-collared businessmen more comfortable in boardrooms than on the set. Talking with the two of them is like talking with old buddies. They are friendly and cordial, and like to wisecrack a bit.

BO3: How did the idea for *Charmed* first come across your desks?

AARON SPELLING: How did we start *Charmed*? . . . Okay. . . That's five years ago. . . .

E. DUKE VINCENT: It is five years ago. . . . The initial idea came from a gal by the name of Connie Burge. She came to us with the idea of doing a story about three sisters who happen to be witches—not about three witches who happen to be sisters. That was a very, very important distinction for all of us because we never believed that a show that did not have that element of companionship and love between the three girls would work. We did the pilot. The network loved the show, and they picked it up and we went roaring into the first year. Brad Kern was hired as our showrunner at that time. He is still with the show and still doing a brilliant job.

AS: Connie is a whiz at creating. She did *Savannah* for us too. And *Savannah* was so different from this that we were stunned when she sent us this. But we love her for it.

BO3: What was it about the fantasy element that attracted you to the project?

EDV: Well, obviously if you're dealing with witches and warlocks and the netherworld, you're automatically, by definition, into a fantasy world. While we make that sort of a pivotal part of the show in every episode, it doesn't drive the episodes. The relationship between the three girls and what they learn about each other from the experiences of a particular episode is what drives the show.

AS: What we had to be careful of—and we don't say this to a lot of people—is we didn't want to say, "Oh look, they're doing *Charlie's Angels* again with three beautiful girls." Nothing is further away. The thing that really excites me about it is the special effects. And Duke here is in charge of that. He does a brilliant job and now he's going to ask for another raise. The special effects are just marvelous . . . just marvelous. If you can combine serious special effects with humor and the sensuality of these girls, I think we've got a hit.

BO3: Would you say this is the most special effects intensive show you've done?

EDV: Not only by far, but by a factor of fifty.

AS: And I've got the debt to prove it.

EDV: We're doing things now that we wouldn't even consider—that weren't feasible ten years ago. We're doing more special effects and we're doing them better because of the technology that's available to us. It's still a very, very expensive way to go, but it is a very integral part of the show.

AS: I love to sit with my wife at home to watch the show. I've already seen it at the office, but when the show's on the air I sit with my wife at home and she goes crazy with the special effects. After all these years with Duke and me, she's still asking, "How did they do that? How did they do that?"

EDV: Interestingly enough we get the same questions from people in the business with shows with special effects.

BO3: How have you found the fan response?

EDV: Oh, it's been superb. We're all over the Internet. It's amazing how close the audience stays to the show. I never realized that audiences pick up on what I call such fragmentary things. I'll give you an example: This year we have a baby on the show. Well, obviously you can't use *one* baby. It's an infant, so you can only shoot him for two hours, so you look for a set of twins or a set of triplets. Even though they are so-called identical, they're really not. We had four inquiries asking "How come you used two different babies in one shot?" I said, "My God, *I* didn't notice that." So they are paying attention and they do respond to us and we do get a lot of mail.

BO3: It's clear that you foster a great work atmosphere on the set.

AS: It starts with Duke. You have to know how you want the cast to feel, and I think, God bless us, with all the shows we've had together—and we've only been together for twenty-two years—Duke never changes. When he goes on the set, he's filled with vitality and treats it like the first hit we've ever had in our lives. And they love him for that. They love him for that. That's why I can't go on the set, because they throw rocks at me.

EDV: Oh, that's not true. Aaron started this way back and taught me how to do it. There always has to be a quarterback on the set—somebody who the rest of the people in the cast and crew look to for advice and for leadership and for inspiration. Of course, in that case we have Alyssa Milano. On every single show, you're always going to find somebody. On *7th Heaven*, obviously it's Stephen Collins. On *90210* it was Jason Priestley. So, what you feel when you go on a set is a tremendous sense of togetherness and camaraderie. It starts on the set with Alyssa and Holly and Rose. They love to be there. Everybody knows they love to be there and they know that they're having fun, so consequently the crew is very responsive to every one of their whims and wishes. So we do the show on time, get those people out of there without horrendous hours, and we do a good show.

AS: And he's gonna get one hell of a phone call when I tell Tori that he went with Jason Priestley.

BO3: We'll balance it out when we write it up.
EDV: That would be good.

BO3: Maybe she was second-string quarterback?
AS: She loves Duke. She wouldn't scream.
EDV: That's my niece.

BO3: With *Charmed* you seem to present a sensual show, but maintain a balance of a family-friendly atmosphere.
AS: And we never use vulgarity.
EDV: No. That's intentional. Obviously the opportunity to do so is there, but we steer away from it for the obvious reasons. It's hard to put dirty words in Alyssa Milano's mouth and keep her looking beautiful.

BO3: What's the show's relationship with The WB like?
AS: We have been really lucky by striking something—I guess it's gold. Years ago it was ABC for Duke and me, and then after that it became FOX with *90210* and *Melrose Place,* and now we have *7th Heaven* and *Charmed* with The WB.

BO3: What are some of your highlights from the show?
EDV: The pickups! No, this year I think we had one of them. We opened the season this year with the episode that we did about the mermaids. I gotta tell you the letters and the Internet exploded. I thought it was a good episode, but I didn't realize that the audience would react that big.
AS: And, just as an observer, I've got to tell you, the audience acted like they'd never seen mermaids before.
EDV: The funny story is the network was so impressed, they called up Aaron, and Aaron called me, and he said, "You're never going to believe the call I just got. They want us to do a series about mermaids!"

BO3: What do you hope for the future?
EDV: Aaron and I always hope a show goes ten years. But you have to have a lot of things happen for a show to do that. To go four, and five, and then into a sixth year is miraculous. That you can keep an audience that long. *7th Heaven* is a minor miracle; *90210 was* a miracle.
AS: Three hundred episodes.
EDV: We kind of got used to it, from the days of *Dynasty* and *The Love Boat.*
AS: I think it will continue. The network is very taken with the ratings it's been getting. They've moved the time slot a couple times now and to be in that Sunday night time slot is difficult, but it continues to do very well.

Back when Brad Kern was in college, his life path had a very different outlook. He was majoring in economics at Cal State, Northridge, and, as he says, pretty much hated where that was taking him. Even though he had no experience with cinematography he, quite by chance, ended up taking a super-eight filmmaking class. Suddenly, as he says, "I had found God." As opposed to the kind of boring drone professors he had in economics and marketing, he had found these passionate people who were teaching with vim and vigor. His entire future changed based on that one class.

Soon after changing majors, Brad directed a student film that won twenty-two international film festivals. Even with that success, he knew that no one was just going to hand him a directing assignment, so he realized that he had better learn how to write. Brad started taking extension classes at UCLA, USC, and AFI.

His first break came when he wrote a *Hill Street Blues* spec script that got him noticed at MTM Enterprises, Inc. and secured him his job on *Remington Steele.* He was with the series for three years, going from staff writer to supervising producer. He credits the series' showrunner and creator, Michael Gleason, as a true mentor.

Years later Brad is now the showrunner of *Charmed* and is responsible for setting the tone of the entire series. That role encompasses more than just writing the episodes, however. By the time he had a moment to sit down to talk to the *Book of Three,* production had already wrapped on the fifth season. There was nothing more to write, but his work was far from over. Brad had to take a break from editing just to speak with us over the phone. He didn't even have the luxury of going back to his office at Spelling Enterprises for the call, but still managed to spend a half hour of his very precious time with us.

Let's start at the beginning. How did you get involved in the series?

BK: Connie Burge created the show and Spelling had sold it as a presentation and it got picked up to series based on the presentation. They were looking for a showrunner to come in and help turn the presentation into a pilot and turn the pilot into a series. I was the executive producer and showrunner on *New York Undercover* and that show had just been canceled. So I just interviewed for *Charmed.*

What was it about the idea that caught your attention?

BK: I was looking to get away from the procedural cop show and was attracted to the fantasy elements and the supernatural canvas as well as the sister relationship. Aaron and The WB were looking for somebody who was interested in all those things. So I helped turn the presentation into a full hour episode and then helped develop the series from that.

Were you into fantasy growing up?

BK: The best part of my growing up was fantasy. Reality sucked. I had an active imagination growing up, and *Charmed* was the first vehicle that I had worked on professionally that allowed me to really channel that imagination into my work. I did *Lois & Clark: The New Adventures of Superman* for a year, but *Charmed* was really where I felt like a kid again.

When writing the show, how do you balance between the fantasy and reality?

BK: The short answer is it starts with the sisters. On every episode we decide what it is we want to learn about one or more of the sisters and what emotional arc we want to put them through. So that starts with authenticity right there. There's a reality to that, and we try very hard to make it real and make their arc and their growth real. The reason I'm starting with the sisters, to answer your question, is because the fantasy has to resonate through the emotional arc that we're working on for each individual episode. So there's a reality, if you will, an authenticity to the fantasy aspect if it is resonating and magnifying the authenticity of what one or more of the sisters is going through.

We can't start with the reality of fantasy because that's an oxymoron. We start with the reality of the girls and then use the fantasy to bring out that reality. Using the elements and tools from witchcraft and the mythological world, and then our own imaginations, we're able to walk that fine line more often than not and make the fantasy elements seem real.

Beyond the fantasy, you also mix comedy and drama. How do you approach those elements in the writing?

BK: We basically value that and judge that on an episode-by-episode basis. It's a very fine balance. We look at a season and see if we've given the show the balance of drama and comedy, both on an episodic basis as well as over the course of the year. I think that the fact that we've got three sisters allows us to go three different directions in any one story. We look for who has the more comedic element, who has the more dramatic element, and who's got the romantic element. Sometimes they can trade off in an episode.

My job is to look at who has done what recently and make sure that we're changing it up so that they're all getting to do something but that the end result is always the balance between comedy and drama. And again, when you have the sisters, inherently sisters are dramatic and funny. Just by forcing them to live under one roof, alienated by the secret and the fact that they have to fight demons on a daily basis . . . that's funny. It's also dramatic because it so adversely affects their life.

Inherent in the concept we've got comedy and drama. We can't take the fantasy too seriously, because for God's sake, they're fighting demons. But we can take the sisters very seriously, and [also] when the demons throw out those serious aspects. The perfect example is Cole and Phoebe's relationship. That was a wonderfully romantic love affair that had a very dark element to it and a very comedic element to it. It's a long way of saying again that we find the balance through the sisters.

Constance Burge has mentioned in the press that she based the show on her own relationship with her sisters. Do you have sisters too?

BK: No, I have an older brother. So, I'm intimately involved with a sibling relationship. Since he's a year older I've been beaten up my whole life. I don't think I could write the show if I didn't have a sibling. I don't have a sister, obviously, but one of my strengths has always been being able to relate to and understand and write female characters.

What do you consider some of the key moments in the sisters' development?

BK: Obviously the death of a sister is huge. As with any family . . . well, let me back up. We start with three disparate sisters, who really don't want to be together because they're growing up and they're spreading their wings and wanting to establish their own lives. One day they wake up and find out they're witches and they can't share that secret with anybody. And now those three disparate sisters are bound together and forced to live under one roof, alienated by the world and forced to share the secret and live together.

That's the first evolutionary step for them, which forces them as sisters to learn to coexist at a time when sisters really are starting to spread apart. Neil Simon always said that's when you have your best comedy. Put three people in a rocket ship and make them orbit around the Earth. They're going to relate and there's going to be conflict and there's going to be fun. That's kind of what we've done in the house. We lock them in the house with a secret. From that point they learned to work together and live together and expose their individual characteristics—their individual characters.

One of the things I'm most proud of is that they're not three interchangeable characters. They are three distinctive characters. This is somewhat because of the writing, but mostly because of their acting. I think they come across as legitimate sisters. So from that foundation, which is already built in conflict, you bring a guy into the house. And do you share that secret with him or don't you share that secret with him? Suddenly that secret could adversely affect the other two sisters. When we had Andy, Prue's first relationship, that was a conflict for the other two sisters to deal with. When Phoebe started to fall in love with Cole, who the other sisters believed was evil (and they turned out to be right), that didn't diminish the love she felt for him. That was a huge evolutionary step for both Phoebe and the sisters to deal with because we've all been with family members who end up making poor dating choices. So this was a metaphor for that.

When Shannen's character died, we wanted to honor that sisterly relationship, rather than treat it like sometimes television does and just move on. So we honored that pain, but brought in a bright light in Rose, both as a human being and as a character. Paige kind of forced Piper and Phoebe to move back into the light and out of the darkness of the mourning a little bit faster, because of who Rose and Paige are.

Then by losing their older sister, Piper was no longer the middle sister and she was no longer solemn, always being the mediator between the two. She was suddenly the older sister and that's a whole different mantle to carry. That's an evolutionary step for her. Phoebe, who was kind of the screw-up, joie-de-vivre character, suddenly was the middle sister, and she had a new role to play, teaching Paige how to be a witch and teaching her the secrets that they've had to work on. Also to begin the long process of accepting a new sister in their lives was another evolutionary step. I think Paige finally finding her place in the shadow of Prue in the sisterly relationship, striking out on her own but a full-fledged sister, has kind of been the final evolutionary step for them. I know it's a very longwinded answer, but that's five years.

We would imagine the actresses' individual strengths eventually find their way into the characters too.

BK: Oh, absolutely. I'd be a bad showrunner and even a worse writer if I didn't listen to the actresses and watch what they like to do, what they don't like to do, and what they do well. The longer the series goes on, the more the actresses become the characters, and then it's my job to make sure that I'm writing what they like. Obviously we never want to change the basis of what makes *Charmed Charmed,* so we're always writing their characters through what the series is.

Alyssa really plays comedy so well, so we try not to put her in the darkness like we did for a while with Cole. We make a choice to put her in the lightness. Alyssa is the Lucy of the twenty-first century, in my opinion. Let's give her stuff. Let's let her play. Let's let her use her shtick. She's so funny. Holly is such a strong actor with such a strong discipline and a detailed eye for her performance. Let's play to that strength whenever possible. Rose can be very emotional and be very quirky and wacky. Let's play to those strengths too. At the same time, we try to shake it all up so that they're not hitting the same notes, so they're not bored. It's very difficult for actors, day in and day out, week in and week out, month in and month out, and now year in and year out to play the same characters. So I'm very sensitive to what they want and try not to write them into ruts.

What would you say Leo adds to the mix?

BK: Balance.

Sanity.

First of all, he's an angel. Brian is an angel and Leo, his character, is an angel. We put an angel into this craziness to give a fulcrum to this teeter-totter. That's kind of what Leo does. He's kind of a calming influence on everybody. We've got three sisters in alternating states of hysteria and dysfunction . . . comedy and drama and melodrama and wackiness. . . . Where is the center? Well, let's put an angel in the mix and that will hopefully keep everything together. So he really is a calming, balancing influence and that's very important to give the sisters, and the show always has kind of a normal place to go to so that we can then extend out beyond it.

What are some of your favorite episodes?

BK: This is going to sound strange, but they're all my babies. In a way I love them all for different reasons. Sometimes I love them for the moments one or more of the actors have found that just tickles me or moves me. Sometimes I love them because the writers have just done an amazing job doing something that I don't get to see too much on television. Sometimes the visual effects . . . I'm amazed on such a short schedule how those geniuses can do that. There's always something in every episode that makes me proud to be part of the show.

I do have favorite shows, which I don't know if the audience finds them to be favorites or not. But I've got seven or eight of my favorites, but that doesn't mean that I don't like lots of others too.

I think shows where we've really done something special or unique in the storytelling process and that worked all the way through to the end are the ones that I'm most proud of.

I think about "Morality Bites," which I think is a lot of people's favorite, where we went to the future and made a strong point about how every little action all of us does in this moment can magnify over time. The girls learn an important lesson in that episode where they realize as witches they are protectors of the innocent, but they had to learn the hard way. There's a difference between being protectors of the innocent and punishers of the guilty. Their job is not to punish the guilty. Their job is to protect the innocent, and when they crossed the line it had horrific consequences over the course of the ten years that led to the future, which they got to see. And they came back and changed their ways.

I liked "Déjà Vu All Over Again" in the first season. It was just a wacky show. It was the show where T. W. King's character died. I liked "That '70s Episode" where we got to go back and meet Mom and Grams when the girls were kids. It was warm and fuzzy and fun. I liked "All Hell Breaks Loose." Obviously losing Shannen's character was hard, but I thought it turned out to be a really powerful episode. In "Charmed Again, Part One" Piper's grieving over the loss of her sister was just so powerful and so real, and it showed the breadth of the series. We could go from wacky leprechauns to real emotion. That was all Holly. That's only up to the beginning of year four, but there are many others.

What's the relationship with The WB like?

BK: The executives at the WB, Jordan Levin and John Litvack in particular, know exactly what they want. They know exactly what their network is and that's where there is a lot of clarity for me personally. I represent the seller. They're the buyer. It's really nice when the buyer tells you exactly what they're looking for. Then I know how to make that pair of shoes. They want shoes that have rhinestones and glitter and are very attractive and hit a certain demographic more so than others. That makes it easier for me to make choices as far as how to help what the direction of the show could be. I think that the clarity that they have as far as what they're looking for—what their network is, what their brand is—distinguishes them from other networks who maybe are in the process for searching for their own identity.

How have you found the fan reaction?

BK: I think they've been incredibly positive and incredibly loyal. I've done a lot of shows in my career, but I've never met a more loyal fan base. The show has been moved four times in five years, into some of the most difficult slots in television history, and fans just go there and they follow us. Every time I get nervous that the network's moving us again, the fans always follow. I think that really says a lot about them. Whenever I'm designing an episode I'm always hyper aware of not wanting to disappoint the fans—because of their loyalty.

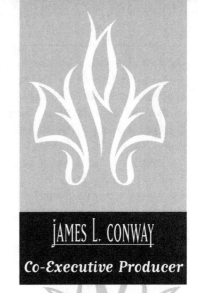

JAMES L. CONWAY
Co-Executive Producer

Jim Conway truly does a balancing act. As a producer and a prolific director, his responsibilities to Spelling Entertainment are many. Outside of Spelling, fans of science fiction and fantasy are probably most familiar with his name from his work directing on each of the modern *Star Trek* series, from *Star Trek: The Next Generation* to *Enterprise*; however, his résumé is far more extensive than simply that entertainment monolith.

Jim was executive vice president of Spelling Entertainment and involved with all the Spelling series from the pilot stage and production stage when Constance Burge came in to pitch the idea for *Charmed*. He's been intimately involved with the series as a consulting producer from the very beginning and named co-executive producer at the start of season five. As a director he worked on one episode a year for the past couple years, finally taking on three episodes in a season when he moved into the co-executive producer position.

From the beginning of his involvement with *Charmed*, the concept struck a chord with the producer-director: "I always loved the idea about a show about three sisters who have magical powers," he says. "It's a great kind of show where it's about wish fulfillment. You wish you could stop time and fix something. Here we empower these women to be able to do just that. The wish-fulfillment aspect of it is terrific when combined with the action element and then the love-life element. It was just a total package and a great idea for a television show."

Aside from giving the audience the opportunity to see their own wishes fulfilled, the series works on many different levels. He credits Brad Kern's leadership for the show's success, noting that the showrunner knows what makes the series work. "Every episode has got arcs for each of the ladies," he explains, "so there's some dramatic movement within each character in each episode, aside from the monsters and the demons and the comedy and all of that. That's what makes the show, for my money, much more fulfilling than a normal television show."

As a producer he and the team have to start from scratch with their first challenge in every week, namely, creating a whole new mythology for the demons of the given episode. What's he going to look like? What's he going to wear? Where does he hang out? What kind of magical power does he have? "Each week that's a whole new challenge," Jim says. "It's a challenge from a writing level when they start the shows and then it's a challenge for us when it comes to actually producing the shows."

But that's only the start of what a unique show like *Charmed* forces the production team to deal with on a weekly basis. "A show like *The Practice* is a terrific TV show," Jim acknowledges. "It's a wonderful drama. But each week they're basically in the courtroom, in their offices, in their houses or apartments, so from a production point of view it's pretty much the same stuff. Same thing goes for *Dawson's Creek* or *90210* or *Melrose Place.* But for *Charmed,* every week is a complete and total challenge because you have to come up with major sets, major wardrobe, major effects, and that's what makes it so much fun to do."

Sure it may be fun, but it's also a lot of work. The shooting company generally works twelve hours a day. "Occasionally they'll go less," Jim says. "Occasionally they'll go over. At this point it's pretty well organized and pretty well planned, so it's a twelve-hour day for the team who actually shoot the shows."

Jim and Producer Jon Paré don't have the early call that the shooting crew does, but their day can often run just as long. As Jim notes, from the moment he comes in to work in the morning "there's a barrage of these meetings and location scouts, and editing that occupy you from the beginning of prep."

The team starts with a concept meeting to get everyone on the same page developing the look of the episode. Then they have individual meetings for costumes, wardrobe, special effects, props, visual effects, stunts, and then the production meetings. "All these meetings," he says. "But it enables you to have a very organized show. It gets shot in twelve hours a day because everything is done ahead of time so when they get out there everybody knows what to do."

Among the usual challenges faced weekly by the production staff, *Charmed* often tackles special episodes the crew knows will be difficult from the start. Among Jim's favorite episodes was one he directed that proved to be one of those unusual challenges from a production standpoint, the fifth season opener, "A Witch's Tail." "Now that was a wonderful show," Jim recalls. "But very complex because we had to build that whole cavern with water in it and have people swimming in the mermaid legs. We had a big second unit, and Jon Paré directed all of the underwater stuff."

Of course going into an episode knowing it will be a challenge doesn't always prepare one for the unexpected. "It was made a little bit more difficult," Jim remembers, "when, a week before we started shooting, we got a call from Alyssa, who had just received the script and read it and said, 'You do know I'm deathly afraid of water?'"

Needless to say, this was a fear of which the producers were entirely unaware.

"So she couldn't go in the ocean," Jim continues. "Although she did get in just a little bit. Suddenly we had enormous challenges to have to try to make it look like she was doing things that she couldn't do and at the same time, we had to keep her comfortable in the times that she *was* doing things. She did get in the tank we had here, but we had to be very careful about that and take care of her. That was a huge shock that complicated an already complicated show."

While the shows themselves certainly stand out in Jim's mind, it's the moments that are created onscreen that he often finds the most touching. Among those favorite moments is one that his producing partner, Jon Paré, directed. As he recalls it was the episode "when Cole died . . . the first time . . . there's a wonderful moment where he and Phoebe look at each other just before they send him away. I actually had tears in my eyes. The actors sold it so well. It was a wonderful moment. I thought that was great."

"There was another moment I loved in one I directed," he adds. "Where Paige goes back into the past and is with her parents, who were killed in a car wreck. I loved the resonance of that whole story. That was a great show for Rose. At the end of that episode, when her parents come back and say they've been watching over her the whole time—I think that was a great show for us."

But it's not just the serious side of *Charmed* the producer appreciates. "I also love when you get a great scene that just makes you laugh out loud," he adds. "Because the girls are so funny. All three of these girls can play comedy so well and the writers can write it. So in some of the scripts, you'll get a scene that is just hysterical."

As is echoed often throughout the interviews for the book, Jim notes that it's the comedy and drama that sell the show as much as the fantasy. Again he cites the core of the show being the real world, not that fantasy one. "It's three sisters who love each other and it's three women who are struggling to find their way in life both in business and love life," Jim explains. "We try to make it all solid, good advice for people to live by. Lessons are learned by both the girls during the show, and hopefully the audience that's watching them. So these girls are role models and they know it as well. They'll read a script and say, 'I can't do this, because this sends the wrong message.' So we're very aware of that sometimes."

As a director Jim approaches each script as if he is making a little movie. It all starts with the mood of the piece, which sets the tone for his direction. "Some of them are sort of light all the way through and you sort of play that as a motif where there's a lot of humor, and you keep it simple," he explains. "Other times it's a very heavy story, but that was mostly fourth-year stuff, not this year so much. When it's a heavier story you tend to have lower angles and longer lenses and you let the camera move along with the storytelling itself. The director's job is to translate the written word to the screen with all the intentions that the writers gave it. Good writers, which we've got, give you a lot of clues to that in the writing."

When dealing with the rigors of both directing and producing, it all comes down to the bottom line. Having to deal with new demons and sets and special effects every week can be a drain on the budget. It's up to Jim and Brad Kern to set that budget for the episodes.

"The scripts are written quite big," Jim admits, when dealing with the budgeting challenge. "Any visual effect can cost five thousand dollars to fifty thousand dollars. We would love to be able to go out on location three or four days a week, but we don't go out that much because that way we're able to spend the money on the sets that are required or the wardrobe or the visual effects. We build a lot of the sets here. Luckily we have a huge stage facility with a lot of swing sets, so we have that ability. But we sort of balance the episodes. If we have an expensive one we look for an inexpensive one. If we go over on one, then we come in under on another."

But no matter how they balance the shows, they all pay off equally when Jim sees the results in his daily life. "Almost everybody I talk to has seen the show or has heard about the show," he says with pride. "I just came from the dentist and the ladies in the dentist's office are rabid fans. They always ask me for new information. When they were watching the show and it looked like we would be losing Cole, they were freaking out. So I find very positive stuff from people."

JON PARÉ
Producer

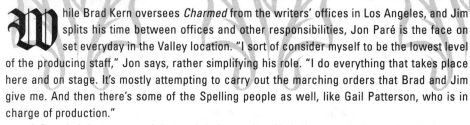

hile Brad Kern oversees *Charmed* from the writers' offices in Los Angeles, and Jim splits his time between offices and other responsibilities, Jon Paré is the face on set everyday in the Valley location. "I sort of consider myself to be the lowest level of the producing staff," Jon says, rather simplifying his role. "I do everything that takes place here and on stage. It's mostly attempting to carry out the marching orders that Brad and Jim give me. And then there's some of the Spelling people as well, like Gail Patterson, who is in charge of production."

J. P., as he's known around the set, is being modest. He is the guy who is the direct link to the seventy-five to eighty people who make the show on stage every day. He's enormously involved with every department at every level at all times. Besides the creative input on wardrobe and sets and special effects, he has to deal with mundane things like hiring and firing, hours, overtime, and all the money. He's also the one who makes sure that each of the episodes meets the budget that Brad and Jim have set, which in itself can often be a daunting task.

With each new show, the production team meets in J. P.'s office to brainstorm over how the episode is going to come together through all their different departments of wardrobe, makeup, sets, props, special effects, stunts, etc. "It makes for a real interesting experience because all of a sudden these ideas start boiling to the top," J. P. says. "It's a very creative process and you realize that all of a sudden you're latching on to a direction in terms of where that particular show can go to."

Even though the creative team is split with the writers in Los Angeles and the production team in the Valley, they often find that the two teams have a similar voice. According to J. P., "Nine times out of ten when you go back and toss it back over the hill and say, 'We came up with this,' you find that's exactly the direction they were conceiving it in as well. So it's really interesting to take the written word and try to execute that and make tangible meaning out of it in terms of how we achieve a particular concept. How do we actually slap it on paper so instead of it being words we make a picture of it? It's very challenging from that point of view."

This is where the team's extensive history in "the business" comes most into play. With the combined decades of talent that meet in J. P.'s office, they have found that they can really work together to solve any problem. "I think it was last year," J. P. recalls. "We were doing the fairy show where we all walked into the concept meeting and we just didn't know how to do it. We just didn't know what to do at the start. And it ended up being one of our best episodes."

It's exactly those kinds of challenges that make *Charmed* such an interesting work environment for the entire crew. "It's really fun trying to put it together," J. P. says. "Particularly after you've been doing it for fifteen or twenty years and you have guys that have been working with Spielberg and the like. Instead of trying to figure out how to do something in the next eight months to make it work, it's how can we prepare it in the next eight hours? Our people usually come in after the latest hundred million–dollar movie that they saw and try and apply it to our little world here and make it work. And for the most part we do. We do a really good job of working together."

But even with all the talent in the room, it doesn't come easily.

"This is the type of show that really requires very exact kind of planning and prep," J. P. explains. "For people not to do their homework and to go on the floor and try to execute one of these scripts, they can really get hurt and they can really get into a lot of trouble. It really takes a lot of homework and when you're on the floor you're checking things off and checking things twice because it really does take a lot of planning."

In the end J. P. knows that after all the work on the look and the effects, it's the moments created on screen that lets him know they succeeded. "It's really hard when you watch television to get an emotional experience from the screen," he admits. "Personally I think it's much easier when you go see a feature and you get involved in the characters and you get that sort of chill in your back at the right minute. I find it really hard to get there watching TV. But on our show there is, on occasion, those moments where we'll see one of these episodes and get that feeling of, 'Wow, we're really communicating.' If you can communicate a feeling where you have an emotional response to it, that's pretty cool. That's hitting the ball out of the park."

J. P. has also been taking more of an active role in creating those moments, first as an assistant director and now as a director. Usually, though, he finds that those moments are there from the start, it's just a matter of bringing them to life. "The first time I read the script was probably the most valuable time," he says. "I would get certain guttural responses. There would be some instinctual responses I would get and I would write them down. And I would find that many times those reactions would carry through to the tenth or eleventh time that I read the script."

"These scripts are so specifically written that you have to read them several times to understand precisely what they're asking of you," he continues. "The first time you read it, you can lose a lot. Even after I've prepped for eight days and read the script dozens of times, when I'm on the set and as soon as I've finished my rehearsal, I usually go right back and read it again to make sure that I'm not missing anything. Because every time you read it, you realize something new."

"You're trying to get the story to talk to you so that when you put the camera somewhere it's a natural organic place and you're not trying to force some action," he continues. "Particularly when you're doing something and you want to have some movement within the scene, you still want to make that appear organic and not forced. Even on our tight schedules—even though our rehearsals might at the most last ten minutes—we're still trying to create as organic an environment as possible and have the camera be as unobtrusive as it might. Then, maybe, you're communicating the most amount of information. The audience is watching what people are saying and not necessarily being distracted by what the camera's doing."

And it's the people at home that keep J. P. both in awe and appreciative of the power of what they're creating. "I'm always amazed the amount of impact television has on people in their lives," he explains. "People really take a lot of these things personally. These people really become important characters in their lives. I remember I was skiing once with a well-known TV star. When we came down for snacks, people came up to this guy and they treated him like they were close relatives, like they were cousins. It was really odd. And he in turn acted like he hadn't seen them for a few weeks. It was really odd, the impact that this has on our culture."

216

Behind the Scenes
The Cast

ALYSSA MILANO
as Phoebe Halliwell

It would be difficult to find someone who has not stumbled across some part of Alyssa Milano's career that has spanned almost three decades—which is an interesting thing to say about a woman who just turned thirty. Following a stint in the touring company of the musical *Annie* when she was eight, Alyssa literally grew up in front of the world as Samantha Micelli on the hit comedy *Who's the Boss?* The series served to launch her career as a child and teen star, allowing her to take on TV movie roles like *The Canterville Ghost* and expand her popularity with the surprisingly popular workout video aimed at kids, *Teen Steam*.

Following her work on *Who's the Boss?* Alyssa continued to work in television and film, taking on more mature roles in projects with broad-based appeal as well as some with a more independent feel. Whether it was in films like *Where the Day Takes You* or TV movies like *Casualties of Love: The Long Island Lolita Story,* she evolved into a dramatic actress known for edgier parts. She also returned to her theater roots by taking on several stage roles throughout the nineties.

Alyssa has also been very active with the Internet, by taking groundbreaking action to protect her rights and the rights of other celebrities on the World Wide Web. She has won several copyright infringement suits, and has dedicated the settlement money to the launch of a new search index on the Web called safesearching.com. The site offers a safe alternative for families to get the best entertainment on the Internet without fear of stumbling across adult content.

Alyssa began her relationship with Spelling Entertainment when she played Jennifer Mancini on *Melrose Place* for two seasons. Aaron Spelling is notorious for the familial relationship he fosters with his many cast members, and their past relationship came in quite handy when he was gearing up for *Charmed*.

In the original presentation for the network, the cast of *Charmed* included another actress in the role of Phoebe. The network liked the piece and everything was set for production when the original actress backed out of the project. Normally losing one of your stars at the last minute would send any producer into a tailspin, but Aaron Spelling calmly picked up the phone and contacted his friend Alyssa Milano, who was working in Hawaii at the time, and asked if she would be interested in the part.

With time being of the essence he immediately sent Alyssa a copy of the original pilot and she knew it was a hit as soon as she saw it. Within days, she signed on to the project and came in to reshoot Phoebe's scenes as the youngest Charmed One.

"Phoebe started off in the series as extremely young and innocent in a quirky and free-spirited way," Alyssa recalls. "She got in trouble quite a bit using love spells and things like that and wasn't really interested in anything but the witchcraft, which, at first, gave her purpose."

Phoebe was definitely searching for her place in life in the early seasons of *Charmed*, but was forced to grow up when Prue died at the end of the third season. "Shifting from being the baby sister to the middle sister is something she's still learning," Alyssa notes. "And it's a little more taxing for her, taking on more responsibilities."

In addition to the responsibilities Phoebe has assumed by season five, she is finally finding a satisfying career as a newspaper advice columnist. But her lessons in love for her readership were little help for herself in dealing with her largest story arc of the series—her tortured relationship with Cole. Alyssa believes that "when Phoebe fell in love with Cole, a demon, it changed her life and she learned a very valuable life lesson—falling in love with someone she shouldn't have fallen in love with in the first place."

Even with Phoebe's real-life concerns of finding her place in the world and dealing with a doomed relationship, Alyssa has managed to bring a lot of comedy to the role. Although she notes that the fourth season did get a little dark when her character married The Source, she has come back to a lighter role through season five. It's the fantasy element of the series that she credits with her favorite moments.

"Anytime I can play something else within my character—like when a ghost inhabited my body—is always a lot of fun to play," she says. "That's the fun thing about this show—you get to be so many things." Behind the scenes Alyssa had the chance to branch out and try different things when, like Holly, she became a producer of the series in the third season.

But the opportunity to have such diversity within a single character can be both a blessing and a curse. One of the standout episodes of *Charmed* is undoubtedly the two-part fifth season opener, "A Witch's Tail," in which Alyssa played a mermaid. Although it would seem exciting to take on such an interesting role, there were some far more practical challenges that came along with the experience. "It was hard when I had to wear a fin and be a mermaid," Alyssa admits. "I had to go in the ocean and a large tank and I'm very afraid of the water." Alyssa managed to combat those fears and impress much of the crew with her ability to work through the demanding scenes.

As Aaron Spelling described her, Alyssa really is the quarterback of this production team.

She sets the tone for production and inspires them to do their best work. In the days following the events of 9/11 she wrote a letter to the cast and crew and gathered everyone to share it so they could come together as one family during those trying times. She is often the voice that speaks for the group.

"I would just have to say that we've gone through many changes over these five years," Alyssa says. "In definitely a good way, and we all really love each other and it's fun to come to work every day. We've overcome so much. We were the little show that could. The fact that we've done as well as we have on so many nights . . . it feels great."

HOLLY MARIE COMBS
as Piper Halliwell

olly Marie Combs is one of only a handful of members of the production from the original *Charmed* pilot to still be with the show in its fifth season. Although it's certainly typical for a series to change as it goes from its original premise through five years of development, it does say a lot for the staying power of the actress who started working in commercials and print ads when she was only ten years old.

After small film roles and work on soap operas in her teens, Holly's breakthrough role came when she was cast as Kimberly Brock on David E. Kelley's Emmy Award–winning series *Picket Fences*. In many ways Kimberly and Piper are similar characters as they have both been the calm, levelheaded members of their respective families and the ones their younger siblings look to for advice.

Following *Picket Fences* Holly starred in several movies made for TV, but she was never far from series television. Holly was already in the process of auditioning for the role of Phoebe when she saw a copy of the script for *Charmed* in the backseat of a friend's car. That friend happened to be Shannen Doherty. Although Shannen hadn't managed to read the script yet, Holly convinced her friend it was worth a look and Shannen instantly connected with the character Prue. Shannen then went in to talk with Aaron Spelling about the part, never forgetting where the original idea came from. After securing the role of Prue she convinced Aaron to hire Holly to play the part of Piper.

In the beginning of the series Piper was the typical middle sister, striving to maintain balance between by-the-book Prue and playful Phoebe. She fell in love with the handyman/Whitelighter and suffered through a bit of a love triangle with the guy next door. Throughout the five seasons of *Charmed* Piper has grown from a slightly put-upon head chef into a mature woman with her own business.

"Piper's key developments definitely are when she started owning and managing P3," Holly says, "which has given her the ability to make more decisions." Those decision-making skills really come in handy in the life-and-death world her character faces every day battling demons. "Of course, becoming the oldest sister and assuming the position of the head of the family and keeping things together has given me the real-life stuff to play in the midst of all this fantasy," she is quick to assert. "My character is definitely going through the life stages by marrying Leo, and becoming a first-time mom to their son Wyatt."

It is that struggle with the real world that makes Piper's life so interesting. She is the only one of the sisters to have a successful long-lasting relationship, although her time with Leo has certainly hit a few bumps in the road. Now she is the mother to a child that is part-witch and part-Whitelighter with unexplored powers all his own. The caregiver part of Piper is something that Holly can easily understand. Although she doesn't yet have any children of her own, Holly's home almost resembles an animal sanctuary with more than a dozen pets that she tends to, including dogs, cats, rabbits, and fish. She also keeps horses at the same stables as her castmate Alyssa Milano.

On the show, baby Wyatt exemplifies the perfect blend of the real-life drama and fantasy element in Piper's life, and Holly loves playing both sides of the equation. "We try to base our show more on fantasy, and it has no bounds, so we can do pretty much anything—like go into the future or into the 1920s and get to wear great wigs and clothes. But the show also tries to focus on sisterhood, family, and real problems, which a lot of people can relate to."

And a lot of people *are* relating. *Charmed* has a following that reaches from children to adults. But it's one particular segment of the fan base that Holly is most protective of. "We have a lot of teenage girls as fans," she notes. "So we attempt to put moral, value, or family messages in the show. I think female empowerment is important, especially during those teenage years." Holly takes that concern for children a step further and is an active spokesperson for the charity Thursday's Child, which helps at-risk teens.

But even within those important messages for the audience, Holly never forgets that the show has its fair share of fun elements. "There's so nothing typical about a day on the set," she admits. "At a recent shoot, I was running around with my pregnant belly, in a robe and with curlers, and the next scene I'm in Rambo gear. In the morning we can do a family scene and I'm crying, and in the afternoon I can be on wires doing karate kicks."

Piper may have the strongest offensive power of the three sisters with her ability to blow up demons, but Holly is still called on to do her fair share of stunt work. "I thought the action on this show was going to be a lot easier than it is," she admits. In almost every episode she and the rest of the cast are called on for fight sequences, or to be flung across a room, or stand next to an explosion. Although she has a stunt double for the more dangerous tasks, Holly is right in there along with her costars getting good and dirty in some very physical scenes.

Holly's commitment to her work may mirror Piper's commitment to her own responsibilities, but that's just one of the areas where the two are alike. Both the actress and the character have a calm, nurturing presence, as several people on set have commented about Holly's own personality.

Even though Holly believes that the character of Piper is funnier than the actress portraying her, many of the crew would disagree. Behind the scenes, there is a definite extension of the onscreen family. The cast and crew often mingle in playful ways. "The atmosphere on set is crazy," Holly admits. "What we do is fun stuff, so it's impossible not to have fun with it."

When pressed on how crazy things can get, the actress shows that she does have a mischievous side. "I started Friday night grape fights early on with some plastic grapes," she admits. "I just started throwing them at the crew one Friday night while we were working late."

Games like that take place to break up the rigors of production work. While on our set visit, we watched as a clothespin was secretly clipped to one person after another as it went around the set. After each victim found that he or she had been tagged, it would discreetly be moved to another. This kind of behavior is typical of this show. Holly and the rest of the cast know that they're all part of the same family and Holly gladly plays along.

Being on *Charmed* has also opened up other opportunities for Holly beyond acting on television. She added a producer credit to her name when she took on that title in the third season of the series. She has also seen her movie work take an interesting turn with an uncredited cameo in the hit film *Ocean's Eleven* in which she gave a tongue-in-cheek portrayal of herself as one of the young, hip Hollywood set.

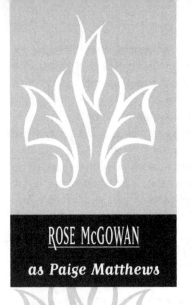

ROSE McGOWAN
as Paige Matthews

n the wake of Shannen Doherty's departure at the end of season three, the producers found they no longer had the Power of Three. Considering that aspect was at the center of the show, they quickly had to come up with a new, never-before-seen sister, and work her into the plot. Enter Rose McGowan and Paige Matthews.

At first it seemed like an unlikely addition to the cast. Rose McGowan was best known for her movie work. Her breakout role came in *The Doom Generation*, for which she was nominated for Best Debut Performance for the Independent Spirit Awards in 1996. Her most notable role, however, was as the doomed best friend in the original *Scream*.

Naturally no one was more surprised at the decision to move into television than Rose herself. "I'm not really a cookie-cutter kind of person," Rose proudly proclaims. "I'm not really from the mold, which I'm grateful for. It's a bit ironic and strange that I am here, but who knows what weird fortunes are at work behind the scenes."

From the moment Paige entered the scene, she added a certain amount of turmoil to the lives of the remaining Charmed Ones, like when she decided to photocopy pages from the *Book of Shadows*. "Sometimes I like being the one that causes all sorts of chaos," Rose admits. "And other times I get bored with apologizing or, rather, I feel like Paige shouldn't apologize anymore. I think it's fun to cause a little disruption in a perfectly oiled machine to show that there's still ways to screw with the main way of doing things."

When describing her character, Rose takes a little help from the press. "The best description of Paige came from a reviewer who said that she's 'goofily vulnerable.' I think that hits the nail on the head. The two things that are trying to meld." She does consider that a bit of a welcome departure for herself. "Whereas probably before this I was perceived as the strong, tough chick, that's definitely not representative of Paige. I think she's strong in personality, but I think she's very soft in a lot of ways and very easily hurt, I would imagine, and not terribly unlike myself in that way. That's definitely a trait we share."

"One of the things that drew me to doing this was the idea of doing comedy and drama within a short space of time," she admits. "Whereas you'd have to do two separate movies to achieve those two things. I've been doing straight-out comedy for a while this year. I was actually thinking about it a couple weeks ago that I would like to ask for more drama to be put in for me because that's an arm that I flex very well and I just haven't had a chance to lately." Rose is quick to note that Brad Kern is very open to comments from the actors, a fact he later confirms.

The chance to do both comedy and drama isn't the only difference between working in film versus television. "Well, you kill yourself and then you get sleep," Rose notes of the filming process. "Here you just kill yourself and kill yourself and kill yourself. But that's an art in its own. It has been easier for me this year because I kind of knew what to expect. Last year was really difficult. Believe it or not, it's very hard to put on all that lip gloss and act cute in a miniskirt when you want to go crawl in a hole."

Paige also has the distinction of being the character Rose has lived with the longest. Whereas in a movie the part is usually over in a few months, Paige has been inside Rose's head for two years. The longevity has had some interesting effects on the actress. "It's funny," she admits. "I'll go shopping and I'll buy something and I'll realize that it's not me, it's a Paige outfit and then I'll bring it to the show and wind up wearing it here—like some crazy multicolored thing that looks like an Easter egg gone mad. That's actually not me, that's Paige."

Rose was also surprised by the audience reaction to the show. "There are a lot of young girls in the audience," she notes. "But there are also sixty-year-old men, sixty-year-old women, thirty-year-old women, thirty-year-old men. It's so across the board. I've never experienced anything like it. That so many different people form a fan base. I really thought it would be all thirteen-years-olds, but it absolutely is not. And I don't know how often that happens with other shows."

When it comes to filming the episodes, some of Rose's past movie work has come in quite handy. The violent fight scene from *Scream* particularly helped in preparing her for all the stunt work she has to do every week on *Charmed*. Unfortunately she wasn't prepared enough for this role.

"I don't feel pain when I'm in the middle of it," Rose notes when talking about the stunt work. "It's just after when I go, 'What the hell happened to me? I look like someone took a two by four. . . .' I always forget when they tell you to flop on the ground and not smack my head. I have hit my head so many times. The camera people wince because they see it bounce really hard on the floor." But even with the bruising and pain involved in stunt work, she's quick to add, "That part's actually fun."

When Rose mentions that the crew winces when she hurts herself, she's not just talking about a natural reaction to seeing someone get hurt. The actress has quite a bond with her coworkers. "I have a great time with the crew," she says. "I always do. It does become a family of sorts. On films you have to give that up pretty quickly, but here it kind of goes on, so it's interesting developing relationships and not just getting to know people very quickly and leaving. It's been quite lovely actually."

So far, Rose is pleased with her decision to make her mark in television. Even though the decision may have been surprising to some—including herself—she looks at it as she has all the other aspects of her working life. "My whole career has been strange and weird," she says. "I just came into the whole thing so backward, being that I first got into a leading role instead of starting out with little parts and working my way up. It's just been a very bizarre thing across the board. I know when I'm older, it's going to all have been an interesting ride."

BRIAN KRAUSE
as Leo Wyatt

Brian Krause made his feature-film debut in *Return to the Blue Lagoon*, and has been balancing work between film and television ever since. He has appeared in several movies, most notably Stephen King's *Sleepwalkers*, and has had roles in several television films as well. With regard to TV series, he has guest-starred on *Walker, Texas Ranger* and was the *seventh* actor to portray Matt Cory on the daytime drama *Another World*.

When Brian originally auditioned for *Charmed,* things didn't go quite as expected, which turned out to be more of a blessing than a curse. "Originally I had auditioned for a different role," Brian recalls. "I auditioned for T. W.'s role as the cop, Andy Trudeau, which thank God I didn't get, because he was killed."

Not getting the part certainly didn't sour Brian to the show, and apparently the producers didn't soon forget him. "I came back a couple months later to read for Leo," he adds. "At the time I was told he was the handyguy/possible boyfriend and would maybe recur. Eventually it just grew and grew. I was really lucky to get called back. It was pretty quick from going in to getting the job."

But just because he had the part didn't mean he would keep it. It took Brian quite a while to feel secure in his job. "It took years till I realized I was going to be around a while," he admits.

"At the end of the first season my character went away and it was possible he wasn't coming back. End of the second season had the same kind of thing. It wasn't until season three that I became a regular. Every year you still kind of wonder if you're coming back." And it was true of the fifth season as well when Leo disappeared and the audience was left to wonder if he was gone for good.

During those five years of development Leo has certainly grown. Although the Whitelighter was close to all his charges, his relationship with the Charmed Ones—and one of them in particular—has obviously affected him and the way he performs his duties. But the experience has also changed him as a man. "Obviously he's got a deeper understanding about women, by getting to know the Charmed Ones," Brian says. "Now he's become a father. That's probably the biggest change of pace in his life over the past sixty years. Now he's a dad and he's at home and a married man."

In fact Leo has probably experienced the most growth of his entire life in the past five years. Looking at Brian Krause, it can be easy to forget that he plays a man who is technically around eighty years old, but that fact is never far from the actor's mind when approaching the role.

228

"I try to view Leo as someone like a grandparent," Brian says. "He's somebody who grew up in the thirties and forties. He's kind of old-school and proper with a high-moral standard and high ethic for honesty. Basically Leo doesn't fit in with today's world as far as being hip and cool. He's basically our grandparent in the body of a late-twenties/early-thirties guy. So he's a little kooky and a little off. He doesn't quite get it all the time. The girls try to keep him up to date. I just try to take it from a view almost like myself, not being the hippest guy in town. It's pretty easy to do."

Brian cites that high moral ground as the basis for many of the decisions that Leo has made on the show going against the wishes of the Elders. "I think it's not so much rebellion as trying to do what's right and always finding the greater good doing what's best for the girls and our Innocents," Brian says. "Sometimes we have to make our own choices and Leo decides to trust the girls' instincts or trust his own and even though it's not by the book all the time, it turns out to always be for the best."

Of all the times he's ignored the wishes of the Elders, none was more meaningful than his marriage to Piper. Brian looks at the love between the two characters as being a little different from most relationships seen among younger characters on television today. "It's not just young love," he says. "It's like any normal married couple. We get along. We have to work together, so that changes the dynamic as far as how much time we spend together. Our characters can drive each other a little nuts, but there's also a lot of stability there and a lot of love and passion. It's different. We play the mom and dad role in a way, and we're young. We send out a good moral message as far as being honest with each other and just really pure."

When pressed to pick a favorite episode, Brian keeps his answer simple. "Every episode that I've been a part of has been a godsend," he says. "I'm blessed to be here. In just about every episode there's a challenge. There's a scene or the entire episode in which you can push the limit a little bit."

Brian has also challenged himself in other ways. In season five, he dabbled with writing in the episode "Sense and Sense Ability," for which he earned a "story by" credit. "I came up with this idea a year and a half to two years ago and kept pushing," he recalls. "Brad Kern liked it. He enjoyed it and thought it was a good episode and we finally got to make it. I like what it's about and the message it puts out there. The girls go deaf, blind, and mute and have to overcome that and learn their message. Each one learns her own thing, but I think the core of the episode is that we can be and do anything we want to be. There's no handicap too great that can stop you from being what you want to be."

Now bitten by the writing bug, Brian doesn't intend to let that aspect of his career simply fade away. "Hopefully next year I'll get a chance to put some more stories out there," he says. "I have a bunch on the burner. All I can do is pitch them and hopefully they'll like it."

Allowing an actor to expand his role in the production is just one of the ways in which *Charmed* is unlike many other series on TV. And it's just one of the reasons why Brian has so enjoyed his experience as being a member of the team. "It's fun," he simply states. "The girls are so funny and have a great attitude every day. You never know what's going to happen one day to the next on the set before we roll. There's just a really good energy here. It's definitely a family with the crew and everybody. It's nice to wake up and know I have such a great place to go to. So many other jobs I've had make you just dread going there because of attitudes and what have you. We don't have that . . . which is charming."

DORIAN GREGORY
as Detective Darryl Morris

orian Gregory started his career in television on *Baywatch Nights* and has also appeared as a guest on numerous other shows, including *Living Single, Moesha,* and *3rd Rock from the Sun.* His diverse career has also included some film work, a spot as guest cohost on a radio talk show, a kickboxing workout video, calendar layouts, and voiceover work. But his most notable role, in addition to his work on *Charmed,* would have to be his work as one of the cohosts of the daytime talk show *The Other Half.*

The actor is also an active humanitarian who serves as spokesperson for the American Diabetes Association. Diagnosed with the disease when he was nine, he now talks to young adults and children to show that there are no boundaries or barriers in life that they cannot overcome.

Dorian started on *Charmed* with the recurring role of Andy Trudeau's partner. At the time he didn't even have a first name—at least as far as the audience knew. "When I first came on, *I* knew his name was Darryl Morris," Dorian quickly asserts. "I think what happened was, Darryl was kind of a stickler about things. He was a very by-the-book kind of guy and he was very much untrusting of all that was going on. So it was very appropriate for him to be called 'Morris' because there was a distance. As things progressed and he started to be more of an ally and grew closer to the family, of course he became Darryl, because that's who he is."

However, the closer Darryl got to the Halliwells, the more his world was systematically turned upside down. "The big thing about Darryl," Dorian says, "was the fact that he thought that everything could be explained away in great detail if you just looked hard enough. So when something comes in and takes away everything that you've ever believed, your whole way of approaching everything is stripped away from you. So that's a process to really strip you of all that you know and redefine your whole outlook on life. It took him four years, which in television time is a long time. It wasn't just, 'Oh, you're witches. Okay, great! Well, I never believed that, but now you're telling me, so that's all good.' That's not what happened."

Although it would seem unlikely that Darryl would ever accept such an outlandish idea and eventually side with the Charmed Ones, Dorian bases his approach to the character on a very simple concept. "His whole thing was about being there for people who had nowhere to turn," he explains. "That's the whole story of these three women. We take that definition to its absolute extreme max. Because when you start talking about demons and evil, you're talking about people who've got nobody to go to because nobody knows about it and nobody wants to hear. And even with the people who do know about it, who knows how to fight it? So take his whole purpose, multiply it by a hundred, and that is what these women embody."

The other aspect that Dorian credits for his character's bond with the Charmed Ones is the theme of family that permeates the show. "Darryl's a family man," he says. "Another big theme about what these women are all about is about family. It doesn't matter what it is. No man, no witch, no magic, no power, no nothing comes in between family. So you've got these two things that are about his entire makeup that these women embody. And now it's like they're family to him.

"What I found beautiful about this whole ride is that this man has got no blood ties to these women," he adds. "He's got no family ties to these women. He's got no particular friendship ties to these women. I mean, his partner died the first year indirectly due to what their world is about. There are no ties other than what they're all about. It's not like we used to go out or they're my cousins or whatever."

Of course he is also the one ally for the Charmed Ones who has no supernatural powers whatsoever. Dorian is quick to point out that is a very important element in making the concept of the series work. "He's got no magical powers and he represents all of us," Dorian explains. "We're just normal people. And he's thrown into this world that's out of control. So the whole joy of this is how do you handle [it] when things just go out of control? How do you handle that consistently on a day to day basis when you've got no power over anything? I think that's a cool message that he embodies. He's in this powerless position and being able to handle it. And being able to not only handle it, but face up to things that he knows could at the flick of a hand destroy him with a fireball. He is able to deal with that and still be strong."

Along with the challenges presented by his character, Dorian also enjoys the work of being part of this ensemble. "Since the beginning of the show each core member of this cast has had a completely different way of doing their thing," he says. "We got five core people, Brian, Alyssa, there was Shannen, Rose, and Holly and myself. Our way of doing things is so different. Sometimes you see an ensemble cast where some of the quirks are the same, but none of us are the same. My favorite moments are just working with each one of them, just picking up on the weird ways they approach the scene and the weird way in which they deliver this moment that we're trying to make real."

"I mean, when you watch Holly," he continues, "the moments in between are just amazing. And Alyssa has this strength and this sensuality and this humor all boiled down in this one person.

231

And you got Rose; she's just straight up quirky. And we got Brian, who's this calm, centering force who's dealing with these three powerful women and still is able to hold on to the strength of being a man. Then you got me. I don't even know how to describe me. The cool part about it is you've got these five beautiful dancers. You've got merengue, you've got some flamenco over here, you've got waltzing over here, and you've got all these dances going at the same time and it looks beautiful."

The work these dancers put into the show certainly finds its way to the screen, and it shows in what they do every week. Dorian first knew that it was working when the initial fan response to the show started coming in, but it's how the reaction has changed that has most interested him. "Everybody loves it," he says. "At the beginning, guys were kind of bashful to admit that they really dug our show. They would pull me off to the side and say 'Oh, my God, this stuff is really cool.' The first year, from the guys' reaction was simply that we've got these three beautiful women doing their thing and now it's so evolved beyond that. It's so evolved into the story line, the content, the magical aspect, and the whole Wicca thing and the witch thing. It's evolved beyond that."

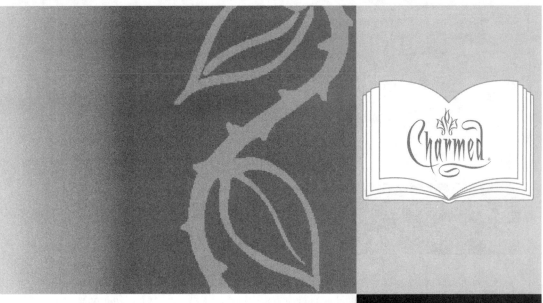

Behind the Scenes
The Crew

NANCY SOLOMON
Script Supervisor

As the script supervisor, Nancy Solomon has one of the jobs that most of the hard-core fans are interested in buzzing about in chat rooms and fan sites as soon as each episode ends. She's the one who has to track the continuity within each episode to make sure the scenes match, the effects are properly placed, and the clocks are set to the right time. In truth, that's an incredible oversimplification of her job description.

This is Nancy's first season on *Charmed,* and after twenty episodes, she's well accustomed to the special needs of the show. But then again, she's proven to be very good at adapting.

Nancy started off her Hollywood career doing video camera operating and then moved into editing. When she "got over that" she started doing stunts for a little bit and wound up blowing out her knee. While she was in physical therapy she decided to jump into script supervising and has been doing that for eight years for commercials and other shows like *JAG, The X-Files, 7th Heaven,* and a plethora of feature films, including *Traffic.*

Coming into *Charmed* just happened to be a result of being at the "right place at the right time." She had filled in for a couple days for the previous script supervisor and apparently impressed the production team with her work. When the time came that they were looking to hire new crew members, she got the call for an interview and was eventually hired for the permanent gig.

In approaching a new episode, as with every other department, for Nancy it starts with the script. "When I first get the script I break it down and go through it to find continuity, things I'm going to have to pay attention to before we even see it," she explains. "Basically, if they're leaving with a jacket, we have to make sure they have that jacket five scenes later." But again, that's the easy part of her task. Considering all the vanquishing and spells being cast, continuity can be a difficult thing to track.

Knowing that other departments are going to depend on her work when it comes time to add the effects, Nancy tries to get a handle on their needs from the start. "To kind of get a heads up on the effects," she explains, "I highlight all the visual effects that we're going to have on the scene so we can find it quickly and make sure that everything gets placed. Although we have a visual effects guy here with us whenever we do big effects shots, I just want to make sure we get all the elements in it. If they throw a potion vial, I have to make sure we get a plate for the explosion and we get a plate for the person exploding and any effects or light cues we're going to need."

A "plate" is basically one of the shots to be used to create the overall effect. Whenever the script calls for a visual effect, the team has to construct it in several layers. Each layer is a plate. One layer may be taking a full shot of the person talking. "Now we're going to vanquish the person," Nancy explains. "He would do this 'Aaaagggghhh!' or whatever he was going to do. That would be one element. Next element would be he walks out of frame and we shoot nobody there. So then they would overlap that and then they can put in any kind of visual effects they're going to do, flames or stars, or whatever. Sometimes, you need to add a third element, which means that we put the person in front of a green screen."

Then the visual effects supervisor, Stephen Lebed, will put all those elements together and add in the computer effects surrounding what had been shot to compose the effect. It's Nancy's responsibility to make sure that they have the required plates. She also makes sure that they have video playback on days they need to match things. For example, if one person is morphing into another, the two people being filmed for the effect need to be in the same position. Nancy is the one who makes sure they are.

Her job also deals with some of the more esoteric demands of filming that aren't quite as simple as tracking a jacket as it moves from scene to scene or setting up for effects. "I keep track of the regular set stuff, making sure all the clocks are all correct. I try to find what time it is. Because it's never really written in the script what time it is. It'll just be day or night so you have to find audio cues in there. If the character says, 'Oh, I'm going off to work,' you have to assume it's around eight or eight thirty. So when I do my breakdown I try to find anything that will give me a cue for what time it is that day." She doesn't just do this for the fans reading the clocks on the walls. Knowing the time of day helps the director of photography when he's lighting a scene because a scene set at dusk looks very different from one filmed at high noon.

But of course most of her job does entail checking on the minutia. "If we're doing a driving shot we want to make sure it looks like they're steering," she says. "Or I'm looking for reflections if we're in the Manor. If we're going by a mirror do we see the boom coming in? Do we see our camera booming down? Did I make sure we don't see any of the crewmembers in there?"

Aside from the fact that it's a part of making good television, Nancy knows that she's also doing this for the fans because, "They watch everything."

In the fifth season the fans had a bit of a treat with the episode "Cat House." It was effectively a "clip show" in which snippets of past episodes were revisited during the course of the hour. However, unlike most clip shows from other series, this episode did not consist of a group of characters sitting around a table going, "Oh, do you remember when we . . ." and then flashback to a clip. No, *Charmed* had to do it a little differently and actually physically placed Phoebe and Paige in Piper's memories that encompassed five years of the series. It doesn't take a genius to realize this was a difficult episode for the script supervisor to have to coordinate.

"We put the characters into scenes that have already taken place, so we have a lot of eighths of a page here and there," Nancy explains. "And we would have them look at the action that was already shot two or three years ago. We had a lot of different elements on that to insert the girls into the whole scene. So they might sneak up behind the couch and we would see them and then we'd shoot over them and we'd see the scene happen. We put a lot of green screen in there. We used a lot of video playback to look at the prerecorded scenes and match angles and lighting. That was probably the most challenging episode this year as far as all of the different things we had to do."

Naturally with a background in stunt work, Nancy has a bit of an edge when it comes to making sure that a scene is properly set for the physical work required in the show. "I probably have more of a clarity of what a stunt's going to require," she explains. "I look at safety first when they do stunts. If Alyssa has a purse, I'll want her to set that purse down before they do the stunt. So somewhere in the dialogue I'll want her to take that off because I don't want a stunt person coming in and having to fly through the air with a purse in their hand."

"It's a challenging show to work on," Nancy admits with pride. "We have a lot of stuff that we're packing into an hour. People don't realize we have almost a hundred effects an episode, which is probably more than any other show that's on TV right now. We have a lot of elements that we shoot in the show that makes it a little more than somebody just talking."

EILISH
Costume Designer

In Hollywood, where people move from job to job every other day, people outside of the *Charmed* set would consider costume designer Eilish almost an institution at Spelling Entertainment because she has been working with Aaron Spelling for over twenty-six years. But that's the thing about working for Aaron Spelling. He inspires such loyalty that Eilish isn't the only one in his company who's been there for decades.

At age twenty Eilish moved to America from Ireland and started work as a governess. After about a year in the States, she met the man who would become her husband. He then introduced her to his neighbor, who dyed fabrics in the Warner Bros. costume department. Eilish had worked for five years in a clothing factory in Ireland and used her background to get a job in the studio's tailor shop. After six weeks she moved over to the "finished end" of costumes and started working on the film *Camelot*.

At the start of her career Eilish did move around Hollywood like most people in the industry. She first got involved with Spelling's company while working for Columbia Television on *Fantasy Island*, when she met Aaron's friend, designer Nolan Miller. Apparently impressed by her work, Nolan suggested to Aaron that she would be a perfect addition to the company. Eilish started working for Spelling on the tail end of *Charlie's Angels* and has been with the company ever since, overseeing such shows as *The Love Boat*, *Hotel*, *Matt Houston*, and the crown jewel of fashionable television series, *Dynasty*.

"There was one time we had like eight productions going," Eilish says of her time spent as head of the Spelling costume department. "It was fabulous. It was crazy, but it worked. It just worked." They would literally have all-day production meetings where she and Aaron stayed in the room as the different productions came and went.

Although Eilish came onto *Charmed* in the second season, she was already well aware of the show. "I remember hearing about it being within the company and how cute it is and these three girls and they're witches and I thought, what a cute concept," she recalls. "Now, I would have to say that *Charmed* is the most fun."

Eilish is quick to note that part of the fun is also because of the demands of the series. "It's a lot of work," she adds. "It's not an easy show. But I think it's an absolute designer's dream. You get to be so creative. That's the fun thing. Besides the three girls we have guest stars and they're demons and they're witches. It's like every week you can't wait to read the script to see what you

have to come up with. Like on this particular show we're doing Titans and Greek mythology. It's wonderful. It's really great."

By season five, each of the girls has had some very interesting outfits to wear, but it's with their everyday attire that Eilish gets to help create the characters. "Phoebe is always very hot and very sexy," Eilish says. "It's almost like Alyssa's so cute she could put on anything. She can pretty much wear anything. But her clothes are more fun."

"Piper is sort of in charge of these three girls," Eilish continues. "She's like the mother. I hate to use the word conservative, but her clothes are just a little more classy—stylish, but classy. She's not into fuss. The clothes are more sensible. Holly herself doesn't like anything too bright, whereas Alyssa can be bright and flowery and stripes and polka dots. It doesn't matter. But Holly likes more classic looks. In the last couple of months Holly's look has changed a little. We have actually been doing a little bit more color and having a little more fun."

"Rose is definitely a beautiful girl with that beautiful red hair," Eilish adds. "I'd say Rose is probably a little more glamorous. The hair's more glam and the makeup's more glam and the clothes go toward the more glamour as opposed to Alyssa, who is more fun. Rose is more into that classic movie star thing. Like we just did an episode where she was singing and I had to do like a forties look. She's just so at home in that outfit."

Eilish does a lot of original designs for the show, but she actually winds up purchasing or renting outfits more often than creating them from scratch. She does a lot of rental for the demon clothes because she's always finding great stuff around Hollywood that's already made for her, which helps when being given only a few days to design an entire show.

One area where Eilish has found success, particularly in dressing the girls, is in some of Los Angeles's many boutique stores. "I like to do boutiques," she admits. "I don't really go to department stores, because then what happens is you'll see it on other shows because that's the easy way to do it. Then if I want something a little antiquey, we'll go to the antique stores or the vintage clothing stores."

Of course, due to the special needs of *Charmed,* Eilish does have to build some clothes from time to time. "In our show, a lot of times we do a lot of doubles and quadruples," she explains. "So that's where we depend on making a lot of clothes. With the stunt doubles or if it's a water scene, then I have to have five or six of that one outfit. Not only do the clothes have to look great on our girls, I also have to make sure that those clothes are going to work for everything they have to do—running, stunts, flying—there's just so many elements they have to do in that costume."

Among the other physical realities of filming is the fact that the Charmed Ones will have a lot of scenes together and can't dress too much alike. "Then I am very, very big on making sure that each girl looks totally different," Eilish adds. "They have to be totally different. If I have one girl in a T-shirt, the other will not be in a T-shirt. They have to have definite differences, especially if they're in one outfit through the whole picture. I think it makes it more interesting to the audience that they see different styles."

One of the benefits of a show like *Charmed* is that Eilish gets to have a lot of fun with dressing the characters in different looks. "One of the favorites that Alyssa did," she recalls, "was when we put her in a 1940s outfit when she was with Cole and he was in an air force dress uniform. She was in this beautiful white forties dress. She had her hair up in a forties do and she had all the gardenias in her hair. It was wonderful. With Rose we did her in a medieval costume. She actually had a couple of changes in her medieval costume. Those were wonderful." But it's not just the fantasy clothes Eilish likes. "There were a couple of Holly's maternity outfits that I thought were so cute and fun. We had a lot of fun with the maternity looks."

Even though she's been involved with some notoriously fashion-driven shows throughout her career, some things still manage to surprise her. One particularly pleasant surprise came while she was walking around in Paris. "I saw these newspaper stands with the girls on all of the magazines in the three comic book hero outfits," she recalls. "That photograph was all over everything. I couldn't believe it. Of all the clothes, that picture showed up the most."

The Charmed Ones do have a following around the world. And the one thing Eilish wants all the fans to know is that the show simply is a lot of fun. "It's a hardworking show," she admits. "But you get pleasure when you work on a show and you work hard and you see it all put together. The girls are so nice to work with. We have incredible guest stars. We have incredible bosses that we work with and I think that's where it all starts. I have to say, working with the people that I do, I'm very grateful. To actually do this show, it's rewarding. And like I say, I think it's just so much fun to see it all put together."

Eilish does love to get the fan response to things, and is especially thrilled to hear when people love her clothes. But she's also quick to let them know that the looks she creates are not impossible to have at home. "I get these calls all the time asking where I got the clothes," she says. "And it's very, very expensive because we're on a television show budget. But I tell them if you're really, really clever you can put these looks together. I have taken T-shirts that were fourteen dollars and ripped them and cut them and put satin bows on them and did flowers and made them look fabulous. So you can do that. You can create these looks and not have to spend a fortune. If you're a good shopper you go and find a basic and then you can get them to that. Just because you see it on television doesn't mean you can't have those looks."

NANETTE NEW

Department Head
Key Makeup

Her mother was a Ziegfield Girl.

Her father opened up the show for George Burns and Gracie Allen.

"I was really born in a trunk," Nanette New announces with glee when recalling her childhood spent touring with her parents. "We're going on three generations. Now my niece is in it. So our whole family's been in the business. It's just been an incredible blessing for me. I love what I do. I'm fifty-eight years old and I've been doing it since I was twenty-two. So I'm very blessed."

The wanderlust of the touring life continued to flow through the veins of this self-proclaimed gypsy when she entered the workforce and began doing makeup on productions all over the country. It was when she finally came back into Los Angeles and started settling down to work in Hollywood that she had the opportunity to meet Aaron Spelling. "That was sixteen years ago," she says. "And I've been with him ever since."

Nanette has worked on many of the Spelling series, and considers *90210* to be a particular highlight. "Jennie Garth was really wonderful," she says, recalling one of her favorites from her past work. "Her and all those kids on *90210*. That was really great for me. I was with them for a long time. But this is my greatest pleasure to be with these three girls right now."

One of the reasons Nanette suspects Aaron Spelling called her in for *Charmed* was because of her experience with young Hollywood. "I think they know I'm good with kids," she says. "And I don't want to call the girls kids, because they're grown up. But, it's just really been a blessing to be with Alyssa, Holly, and Rose. They're three of the greatest girls I've ever met. I feel like they're my daughters in some ways. And they're the teachers at times too. They keep me really vital and young. I'm just as silly and stupid as they are sometimes. I use that word because sometimes we have 'stupid attacks' and act so silly sometimes. It's so much fun."

When describing her take on doing makeup for the Charmed Ones, Nanette knows that it's important to keep things simple. "We don't use a lot of makeup on these girls," she admits. "They're very fresh. They're very natural. My expertise comes in because I'm a whiz at lighting and I know what they need and when they don't need it. I think that's kind of a nice happy medium."

The makeup artist knows that she's lucky to have such a wonderful starting point when she approaches her work. "The girls really are so beautiful. They set a lot of trends and I think that the trend that they're setting is really terrific. They keep it pretty natural, which is really beautiful. I think the key to makeup is good skin. And they all have beautiful skin. Holly doesn't even need to wear base."

What Nanette loves most about her job is the fact that the makeup department gets to run the whole gamut of looks, and she credits her makeup team as being some of the best people she's been around in her life. The three members of the team do makeup for all the guest stars, and each of them has their own Charmed One. Nanette oversees Rose's makeup, while Bret Mardock is Alyssa's makeup artist and Ani Malony does Holly. "It's the greatest team you've ever seen," Nanette boasts. "And we all love each other and we all work together and we all help each and we tag team." And when the demon designs tend toward the more intricate, the team calls in special effects makeup artist Todd Tucker for an assist.

"We have all kinds of looks," Nanette adds. "Sometimes they have to be very, very glamorous, too. It just depends on the script." But Nanette explains the real talent of the work of a makeup artist comes when they have to change those looks throughout one day of shooting.

"This is what people don't know," she says. "Which I think is so wonderful about what we do and what makes us artists and why I believe we're so good at our craft. We often will have two scenes that the girls have to look very natural and then they throw in one scene where they have to be in P3 and look absolutely drop dead, elegant, gorgeous, magazine makeup. So we have to go from the natural look to the other look and then back to the natural look, so we might have three and four changes a day. There's a lot of work that goes into it. There's a lot of continuity that people don't know."

"We don't just walk in and make them look beautiful," she says. "I mean, they walk into the makeup trailer in the morning and already look beautiful. They really do. But we have to change them, and that's where our expertise comes in. How fast we can do that. We usually have twenty minutes, maybe, between scenes that we have to do that changeover. So we get into quite a routine."

The work doesn't end just because an actress is out of the makeup chair. The makeup artists are constantly on set touching up the cast before every single shot because the lighting changes often, which usually requires a different look. "So you have to take the blush down," Nanette explains. "Or you have to add the blush. There's always something we need to 'tweak'—as they call it in the business. They tweak the lights. We tweak the makeup."

Nanette is aware that the show emanates from the Charmed Ones, and their looks set the tone. To paraphrase a familiar saying, Nanette notes that, "If these girls don't look good, the show doesn't look good." And she works very closely with Eilish in the costume department to make sure the show looks good.

"Eilish is fabulous," Nanette says. "We see the costumes and know what kind of look they're going to have. We have a girl today playing a very evil woman, and her costume had a very evil look to it. So we went with an evil look on her and gave her very dramatic eyes. That's when the makeup part comes in. She's a very sweet-looking girl and we made her look very edgy, like she could come out and kill you at any moment. And that depends on how her eyes would be—what kind of a line she would have on her eyes. So we gave her catlike eyes and kind of dark smoky eyes so she would look like what she is, an evil woman."

One of her favorite looks for the girls was when Paige had to play herself at sixteen in "A Paige from the Past." As Nanette recalls, "We had a short little crop wig on her and very little makeup. All we had was this makeup that made her look like a little girl. She, of course, suggested—because she's really good at that—that she would wear braces. So we got her braces and that made the whole look. That was one of my favorite things. I think my other favorite look on Rose was when she wore the rubber dress and all the grips and electricians could hardly work that day because of how she looked."

"Holly is such a natural beauty," she adds. "She looks like the little girl next door and then all of a sudden to see her in a Chanel outfit looking like this drop dead—she put Wonder Woman to shame. She really looked absolutely amazing and sexy. She could have been on the cover of any magazine. She just looked like the sex queen. And to see little Holly walk out like that, even the crew members were falling over."

"Of course when Alyssa was the mermaid, nobody could work," she adds. "The lighting and everything was a little slow that day because there was everybody just staring at the mermaid. Believe me, she really looked like a mermaid. Nobody ever knows what they're going to look like on this show from one script to the other. And it's hard, but it keeps you on your toes."

Nanette isn't kidding when she says nobody knows what they're going to look like. She only gets a new script about five or six days in advance of filming the episode. Although the scripts do come out earlier than that she and her team are so deeply ensconced in the show they're already filming that they don't get to look at the new one until that time. Of course, Jon Paré will always call them and give a heads up if they have something particularly difficult coming up.

Then she gets together with the rest of the production team to discuss the look of the upcoming episode. "Eilish will let us know what the costumes look like," she says, noting the most important part of their preparation. "We just had a group of women that came in that we had to make look like 1800s, and a lot of work goes into that with the wig building and all that stuff. So we needed a week and a half to get that show off the ground."

It should be clear by this point that Nanette loves her job. Her natural exuberance for her work and life in general are just contagious. And she loves the warm environment in which she works, which is a tone that is often set by the stars. "Alyssa wrote us all this wonderful letter after 9/11 and just being here with everyone after that," she says. "And this is going to sound really trivial, but just to get the Krispy Kreme doughnuts that Rose brings us once a week—it's a pretty cool thing. And Holly will suddenly spring for In and Out burgers for everybody. They make sure that we have great wrap parties and beautiful gifts. They take care of us. That's very special."

TODD TUCKER
Special Effects Makeup

243

Growing up, Todd Tucker was always expressing his creative side. Like most children, he loved to draw, but his interest grew beyond simple crayon designs to be put up on refrigerator doors. He spent a lot of time doing illustrations as a kid, and even considered becoming a cartoonist. By the time he was in high school, his interests had shifted to the art of special effects makeup, which was just starting to emerge as a serious industry as he was about to emerge into the world.

"I was looking around for schools that taught how to do the makeup and all that stuff," he recalls. "But there weren't a lot of schools for that back then. So I met up with a couple friends of mine that were doing makeup effects at the time and they pretty much taught me everything I needed to know within a year—well, everything that they could teach me within a year."

Unfortunately, Todd lost his mentors after that year because they moved to Hollywood and started working professionally. Of course that didn't stop Todd. He continued working on his designs and practicing sculpting and painting and the makeup process. Once he had built a portfolio, he too made the move to Hollywood in 1990 and started working professionally himself.

Todd now works at Keith Vanderlaan's Captive Audience, a special effects makeup house, and has done a lot of films and television. He's worked as an effects artist on *Men in Black, Blade,* and *Nurse Betty* and has been part of the Academy Award–winning makeup teams of the films *Bram Stoker's Dracula* and *Mrs. Doubtfire.*

At the start of season three, the *Charmed* production office called up Captive Audience's shop, looking for Todd. He came on and met the crew and the cast and immediately fell in sync with the production and has been working with them ever since, providing the look of their more intricate demons and special props.

Naturally his work with each episode begins with the script. But that's also where the challenges begin, merely due to the nature of television production. "Usually they start shooting within a week of when we get the script," he explains. "So, whenever we know we're going to do a makeup or some kind of effect, the turnaround is really fast. We try to lock down the design of what it is going to be as quickly as we can so that we can start making it and have it ready to shoot, usually days later. You really have to test your skills to come up with the best product in the shortest amount of time."

Before they can lock in the design, Todd has to develop it, which is where that background in drawing comes into play. But he never lets the time crunch limit his ideas. "I like to bring a variation of ideas to the board," he says. "I always come with two or three different ideas or designs ranging from a more over-the-top look to a more subtle one so that we can sit there and look at it and creatively come up with what works best for the episode and the show. The main goal is to make sure that it all works together, so the look, the writing, and everything just works as one."

But just what is that magical formula he follows to create the very specific look of *Charmed*?

"We try to keep everything very subtle," he explains. "We're not creating monsters. We're creating demons and ghosts and more fantasy elements. It changes a lot, but it's very much in the world of fantasy as opposed to the world of horror. We're doing fantasy elements, because the show is a magical fantasy show. We're trying to keep from going over the top so it has more believable characters and a more believable world. We don't want to go to the point where we've had a certain look so far and all of a sudden we throw something in that had never been seen before and possibly doesn't fit."

And where does he get that guidance? Again, it all goes back to the script. Todd reads the script and talks to the creators to find out what direction they want him to take a character. But the script is often just a jumping-off point. "It can be very broad," Todd notes. "When you're reading the script and it says 'lizard demon,' there's a lot of ways to depict that. It could be a guy that looks like a lizard, it could be a guy that just looks creepy, or it could be a guy that only has contacts that make his eyes look reptilian, which ultimately is what we ended up doing." This is why he usually brings three different ideas to the board to give options to the producers depending on how they want to play the look.

Even though he is dealing with fantasy, Todd still has to rely on plenty of research from the real world. Using the "lizard demon" as an example, he had a case where it just wasn't a simple case of making a man look like a lizard. There are literally thousands of breeds of lizards, which required Todd to look up references on the different aspects or elements of the reptiles that he could use within a makeup to veer it in that direction. But after all that research and work, it just came down to what was in the actor's eyes.

If the lizard demon was one of the easier applications, then Todd would count the poltergeist portrayed by Sophia Crawford as the most difficult. "I think her whole makeup application was two and a half hours," he recalls. "It can get a lot worse, but on a TV time schedule you have to do things really quickly. So that was a luxury to have that much time. But she looked really, really creepy and she did a great job. That was probably one of the scarier creatures we've built for the show."

It is with the cases of heavy demon makeup where it really helps to have actors who are good sports. Todd sites Sophia's willingness to be put through the rigors of the makeup process as the main reason the end result came out so well. "She was great. She came in and was ready to let me do anything I needed to do to make her look as scary as I needed her to look. We did finger extensions and painted her arms, shoulders, and face to look dead ghost white with veins going through it. Then we did a full prosthetic face application, lenses and teeth and wig. That was the most time-consuming makeup that we've done on the show."

Although Todd spoke of the importance of maintaining a consistent look with his designs, he still gives himself plenty of room for creativity. Whether the change is seemingly simple like finding the right lenses for lizard eyes or more involved like the poltergeist, Todd has created a host of good and evil characters for the show.

"One of my favorite characters is the elf nanny," he admits. "I think she's a great actress and she really played a good part. For her we kind of came up with a couple different looks and did three

244

or four different makeup tests. Originally there was talk about trying to make her look greenish, but we veered away from that and we went for a very elegant, very beautiful elf nanny. We gave her very elegant ears and did her makeup very soft." And once again, much of the look was in her eyes.

In lieu of green skin, Todd made the decision to give her really vibrant green eyes. Professional Vision and Care provides all the designed contact lenses for *Charmed* and they are often an important component in creating the character. "We got some really great green eyes," Todd says. "So when you put the eyes in we did the makeup and the hair and had the ears showing, I felt like her character really came together. I think a lot of people remember that character."

During the process of the design coming together, Todd is also helping the character come together. Although Todd is quick to credit the actors for their portrayals, there is an element of his designs that helps the actors find their characters. "Their look can definitely dictate where they're going to go with the character," he explains. "Originally when we had cast the elf nanny, she was going to be a much older lady and we were going to make her look a little creepier. Then once we cast Niki Botelho in the part, she came in and she was such a pretty girl that we thought it would be a shame to try so hard to make her look the original way when we could go with a much more beautiful elf look. That obviously dictated that her character would be more that way as opposed to the way the script originally read, which was a much harsher and tougher character. Of course, the actor or actress brings so much to it. They see themselves and find that character."

Todd's job responsibilities are not simply limited to applying makeup on the actors. He is also charged with all manner of special creations, including the foam pregnant belly Holly wore under her clothes, the animatronic baby that has been seen on the show, a unicorn horn placed on a horse, as well as numerous props. "There was one episode where Paige was being attacked by a gang of bats," he says, referring to "Bite Me." "A lot of the bats were CG, but we did a biting bat for close-up shots, then we just angled it five hundred different ways so it looked like all these different bats were attacking her. Then we cut to a far shot and saw these things just flying all over the place. It worked really well. I remember it being pretty graphic."

Todd's work is not just behind the scenes. He often plays the creatures he's creating. Usually if there is a creature with heavy prosthetics the production casts Todd in the part. He's even been one of the embodiments of The Source. But it was another role that was rather light on makeup that he counts among his favorites: the comic book-esque supervillain, The Aggressor. "That was a lot of fun," he recalls. "That was probably the most fun of any of the characters because who doesn't want to play a bad superhero?"

Even with the hectic schedule, Todd wouldn't trade his work on *Charmed* for anything. "I've worked on probably a hundred features and maybe three television shows," he says. "The crew and the cast of this show are a family—more so than I've ever seen on any other show. It's one of the coolest, most down-to-earth groups of people I've worked with. I love working on this show. The fact that they give me the opportunity to act in certain episodes and the fact that what I'm doing changes so much from show to show, the variety is really fun to play with. As long as they have me, I'll continue to make as many wacky, weird things as they want."

AUDREY FUTTERMAN-STERN
Department Head
Key Hairstylist

udrey Futterman-Stern has been a hairstylist for over twenty-five years, but that was not always her chosen profession. She started out as a classical violinist in New York and was actually fairly successful in that field. She had been playing competitions and was offered a position with the Edmonton Symphony Orchestra, but chose not to take it. Instead, she says, she put her fiddle away and moved out to California to live with her sister.

But what to do when she got there?

As Audrey explains, she got into hairstyling for very practical reasons. "I had remembered meeting a gentleman who had a store that was in New York. It was so cool. He was making a ton of money. He had parties going on all the time. It was the complete opposite from what I had been used to. I mean, classical violin is a little boring. All I would do was practice, practice, practice, practice." Audrey was twenty-one years old and not really sure what she was going to do with her life when, as she says, "All of the sudden I thought about him and I went 'Hairdressing! Yeah. That's what I want to do!'"

Audrey attended beauty school, got her license, and was off to a pretty good start considering her very first job in a salon was at Vidal Sassoon. "I had two teachers at the beauty school that were famous colorists," she explains. "They'd pick out people that they thought could be somebody that could advance themselves in their career. So they knew all the guys at Sassoon."

After working in Beverly Hills for a while, Audrey moved up to San Francisco and opened a few of her own salons. She had a list of private clientele that included some industry people in San Francisco who worked in local films and television. Sometimes actors and actresses would come up from Los Angeles needing a stylist too. Audrey eventually met a hairdresser who was from around Los Angeles who turned her onto her first film.

Now it actually took some prodding to get Audrey to reluctantly admit to the title of the first film she worked on that got her into the union, so we won't be so tacky as to announce its name here. But she did drop some clues. "I can't repeat—," she started, with a little embarrassment. "It's a terrible film. Well, it's not that bad. . . . But it was pretty bad. And this was the eighties, so it was big hair. Lea Thompson had crimped hair and we dyed it . . . and there were these ducks."

But the shift into film work was not an easy decision. "I had a great business going on with salons and it was fun," she recalls. "I didn't know if I wanted to do it. But I would come down to L.A. every now and then and I'd look up some people." Eventually she made the move back to Los Angeles and did makeup and hair in Roger Corman films before moving on to other film work.

"Period films I loved," she says. "Films were my thing. And then I started getting into wigs, and wigs became my specialty. Afterward I was with Tracey Ullman for fifteen years and I got the two Emmys from her. I was like, 'Okay, I think I've hit where I want to be.'"

Then Audrey got married and had a child and decided she wanted to slow down a little bit. "I couldn't travel as much," she says. "I didn't want to. So I started getting into TV and I got turned on to *Charmed.* I came in on the third season and I've been here since then."

Walking onto the set, Audrey immediately found herself in a friendly atmosphere. "I've known Eilish from *Murder, She Wrote*," she explains. "It's funny with the business, no matter if you work in film or TV, everybody ends up meeting each other. The girls are just so delicious and so wonderful. We're all so comfortable with each other. It's nice to come to the same place every day. It's funny. When you're young you want to go here and there and you're like 'I don't want to do nine to five.' Now, it's like, 'Give me a nine to five! I'll take a nine to five!'"

Audrey is responsible for Alyssa's, Holly's, and Brian's hair while her assistant, Lana Heying does Rose, and they trade off with the day players. Like the rest of the team, Audrey starts by breaking down the script to see if the girls are going to be doing any changes. "Like on this one and the next one," she says, referring to the two-part season finale, "Oh, My Goddess." "They go into it looking like goddesses. So I asked myself if wigs were going to be involved, and ultimately the answer was 'yes.' Usually we do like to try and change things up. Even if they're going undercover, it's fun to give them a little bit of a different look."

"So I do that breakdown," she continues. "And if there's nothing special like that there's still their everyday look. If there's going to be three days that the episode takes place in, then there's maybe three different looks that they might have between what they're doing in the day or if they're going to the club." She also has to take the elements into consideration on the rare occasions they go on location, for instance, if it's really humid, she'll use the actresses' real hair as opposed to wigs.

When discussing the look of each of the Charmed Ones, Audrey echoes some of what Eilish and Nanette have said before her. "Alyssa is actually who I was hired to do for the show," she explains. "She's the sexy, fun, hip look that you can work with. You can do almost anything and everything. Because her character in the show is an outgoing character, we like to show that in her hair, too. We like to present new and fun hairstyles that kids today will want to look at and say, 'That looks like that can be really fun.'"

The viewer reaction is an integral part of Audrey's thought process when she's designing the styles for the hair. When Audrey first came onto the show she admits the styles were a little bit more complicated and technical. She explains, "Then I realized that they looked good and it was great, but I didn't think that maybe the audience would feel like they could possibly do it on themselves. I decided to bring on something that they could possibly do and that would be fun. That's what we like to present to people."

Audrey continues discussing the individual looks with Holly. "She is the earth girl. She's the grounded one. She's the mother. She's the sister that holds everything together. So, she's just simplistically beautiful. Radiance in her own self and her hair obviously says that. She's got gorgeous hair. To do less with her is probably better and it looks good on her too. It's a really smooth transition from who Holly is to who Piper is. If she had it her way, she would probably wear jeans and T-shirts everyday on the show. That's her."

"Rose is the antithesis of a modern movie star look," she continues. "That's the way that I see her. And I see that in her own personality as well. She just exudes this classic beauty about her. She photographs like that as well. What really does look good with her is to do simple classic old styles. They're great. She does fun things too, but doesn't go over as much as to where Alyssa can pull it off. Rose is so into deco and the old movie stars. It's nice to bring that out."

Audrey is well aware of the importance of balancing the needs of the actress and the character: "The actresses just feel so much more comfortable in themselves when they look at themselves and know they've got their character," she says. "But then when they look at themselves and they really like the look because it really represents something of themselves . . . I guess one of the things I've learned over the years is you have to keep whatever you can that represents their heart still to show on their head."

PAUL STAHELI
Production Designer

ike Brad Kern and Audrey Futterman-Stern, Paul Staheli was also on a different life path when he got the entertainment bug. He was attending college on a football scholarship and studying forestry when his girlfriend—who eventually became his wife—talked him into trying out for a play. Well, Paul found the decision to shift focus easier than he expected. "There were more girls in the theater department than there were in the forestry department," he says with a chuckle. "So I changed majors. Then I took a basic design class and the teacher said, 'I think you've got some talent.'"

Based on his teacher's encouragement, Paul pursued that area of study and graduated in theater design. He was in the live stage business for the first twelve years of his professional career and then moved into film because, as he quite succinctly puts it, "You can't make a reasonable living in live stage. I realized that after I had my one and only Broadway show and still couldn't make a living."

The first TV series he did was *The Life and Times of Grizzly Adams,* which was filmed in Utah. This was more or less fine with him because that's the part of the country Paul came from. After that he did freelance work, which brought him to Viacom, the company that now owns Spelling Entertainment.

"In 1986 Viacom hired me to production-design a movie of the week they were doing in Colorado," he explains. "I did that and about three months later Viacom Productions brought the Perry Mason movies to Colorado, which lasted for seven years. So I was there for seven years doing all the Perry Mason movies. Plus at that time I also did the *Father Dowling Mysteries* in Colorado and then they brought *Diagnosis Murder* there. But after eight episodes, Dick Van Dyke, who was the star, wanted to move back home. So we moved to Los Angeles and I did *Diagnosis Murder* for six years and got really, really bored. Then Spelling offered me a show in Florida and I thought that would be fun and then they offered me *Charmed.*"

Paul came into *Charmed* in the third season and immediately found the gig more exciting than previous projects. "For a designer it's a great show," he explains. "The reason I got bored with *Diagnosis Murder*—which was a fun show with great people—was I would design living rooms and offices, the same old thing week after week, whereas here we do demons and where demons hang out. There's a lot of fantasy and it's fun for a designer. For some reason it's much more interesting to do a sewer than it is to do a doctor's office. This week we're doing an ice cave. That's fun. And now we even know what heaven looks like."

Once again the design process begins with the almighty script. "You see pictures if you're a designer." He explains how inspiration strikes as he does his first read of the episode. "I think if you're a filmmaker you have to see pictures, if you're in the creative end of it. Since film is a collaborative process, then we have initial creative meetings and you see how well your concepts mesh with those of the other creators, director, producers, visual effects artists. Sometimes people won't have any idea and we bounce things off each other, or they will have a definite idea and then you meld the concepts together, or ultimately the director and producers have the say."

After he has his ideas in line, Paul usually tries to build a small, often crude, model simply to give the design a three-dimensional form so the production team has an easier time discussing it. "A picture on paper is okay," he says. "But that doesn't show space relationships, so I try to do little models."

But just because he has some more freedom with the fantasy element doesn't mean that it's easier than dealing with real-world sets. "A newspaper office you need to do modern or period, basically," he explains. "Fantasy is really more based on a lot of research. If you notice my bookcase, I've got a lot of mythology books and that sort of thing. If you're going to do heaven, I don't know that you necessarily want to do a version of heaven that doesn't look like heaven out there to all those people who believe in heaven. So you have to research that. That's more interesting."

But it's not just re-creating heaven that he finds challenging, because he's also doing a lot of hell. "I think most people think demons live underground," he continues. "So, the challenge there is that underground could look like a mine or it could look like a sewer, or it could look like an ice cave. It's just more creative. It's more fun. I truly think the creative process happens in a split second. Sometimes those split seconds don't come. Then you've just got to slog it out."

"Writers will always tell you they only write what they know, and I think it's the same with designers." He adds, "I don't think you can conceive of something with which you have no experience . . . unless you're on LSD, maybe you can there. I think any design concept is based on a former visual or former experience or certainly elements of it. I mean, I've never really seen an ice cave, but I've seen the inside of cold storage lockers and I come from a winter climate so I've seen icicles and stuff like that, but I've never seen an ice cave. So that came from somewhere, but I think that's just the culmination of a whole bunch of elements."

Maybe it's his time spent growing up in a cold climate, but Paul's mind keeps going back to ice and snow, as is evident when he talks about some of his favorite work. "My first season here we did a snowscape with the evil ice-cream man," he recalls, speaking of "We All Scream for Ice Cream." "I was really quite fond of that snowscape with the playground and the little skating pond. Then we did another one with a drop that was almost a Tibetan mountain with foliage growing on it and we did a bridge that led into a cliff and through the opening in the cliff was a vortex. I quite liked that one."

But Paul's interests don't just lie in the demon dimensions. "We hardly ever filmed it," he says. "But, in terms of a more traditional set, when Paige first came on the show she worked at a social service office. I quite liked that set for an interior."

Since Paul came in on the third season, he naturally inherited the main sets of Halliwell Manor, but he has nothing but praise for the original designer, Dean Mitzner. "They're brilliant sets," Paul says. "And it's an honor and a privilege to work with them. I have nothing but great respect for those sets. They're beautiful. There's not a thing I would want to do different on them,

so I don't mess with them. I just try to maintain them in their glory. I do new stuff when I need to, but those sets are beautiful."

Whether it be an interior, exterior, newspaper office, or heaven, Paul keeps himself grounded on the role of the scenery in the process. "If you have really, really good actors and a really, really good script, the only piece of scenery you need is a lightbulb to see the actors," he says. "Scenery should help set the tone and so on, but it should never be obvious. When I took Scene Design 101, my teacher told me that scenery should never be obvious and never to make the mistake of having a great design and trying to fit a show to it."

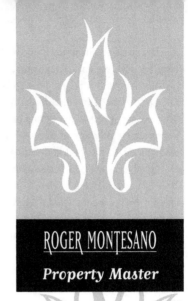

ROGER MONTESANO
Property Master

oger Montesano is yet another member of the production team with a rich Hollywood history. He's been in the entertainment industry for thirty-eight years, after his father-in-law, who was a set decorator, helped him break in. The first show he did set dressing for was a modest little hit called *I-Spy*, starring Robert Culp and Bill Cosby. Then he started prop mastering and worked on *Starsky and Hutch* for Spelling. He also did the original *Love Boat*, which he remembers as "a ten-year run with some nice trips." More recently, he worked on *Full House* for eight years and knows that he's been pretty lucky to keep getting such long-running and notable shows to work on.

We met with Roger in his office, which was loaded down with scrolls and talismans and other such mystical objects. He has been props master for the show since it started and enjoys the challenges of the demanding series. "On this show we do a lot of construction because it's so far out," he says, regarding the unique props he's had to create. "A lot of this stuff has to be made. For instance, these scrolls, we burn them. So I had to have at least ten or twenty scrolls because we're going to put them in and the effects guys are going to set them on fire."

"Then there's breakaways," he says, referring to props that have to be built so that they fall apart upon impact. "We have fights and stuff, so I use a lot of breakaways that we manufacture. There's a place I go to that has breakaway lamps and vases and that kind of stuff, but a lot of stuff is made in our effects department."

Naturally the most important prop is the Book of Shadows. "For this show, the book was our biggest challenge," he explains. "When I did the pilot our producer was saying, 'Now I need a big book and we need a lot of pages in it and hopefully the show will go five to ten years and the girls are going to use this book all the time.' But still, I just didn't feel in the pilot that the book was going to be such a key plot element and it became a *very* key plot. It's in every show and the girls go in there and look and they find their demons and they find their spells and all that stuff. That was quite a challenge to get it done so quickly for the pilot."

"There're actually two books," he explains. And they are both kept under lock and key when not in use, usually guarded by Assistant Prop Master, Christy McGeachy. "We have a third book that the effects guys put a vibrating device in because sometimes it moves and stuff. Then we have a foam book in case we want to slide it across the room or something. So we actually have four books."

Of course as the series grew, so did the *Book of Shadows.* "When we first started on the pilot," Roger recalls, "we got with the producer and she told us what they wanted to see in the book. I hired an artist to do it and he just did a couple pages, but now we have over a hundred pages."

For the past two years Roger has been using artist Dan Haberkorn to create the new pages. "He'll come out and take a picture of our actor," Roger explains. "Eilish will show us the costume the actor is going to wear and Dan will try to get here to see him in costume and take a picture of him in costume. He was a great find and he helps me out a great deal."

Another prop that's been seeing a lot of screen time lately is the scrying crystal the Charmed Ones use as a locating device. "The scrying crystal is basically a crystal on a string," he explains simply. "We have a map that the girls hold and we usually put a magnet under the map so when the crystal gets close the magnet just goes *shoop,* right to the spot. It works out pretty well."

Although the crystal is one of the more simple props, Roger explains that even the seemingly least complicated items can prove to have their own difficulties as well. "We have a lot of athames, which are like daggers," he explains, citing just one of the other challenges of the show. "We have so many of them, I try to get different types and I'm either repainting them or putting jewels on them or something to make them look a little different so we don't see the same thing every week. My biggest problem is I need rubber ones or retractable ones because someone always gets stabbed. So it's hard to find those. I either have to send them out to be manufactured to get retractables or ones made of rubber, and that's my biggest problem, because of our time frame. Everything's a rush."

Even with the time constraints, Roger does take the time to make sure the props he uses are all well researched. "There's a lot of these Wicca books that I go into and try to get information from them," he explains. "Our producers don't really want us to go on the real dark side, because the girls want to have fun with it and that's not our show."

With time travel, however, there's only a certain amount of research that can be done. "Going back in time is not too bad," he says, "because there's a lot of prop houses that I can get stuff from. It's the future stuff that is kind of tough. Stuff has to be made. We have the season finale where Chris comes from the future. So the future is going to have weird-looking glasses or watches and other accessories. I had a rough time getting what I thought was futuristic, but eventually showed him a couple choices and he went with one of them."

But it's not just the fictional future that's on Roger's mind. "Everybody here is great," he says regarding the production team. "I've been on *Charmed* since the pilot. I just turned sixty last year and I'm hoping I can last to sixty-two or sixty-three. So hopefully *Charmed* will go at least another couple years and I can go out on that. That would be pretty good."

oon Orsatti is a third-generation stuntman whose grandfather doubled Buster Keaton. But having the family connection certainly helped Noon in more than just having the same last name. As he explains, "I just held on to the coattails of my father and was on the set all the time with him and learned quite a bit.

"I think working with my father was a great experience," he continues. "We did a ton of TV shows from all the Bochco shows like *Hill Street Blues* and we did *Remington Steele* and all those really fun shows." When he wasn't working with his father, Noon got into some even bigger TV stunt work on shows like *The Fall Guy*—a show that was all about stunts since the lead character was a former stuntman.

It was working with his father once again that got him into *Charmed*. "My father got a call to do the reshoots for the pilot, when we changed to Alyssa," Noon explains. "We started at that point. My dad did pretty much the first season and I came in here and there since I was still coordinating *The Pretender*. On the second season my dad went over to do a feature and left me the reins and never looked back."

Following a reading of the script and the preliminary production meetings, Noon continues his work setting up the stunts by walking the set to see exactly where everything can happen. With all the demon battles in just about every single episode, Noon credits his crew with the amazing job they do week after week. Dorenda Moore has been doubling Alyssa since the end of season one, Dana Reed doubled Shannen since the end of year one, but now she's doubling Rose, and Nancy Thurston has been doubling Holly since season two. "They're all fantastic athletes in their own right," he says with pride over his team.

"Then I have David Huggins, who's been my confidante in terms of wire rigging," Noon continues. "Because we do a ton of rigging and wire work flying the demons, flying the people, and flying ourselves. After I know everything there is to know about the gag, then I'll bring him into the mix and we'll start to suss it out and figure out how to do it safely and how to do it efficiently."

As for the so-called average amount of stunts per episode, Noon already has an answer at the ready. "Season one, there was maybe one day a week. Season two there were maybe two days a week. Season three, three days a week . . . and so on and so on. Now that it's our fifth season, they bring me in about five days an episode and we have eight-day episodes. Hopefully next year I'll do six days and won't have to worry about doing other shows."

Noon would be quite content to work solely on *Charmed* since the production really fosters a team atmosphere behind the scenes. The producers and directors actually let the people in special effects, visual effects, and stunts have a creative influence in terms of prepping the scenes. That way each member on the team gets to contribute to the overall look of the show. Noon even had the opportunity to direct the second unit for the last couple episodes of season five.

With regard to stunt work, Noon allows the script to dictate the overall direction of his choreography in terms of the fighting styles of the Charmed Ones. "The very first season," he explains, "Phoebe had a really passive power in terms of the show. We had to give her a little edge, so they went with the martial art thing. We started it out by her buying a punching robot and made her a quick learner. She went from that to like a fourth-degree black belt in Tae Kwon Do and that's kind of the style we've kept her to."

"Piper gained her power of freezing and now blowing demons up," Noon explains. "So she really hasn't had to do too much nitty-gritty stuff. Rose, for the first few times she's been fighting, is more of a judo type. She's flipped a couple guys but she's got a great deal of power, so she doesn't have to do much of the fisticuffs either. She can orb in and orb out, but when she's been confronted she can do the hand locks, arm bars, and that kind of thing."

As for challenges, Noon pretty much lists every season finale for the series. "We haven't done that so much this season," he admits. "But in the past seasons it was always the three girls versus a demon or more for the coup de grâce. So usually you had six elements—six people—who had to go somewhere and do something. It was a bit of a challenge for me to be able to visualize the scene and shoot it and have so many cuts to tell the story, but not kill us with overtime."

As for highlights, he starts with "Wrestling with Demons" in which the production got an assist from the WWE. "Alyssa and Shannen were fighting Scott Steiner and Booker T, these huge wrestlers," he recalls. "And in that one we were able to take it really to the max of these girls' abilities. Both the girls played along really well and so did the wrestlers. I was surprised because we choreographed this entire scene without knowing if they were going to be into it or not. We were rehearsing the girls on wires and the whole thing, never knowing what these guys were all about. And they totally went for it. That was definitely one of the fun ones."

But it's not just the Charmed Ones and their doubles that are being flung around the sets. Noon has had his fair share of screen time too, although his "face time" usually works best if he goes unnoticed. "Whenever they needed a face to throw in there or when we were light a body, or have somebody getting run over by a demon, I just throw myself in there," he explains. "I think there was actually one episode where I was three different people. It was a very background kind of thing. I was a demon who was running away from the girls, I was driving a car that hit a kid on a skateboard, and I might have played a cop as well."

With people flying around the set and being set on fire, one of the major concerns in Noon's job is, naturally, safety. Every stunt presents its own challenges and safety issues. "In terms of car work," Noon explains, "you want to make sure that the airbags aren't going to deploy on you and the gas tank's not going to get ruptured and explode. In terms of fights you need to make sure that everything is well choreographed and you know who's throwing the right and the left."

One of the best advancements in stunt work in recent years is in wire work. When talking about this newly evolving process, Noon isn't just referring to the Hong Kong–style of fighting in which all the stunt people are rigged for battle to allow them to do jumps and aerial acrobatics. Much of the wire work done on *Charmed* is simply to guide the stunt people as they fly across a room or are hit by a car. The benefits of this are numerous, as Noon explains. "We have the time to practice exactly what we're going to do before we do it on the set. You don't want to come slamming somebody into a wall at Mach three when you could do it just as effectively at a slower speed. A lot of times we use machines that are going to give you an exact replication every time with the wire work."

But even with the use of wires, stunt work is still a dangerous profession. Throughout his career, Noon has suffered several broken bones and various injuries, but as he says, "It comes with the territory. . . . Worst one was when I got blown up on a show—and when I say 'blown up'—I was next to a bomb. It went off a little larger than everybody had anticipated. I was out of work for eight months. Ears are still ringing, twenty-one years later."

RANDY CABRAL
SFX Coordinator

"If we build it, they will blow it up."

Randy Cabral is referring to the writers' penchant for developing extensive battle scenes that are often set in Halliwell Manor. He notes that every window in the Manor has been blown out at least once and every piece of furniture has been blown up. As special effects coordinator, Randy is in charge of all that destruction as well as creating all the practical elements of wind, rain, and fire. It's a job he claims to have gotten into completely by accident.

"Myself and my entire crew are second- and third-generation effects guys," he explains. "It just happens. Our fathers were special effects men and we just followed suit." After decades of film work, *Charmed* is the first TV series Randy has done since the seventies. "They'd been after me for years to come and work on a TV show and I hadn't worked on one since *The Hulk*. We'd been doing big features and we were all over the United States. It was getting to be where the dog would growl at me when I came home because I'd be gone for six months at a crack. Finally my wife said, 'Look, why don't you find something closer to home?'"

Randy decided to try this show called *Charmed* that had been contacting him with interest. "It has been a godsend," he claims. "It has really been a great adventure. Whenever we got scripts prior to this, it would be like everything that has ever been done. All you need to do is go look at some old footage from a movie and every earthquake, every hurricane, every flood—it's been done. You can pick up the phone and call someone and say how'd you do that? Until we got to *Charmed*."

"This show is a whole different thing," he continues. "We're doing stuff that's never even been thought of for TV. The fun part about this is we're using all that experience and all that knowledge from every feature we know and we're trying to give *Charmed* at least one or two feature effect shots per episode. When I took this job, I hadn't worked on a TV show in years and I would run up against stuff people would be saying and I'd hate to hear it. 'Oh, don't worry about this. It's only TV.' It would drive me nuts. To this day, I hate to hear that, 'It's only TV,' because to me it's not. You can always make it better. That's what we strive to do."

After Randy breaks down a script and looks at what their "gags" are he meets with the visual effects department to discuss the realities of filming for television. Since TV moves so much faster than a feature he doesn't really have the time for take three. "You've got to get it right the first time," he explains. "In that respect you've got to be honest with yourself. It's great to read hellacious snowstorms or wind storms or army scenes, but you've got a half hour to shoot it." So sometimes, Randy has to give in and allow for some of that to be created digitally.

Even when dealing with the limitations of the television schedule, Randy still manages to amaze himself with his team's work. "We did one episode where we did Guadalcanal in four hours. We cleared all the cars out of the parking lot, brought in a dozen dump trucks, and put sand everywhere. Then we made a 1940s Chris-Craft boat into a PT boat. It was hilarious. We actually shot Guadalcanal. We brought in the palm trees and did all kinds of explosions and shot the whole thing in four hours—in a parking lot. It's a rush."

Considering he's constantly doing explosions around the cast members, Randy considers gaining their trust to be among the highlights of his experiences on the show. "I gain their confidence when I tell them where to stand and that they'll be one hundred percent safe, and then I blow off a hellacious explosion that scares everybody," Randy notes. "But they have the trust in you and they don't even blink."

It helps that the actors and stunt people are also very willing to go along with what needs to be done to get the shot. "We try to get away with as much as we can," Randy says. "We did one episode recently where Brian was in a big tank that he couldn't get out of. We filled the tank with about five hundred gallons of water and then, with our stunt guy in it, blew out the glass and had him blown out of the tank along with the water onto the set. There wasn't one hair on his head damaged or hurt or anything like that. That kind of thing is fun to do because when you get the script, they look at it and go, 'This can't be done. This would kill somebody.' It's fun to say, 'Well, you know, I think we can do this.' They look at you like you're nuts."

Going back to the Manor set, Randy says it again: "Since the original pilot we have literally blown out every window in the house, every piece of furniture, the banister, the ceilings, the floors. We've practically blown everything out and rebuilt it, and we do that on a weekly basis. In fact you can go behind the set and we've got extra stairs, extra doors, extra everything. Any place a director decides to point and say, 'Oh, I would love to have a demon come out of that closet,' I happen to have one."

According to Randy, blowing up everything on such a consistent basis is the hardest part of working on TV. "It's more challenging to do a TV show than it is to do a feature," he says. "On a feature you've got a big crew and a lot of money and you got your big shots. You get two or three big huge shots and the rest of it is you've got time in between to set those up. Then it's clean up and onto your next gig. Here it's such a challenge just to meet—you've got a hurricane today, you've got a snowstorm tomorrow, you're blowing up half the Manor the following day. Just to keep on schedule is a roller coaster."

That schedule also proves to be the biggest stumbling block. On the second day visiting the set during the filming of "Oh, My Goddess," Randy had to deal with one of those time-consuming challenges. As a storm rages on outside the manor, there is a brief shot of part of a tree crashing through a window in the living room. The shot that takes up about one second on screen took over a half hour and three takes just to get right because neither the window nor the tree were cooperating. But everyone on set was quick to point out this was a rare delay.

"You can have the greatest effect of all," Randy notes. "But if you don't have the time to shoot it, that's just one of the things you have to deal with. It gets to you every once in a while, but by and large we usually get everything in the first take. If you hold them up, even for five minutes, to put another pane of glass in, the five minutes is Purgatory because everybody is just looking at their watches. What's good here is that everybody respects everybody so much and they trust the fact that you can pull it off, and that's the good part about doing this."

Randy credits his special effects team of John Gray, Vince Borgese, Bruce Knechtges, and Mike Arbogast as the reason he can consistently get the best effects in the proper amount of time. "The neat thing about this show is I have the same talent pool for this TV show as I would for working with Steven Spielberg," Randy says. "For instance, I worked with Mike's dad on some of the *Jaws* movies fifteen to twenty years ago. Here, we build just about every prop. Everything is such a specialty that our prop guy doesn't have the time to go outside to find this stuff. We literally build just about everything here. That doesn't happen very often for a TV show, because they just don't have the talent. If it wasn't for my guys I would be dead here."

PETER CHOMSKY
Co-Producer

Peter Chomsky is the person who oversees postproduction of all the episodes and is ultimately responsible for bringing all of the elements of the show together. From editing to sound to music, he is the one who puts the final touches on the episode and oftentimes is under such tight time constraints that he delivers the show to the network the day before it's scheduled to hit the airwaves.

Peter first got into postproduction when he was in college, when he took an internship working with the editors on the miniseries *Peter the Great*. When he graduated from college, he contacted NBC productions, where he had done the internship, and got a job as a production assistant. From there he got into their postproduction department and became a coordinator; then he became manager of postproduction.

He was with NBC for ten years and was a production supervisor by the time he left. From there, he went freelance and landed on *Sliders* in its first season on the SciFi Channel. Since that production wasn't sure if they were coming back or not, he took the job on *Charmed* when the pilot had just been picked up for series. "After seeing the pilot I really thought something was going to happen with this show," he recalls. "And here I am at the end of the fifth season and we're still going."

Peter works very closely with the visual effects producer and visual effects supervisor to get a breakdown of all the effects shots on the show so he can come up with a budget. "In the first season when we were figuring out the show," Peter recalls, "a heavy visual effects show might be thirty-five visual effects. Now in season five we average about a hundred visual effects throughout an episode. It can get pretty crazy. I get two days to mix the show and on my second and last day of the mix, I might still be revising some visual effects I'm still putting into the show, which will then deliver the next day where it will air in Canada that night. It's a very tight turnaround."

While production is still shooting the show, the editors start cutting each day that they get dailies. "About five days after production wraps, the editor will cut the entire show together," Peter says. "The director will have been in working with them and in five to seven days we'll screen it. Based upon a screening, the show might be longer than the format length or it might be shorter. We'll get it cut to the length that the network will allow us to deliver."

Peter credits The WB with the flexibility to allow them to deliver the best show possible. Oftentimes a network is very specific about an episode's length, right down to the second. However,

The WB allows *Charmed* to come in a minute or two under at times instead of forcing them to add pointless filler to meet the time commitment.

"Once we've shown it to the network and they've given us their notes and we've locked the picture," Peter continues, "I'll go over with the locked picture and spot all the visual effects with the artists and say, 'Okay, here we want to blow up the demon. Here's where Paige orbs in, Leo orbs out. We do the magic spell.' And we add in all the different things that we've already prepared. The artists usually have between five and ten working days to turn around about a hundred visual effects."

Peter also works with the sound department and "spots" the show for the sound designers so they can create the audio to go with the visual effects. "I have to do a lot of voiceover work with the girls if there are lines that need to be added," he explains. "Or sometimes we'll have rain in the background on the windows and it's so noisy that I have to replace all the dialogue."

Peter also spots the music with the composer and tells him which scenes to score. "We get about anywhere from five to ten days for visual effects, sound effects, and music to get all their stuff together before I get to the mixing stage," he continues. "Then I mix the show in two days to get it delivered. During that time I also sit in with a color timer and we'll be dropping in the visual effects as they get finished and color-time the show so it's got all the shots so that it looks as good as it does. It's a challenge. I remember when I first signed on to do the show I was thinking, 'I know it's a show about magic, but it won't be like they're going to get more and more powers all the time, will it?'"

Well, needless to say, the Charmed Ones did grow in their powers, as did the demons they faced. Over the course of five seasons, this has led to some intensive visual effects. "One of my favorite episodes is probably the episode where Paige becomes a vampire," Peter says. "We did almost all the vampire bats in 3-D. It was a fun episode and I was very, very happy with how the visual effects turned out."

Naturally he lists another one of his favorites being the one that was such a challenge for Nancy Solomon. It was equally difficult for the postproduction team. "I really enjoyed the episode that we recently did called 'Cat House,'" he notes, "in which Leo and Piper go into marriage counseling and, in so doing, go back into all their memories and cast Phoebe and Paige back in time to all those memories. That was a huge challenge. Working with Brad Kern to figure out what clips he wanted to use and for him to write that episode and for us to go back into all these old episodes and pull the material and put it together into a whole new show. It was quite a challenge, and I really enjoyed that."

After over a hundred episodes, Peter and the team also find that one of the challenges is simply to outdo themselves. "When it comes to the different vanquishes we really try to come up with new looks and do different things," he explains. "Sometimes we just blow them up and we try to find fire elements that are as organic and natural as we can to fit the motion of the actor who's playing the demon that we're blowing up. At times we try to come up with completely different looks. It's a challenge because we never want to have the same effect over and over when it comes to a vanquish. We try to differentiate it as much as we can."

In addition to the visuals, Peter also works with the composers and music supervisor, Celeste Ray, to add the aural tones to the show. Obviously much of the musical composition follows the tone of the script, but the music component does affect the overall mood. "There are certain scenes that the girls play so well and it works so well that I won't even play music, even though it's a very emotional scene. There's other scenes where we'll support it with a composer and we'll underscore. It's fun having the balance. I think some of our best episodes are when they've got a pretty even balance of both."

Whether it is due to the sound, visuals, or just general response to the show, Peter loves to hear from the fans. "I get a kick out of when I look on the Internet to get some of the comments and the reactions. It's fun. I'll look at the boards and I'll appreciate the criticism, and I'll certainly appreciate the accolades when people enjoy it. It's a show that's out there to entertain people. It's fantasy. It's fun. We play drama. We play real moments with the sisters that I think everybody can relate to, which keeps it grounded. All those ingredients put together I think make for a fun hour of entertainment. That's why we're here."

Stephen Lebed
Visual Effects Supervisor

Steve Lebed wanted to do visual effects his entire life. "My dad got me started building models of tanks and airplanes from kits as a kid," he recalls. "After building the models I'd rearrange the parts and glue them together and build spaceships and whatnot. I found I really liked doing that. I went to a lot of movies of course and saw *Star Wars* and *Star Trek* and everything and realized that these guys were getting paid to build models, the thing I really loved doing."

Considering that Steve was also into photography it just seemed like the ideal job for him to get into. So he started doing research, reading up on visual effects and where to find work. Nowadays there are entire magazines devoted to that line of work, but back when Steve was looking, there was very little information to be found. "Occasionally," he recalls, "in a magazine they might have a little blurb on the guys who did the effects and I'd tear those out and save all those clippings. I basically wanted to learn all the aspects of it."

He eventually moved to Los Angeles and got his first job as a model builder, working on some TV commercials and other projects, and eventually ended up working at David Stipes Productions. "David took me under his wing," Steve says, "and showed me motion control and taught me camera work and everything. He taught me everything I know about visual effects. And then from there I just started working job to job."

Steve worked as a motion control programmer, a cameraman, a model builder, and a prop maker. "I had a chance to do a little bit of everything in special effects," he says. "And then eventually worked my way to here."

As Steve grew and learned, the industry changed as well. Productions were focusing less and less on physical models and more and more on computer models. "The last motion control job that I had done was *Independence Day,*" he says. "After that movie was finished I had the opportunity to move on to other features or get out of it and try computer animation. I decided to abandon the motion control part of it and just take a stab at computer animation. I started getting heavily into that and ended up getting a job as an animator and worked my way up to computer graphics supervisor and eventually as a visual effects supervisor."

Steve came into *Charmed* on the sixth episode of the first season and has been supervising the design of their visual effects over all five seasons. In regard to the effects, Steve echoes the words of his coworkers when he says it all starts with his first impressions of the script. "I'll read the script and try to get the tone of the writing and try to get a sense of where the writer wants to go with the story," he explains. "I'll try to pick up clues in terms of how the script will describe an effect. A lot of times the writer doesn't have a specific idea, but may just throw a couple adjectives in there that help carry the story. Those things might spark something and give me an idea of how fast, or how slow, or how colorful, or how bland an effect may need to be."

From that point he starts his own breakdown outlining every effect in the show by listing if a character explodes or whatever occurs. There also might be other effects that aren't as obvious. For instance the script may call for a location that the production can't go to. In that case Steve will have to work with a green screen to drop in a location later. "Once I have my list done, then we have our meetings," he says. "We'll talk with the director and try to get an idea of what he sees and try to fit our work into his particular shooting style so the effects can seamlessly fit into the show."

Once they've had their production meeting Steve goes back to his office and starts breaking down how the team is going to accomplish what it is that they're going to do. "A lot of it is just trying to be unique while still balancing what the production needs are," he says. "Is what they're asking for doable in the time that we have?"

More often than not, they make it happen. Steve agrees with Peter that the effects have grown considerably since the first season. "We started off our first season and had maybe like twenty to thirty effects shots in an average episode. In the second season it climbed to forty and in the third season it climbed a little bit more. And now we're averaging around over eighty. We've had shows that have gone over a hundred for a one-hour episode." He even set a new personal record for the show when the final hour of the fifth season hit one hundred twenty effects.

One of the most familiar shots unique to *Charmed* is the orbing ability of the Whitelighters, starting with Leo. "When we first discovered that Leo was going to be a Whitelighter," Steve recalls, "I don't think that we even had a name for the effect or a description of it. I think it just said 'Leo disappears.' So for me I just went off the name Whitelighter. To me it seemed like it should be much light."

Although it's a little unclear where the origin of the "orbing" concept came from, Steve was clear from the start that the idea was that when Leo disappeared he was disappearing into the light. "Originally the plan was we would have light squares flaring around so everything was bright," he recalls. "But the squares ended up getting tightened down to where they just became balls of light and it just kind of stuck. They ended up doing a swirl around him as particles and before you know it the name just kind of stuck and it became 'orbing.' It's our transporter effect."

And, like the transportation effect so familiar with *Star Trek,* orbing has become a signature of *Charmed.* "Anytime you see Leo or Paige or anybody else orbing on the show, that isn't just some effect that's just scanned down," he is quick to add. "Every time we do that effect, we're physically going into that specific shot and shooting frames. We don't push a button and add the orbing effect. It would be nice. I'm sure the artist would love to not have to sit there and do it. But it's to their credit. They hand animate all the little balls that are spinning around, all the particles and stuff and fills in the glowing color that eventually stretches and floats away. It's all done by hand."

The effect has even evolved so that it has become as much a part of the show as the sets or the costumes. "The writers have been writing effects in such a way that it's become part of the background," Steve says. "Now Leo will go orb somewhere and we'll shoot that in such a way that it's as common as him turning around and walking out the door. We don't focus on it. We don't pay attention to it. It kind of just happens in the background. That's kind of nice because it makes the world feel that much more real. It's not, 'Here's the effect shot.' Now it really feels like it's part of the show—like they actually have this ability."

"All of the artists who work on this show do a really great job," Steve says with pride. "They put a lot of hard hours into it. Every time I see a show when it airs and I watch an effect, I get more and more impressed with the level of work that goes into it. We're not getting any more time to do the effects and we don't have any more artists than we had before. These guys are doing multiple shots a day and they're keeping them at a high level of quality and adding their own touches to it."

CELESTE RAY

Vice President of Music for Paramount Pictures Group

usic Supervisor Celeste Ray started her career in the most logical of places—working at a record label. In 1982 she was hired as Director of Music for Embassy Pictures, where she worked on movies like *This Is Spinal Tap, Stand by Me*, and numerous others.

Ten years after she moved from records to films, Ken Miller, the Senior Vice President of Post Production at Spelling Entertainment, called her up and asked her to get involved with some of the shows that they had. "That was so fabulous for me," she says. "Because of the creative input of Aaron Spelling and Duke Vincent. It was 1992 and at that time, *Beverly Hills, 90210* was a top priority for Aaron Spelling. After that I worked on *Melrose Place* and other shows."

She started working independently for Spelling at first, but eventually moved out of film work and into the company full-time. "The difference between movies and TV is that with movies you have a script and it may be about a year and a half later that the movie is mixing," she says. "It's not even released. It might be released two years after you have the script in hand. With that in mind, when the music person gets involved, the music landscape changes so much in a year to a year and a half. You can start out picking music for a movie and by the time it comes to mix, the music's completely changed. Often you're picking and repicking and pitching and repitching music cues for scenes right up until the very last minute."

"What I loved about starting to work with Spelling Entertainment is that it was very immediate," she continues. "We'll have a spotting session where we're mixing the show and one to two weeks after that we're airing. You really have to put your time and energy into moving quickly, but what's really good about that is the promotional synergy that we have with the record labels and the publishers." Under Aaron Spelling and Duke Vincent's direction to have contemporary songs in their shows, Celeste and the music department have the ability to help break new artists as well as support existing songs that are on the pop and alternative charts.

Much of Celeste's personal oversight is for the Spelling projects, although she is now technically Vice President of Music for Paramount Pictures Television Group and oversees quite a large staff. As far as her work with Spelling is concerned, she's contributed to a lot of their efforts. In fact, when she started out there, she was overseeing *Models Inc.*, *Melrose Place*, *Burke's Law*, *Robin's Hoods*, *Kindred*, and *Malibu Shores* all at once as well as helping Ken Miller with *90210*. "It was a lot of creative placement. Because Spelling Television likes to focus on bands in the clubs we oftentimes tie in a club atmosphere. It really gives us an opportunity to put a lot of bands on the shows."

Whether the music is in the background or being performed on stage at P3, Celeste never lets the band overshadow the episode. "Each song to me has a significance," she says. "I like to pick songs where the lyrics have some subliminal message or it even has a specific message. When Michelle Branch came in on the hundredth episode and sang on camera 'Good-Bye to You,' that was subliminally good-bye to Cole. It tied in really nicely. For the fans I think that they probably picked up on that. For our opening credit sequences, music-wise we always like to find songs that are counterpointing or giving some idea of what's going to happen in the show. We don't just pick a song because it happens to be a hit."

In addition to the pop songs and bands, Celeste is responsible for hiring composers to create the underscore. Jay Gruska and J. P. Robinson are the show's composers, who switch off composing duties every other episode.

Once Celeste receives the locked print of the episode, they meet for a spotting session. "That's a group effort," she explains. "Our producers attend the spotting session, along with our music editor, Nino Centurion, and our composer for the episode. At that time we spot each individual cue that goes into the show. Each cue has a cue number and those notes go to the composer. That's where we say, 'Right there, where Piper turns and she's telling Phoebe the importance of being the Charmed Ones,' at this point, this is something we need to underpin. That's where the composer comes in and colors the scene with something that's going to support that dialogue."

After the spotting session, Nino gives the meeting notes to the composer and the composer scores the episode. The composer then delivers the music to Peter Chomsky, who supervises the mix. They also take the songs that Celeste procures and adds them as well. "Brad is very involved with the music," Celeste adds. "He's very interested and calls me up and says, 'I want hot music. Hot hit music!' So whatever he signs off on, we go ahead and send down to the stage and Peter mixes the show together. It's a group effort."

Having a club on the show not only gives *Charmed* the opportunity to book bands, but it also adds an interesting setting to place the action. Celeste is very aware of the fact that even though the space can be used to showcase talent, it is never the primary goal of the club.

"There's two different issues with P3," she says. "One is when you have a scene with very important dialogue, we need to set a mood for the club and the most important thing about that is you can hear what they're saying. In those times what we often do is we use popular songs where you've got some vocal in there, but you've also got the beat so it's not fighting with the dialogue. Sometimes we'll go for an independent artist who is going to be more in the ambient rave/dance material so it's not competing with the dialogue. It gives us the underscore effect of a source cue in the club."

The other issue with P3 comes when it's time to book a band. "As far as the on-camera bands go," she says, "we like to go for the alternative pop. We like bands like Barenaked Ladies and Goo Goo Dolls. We had Pat Benatar and Neil Giraldo on and the girls really liked that. We like female vocalists because we like to support women's empowerment. And Pat Benatar is certainly the embodiment of that.

"All the bands that come on are really excited to come on," Celeste adds. "They really seem to get P3 and realize that although it's not a big club in San Francisco, there's a good reason for them to be at the club. In fact, sometimes I feel like I'm booking an actual club. It's been really a great joy to work for *Charmed*."